BREAD FOR THE JOURNEY

The American Society of Missiology Series, in collaboration with Orbis Books, seeks to publish scholarly works of high merit and wide interest on numerous aspects of missiology—the study of mission. Able presentations on new and creative approaches to the practice and understanding of mission will receive close attention.

**Previously published in
The American Society of Missiology Series**

American Society of Missiology Series, No. 17

BREAD FOR THE JOURNEY

*The Mission of Transformation
and the
Transformation of Mission*

Anthony J. Gittins

ORBIS BOOKS

Maryknoll, New York 10545

Copyright © 1993 by Anthony J. Gittins
Chapter 7 draws on the author's *Mende Religion* (Nettetal, W. Germany: Steyler Verlag, 1987) and is used with the permission of the publisher
All rights reserved
Manufactured in the United States of America

Library of Congress Cataloging-in-Publication Data

Gittins, Anthony J., 1943-
    Bread for the journey : the mission of transformation and the
transformation of mission / Anthony J. Gittins.
        p.   cm. — (American Society of Missiology series ; no. 17)
    ISBN 0-88344-857-2 (pbk.)
    1. Missions.   2. Missions — Anthropological aspects.   I. Title.
II. Series.
BV2061.G58   1993
266'.001 — dc20   92-42152
                                                            CIP

For Genesis House:
A House of Nurturing,
A House of Transformation;

For all the women
who have come seeking
rehabilitation and new life;

For Edwina, Judy, and Ted,
who took the risk in faith,
and lit the fire;

For Depaul who fanned the flame;

And for all those who have offered
counsel, expertise,
moral support,
and above all, love;

This book is respectfully dedicated.

Contents

Preface to the Series

The purpose of the ASM Series—now in existence since 1980—is to publish, without regard for disciplinary, national, or denominational boundaries, scholarly works of high quality and wide interest on missiological themes from the entire spectrum of scholarly pursuits, e.g., biblical studies, theology, history, history of religions, cultural anthropology, linguistics, art, education, political science, economics, and development, to name only the major components. Always the focus will be on Christian mission.

By "mission" in this context is meant a passage over the boundary between faith in Jesus Christ and its absence. In this understanding of mission, the basic functions of Christian proclamation, dialogue, witness, service, worship, and nurture are of special concern. How does the transition from one cultural context to another influence the shape and interaction between these dynamic functions? Cultural and religious plurality are recognized as fundamental characteristics of the six-continent missionary context in East and West, North and South.

Missiologists know that they need the other disciplines. And those in other disciplines need missiology, perhaps more than they sometimes realize. Neither the insider's nor the outsider's view is complete in itself. The world Christian mission has through two millennia amassed a rich and well-documented body of experience to share with other disciplines. The complementary relation between missiology and other learned disciplines is a key of this Series, and interaction will be its hallmark.

The promotion of scholarly dialogue among missiologists may, at times, involve the publication of views and positions that other missiologists cannot accept, and with which members of the Editorial Committee do not agree. Manuscripts published in this series reflect the opinions of their authors and are not meant to represent the position of the American Society of Missiology or of the Editorial Committee for the ASM Series. The committee's selection of texts is guided by such criteria as intrinsic worth, readability, relative brevity, freedom from excessive scholarly apparatus, and accessibility to a broad range of interested persons and not merely to experts or specialists.

On behalf of the membership of the American Society of Missiology we express our deep thanks to the staff of Orbis Books, whose steadfast support over a decade for this joint publishing venture has enabled it to mature and bear scholarly fruit.

James A. Scherer, Chair
Mary Motte, FMM
Charles R. Taber
ASM Series Editorial Committee

Foreword

To sit in the Groves of Academe or high in an Ivory Tower and to write a book about engagement in mission and commitment to those at the very edges of society may seem almost contradictory pursuits. Indeed the tension between flight from the world and active apostolic ministry can sometimes be acutely painful. Yet it is possible to maintain a creative tension and to discover that disciplined, critical thinking and genuine pastoral and missionary involvement are quite compatible. More than that, the call to mission and the call to reflection and to learning are complementary; either is incomplete or partial without the other.

The classroom, the city, and many far-flung places were the initial contexts for much of this book, but the University of Oxford was where they began to take shape. The last days of a warm and green English summer that passed gently into a golden Cotswold autumn afforded inspiration and quiet; and Campion Hall proved a most congenial place for writing. The graciousness of the Master and the wider community there is warmly acknowledged.

Genesis House, a modest row-house in Uptown Chicago, was never far from my consciousness, and one hopes its ethos contributed some verisimilitude to these pages. Genesis, as it is called, opened its door in 1984 as a place where bewildered and abused women could come for coffee and sympathy. Edwina, Judy, and Ted gave it stability and several years of their lives. Since then its work has expanded. Newspapers and television have devoted attention to its pioneering efforts. Many women have found respite; some have found the beginnings of new life.

But on the fringes of Genesis House, and acting in at least an ancillary capacity, some people have watched and been amazed and edified; they have seen that the healing process does not discriminate and grace does not flow in a single direction. Visitors with no personal history of abuse and no obvious need for rehabilitation have been touched by acts of kindness as much as they have been appalled by tales of inhumanity. Genesis House, and similar communities, have undertaken, from vulnerable and marginal positions, the mission of transformation. Genesis House has a precious gift to offer the church and those who take their Christian faith seriously. Insofar as these have discovered, through Genesis House, the power of grace far from the centers, they have been and can still be swept up in an authentic and inspired transformation of mission.

In deference to an ecumenical readership, and in acknowledgment of some inconsistency in current nomenclature, I have paired the terms "missionary" (as a noun) and "evangelization," and used them in the odd-numbered chapters. "Missioner" and "evangelism" are likewise paired, and used in the even-numbered chapters. As an adjective, the word "missionary" is used throughout.

Quotations drawn from works by other authors have *not been modified* to use inclusive language, although at times it has been painful not to do so. They appear here as they are in the original work.

Introduction

READING AND REFERENCE

My mother used to tell a story of the time she worked in a library. One day a slightly disoriented and unsteady figure approached the desk. In a stage whisper that must have echoed round the library stacks, he inquired in a thick and engaging brogue, with heavy emphasis: "Have ye got any *readin'* books?"

There are "readin' books" and there are other books: reference books, pictorial books, "how to" books, theology books; many are worthy and a few are excellent. But some books that are intended to be read are not—though they might be bought in large quantities and displayed on many a shelf.

Bread for the Journey is intended as a "readin' book." My impression is that busy missioners find scholarly works tedious, theoretical, or overly speculative. Such books might be power-packed, like vitamins, but are not appetizing or nourishing; we cannot live on vitamins alone. And though there is no substitute for quality scholarship, it need not be unpalatable or constitute one's total diet.

It seems that many Christians today, accepting the challenge to mission, are more convinced about the basic theological justification than they are competent to judge appropriate missiological tactics. There comes a point when they would betray their ignorance if they were to probe more deeply and to ask some fundamental questions about the aims and methods of Christian mission; in any case there seem to be so many approaches, arguments, and justifications that it is probably easier simply to be swept up into the mainstream. Consequently, basic questions sometimes remain unasked and postings are perhaps too readily accepted in distant local churches. But there are others, maybe clearer about their instrumentality in mission, very sensitive to other people, and theologically sophisticated themselves, who are no less confused after a period of time; for them it is the inappropriateness of missionary methods or the intransigence of dogmatic formulations of church discipline that grate and frustrate. For people with such perspectives or questions as these, the following pages are offered.

THE MATTER OF MISSION

If mission is to proceed in a way compatible with the intention of Jesus and the legitimate claims of persons, then the issue of missionary tactics and cross-cultural modifications of Christian life and liturgy must be faced, and urgently. Epitomizing the current challenge to Christian mission is what Roman Catholics are increasingly calling "inculturation" and many other Christians refer to as "contextualization." These, with variations in detail, concern the way in which—given that messages must be both "translated" and "appropriated" or received—the Gospel can become truly incarnated in the lives of myriad social groups across the face of the earth. It is not a question of relativizing the Gospel, but it is a matter of not imagining that people are blank slates on which anything can be written by any passing scribe.

People reflect their cultural heritage and human context; their knowledge and experience are mediated to them through their language and culture. Anyone wishing to communicate in an adequate fashion absolutely must take these things seriously. The Gospel must challenge culture, but it must not crush it; to crush a culture is to maim its people. People are called to respond to the Gospel in the here and now: wherever they are. This means that a task of mission is encounter: a respectful engagement and dialogue with people wherever they are. And if *they* are not where *we* are, we must go in the spirit of Jesus and seek them, not to make them like we are, but to offer them a glimpse of Jesus and to invite them to follow him.

It is very difficult to meet other people with respect and concern, to want to offer appropriate gifts and yet to ensure that we neither smother nor impose on them. But this too is a task of whoever undertakes the mission of Jesus. He did not force people to do exactly as he did; rather, he pointed them in the same direction he was going and offered to accompany them or to call them to him. He wanted each person to become the person he or she was called to be, not someone else. His task was to liberate people from the chains that prevented that transformation. His life was a journey; his mission was to meet people on their journeys; our mission is to extend his mission. Only if we first encounter people and prove trustworthy can we presume to call them to walk a different path; only if they see a different path as leading to their destination will they choose it and stick to it. In these pages we will consider the legitimate demands of the people to whom we are sent in mission.

BROKEN LIVES, HEALED LIVES

Arguably none of us finishes up where we imagined, ten or twenty years ago, we would be. For every person the future contains unpredictable elements. But, thank God, most of us can trace a thread back down the years that gives continuity to our life's journey. The presence of such a thread indicates what we will describe as "radical continuity" as distinct from "radical disjunction." A good deal of the literature on conversion as a sociological and spiritual phenomenon has treated it as an example of radical disjunction: a cutting of the thread that has run through our life and the beginning of a completely new journey. But in recent times we have been invited to consider life as more commonly a process of radical continuity: not without change or transformation but not necessarily demanding a severing of our very roots.

"Mission in reverse" will be discussed as an attitudinal approach to mission that will ensure, insofar as possible, that radical continuity constitutes the leitmotif of the response to mission, whether on the part of the person who comes as the guest of another or of the host who receives the guest. The attitude that characterizes mission in reverse will sensitize the outsider to local cultural and social values in such a way that the missionary outreach may become a healing touch rather than a destructive gesture.

A certain kind of mission work in the past tended to look for radical disjunction as the only authentic sign of conversion in local people, and called others to repudiate their history and family rather too readily. This completely undermined the place of culture and socialization (the process of growing-up and learning about one's place in relation to others) in people's lives and demanded major trauma as a normal sign of initial commitment to Jesus. But the example of St. Paul is not typical of the effect of conversion; the example of Peter, James, and John—who, after the crucifixion, were ready to return to fishing (Jn 21:3)—or indeed of Mary and Joseph are surely just as authentic.

With perhaps a greater understanding, and, it is hoped, an increasing respect for authentic human values as embodied in people and their social groups even before they have heard the Gospel, those engaged in mission today should be rather more inclined to discern Gospel values in all societies and to grant that the process of conversion commonly builds upon such values. Gospel values are rooted in cultures, are not explicitly Christian, yet are quite compatible with the Gospel of Jesus. Increasingly, missionaries are attempting to proclaim the Gospel in such a way that it encounters, converges with, and where possible, builds on rather than undermines the best human values in various cultures. The following pages consider the importance of people's social contexts and cultural heritage in relation to their response to the Gospel.

CONVERSION AND MISSION

Cultures challenge expatriate missionaries to reevaluate some of their own assumptions about authentic Christianity and frequently remind the expatriate that pre-Christian societies practice some of the so-called Christian values better than do ostensibly committed Christians. Missionary activity should therefore not only call other people to conversion and transformation, but through real engagement with people of other cultures it should call missioners themselves. As Pope John Paul II writes in *Redemptoris Missio*:

> The church serves the kingdom by spreading throughout the world the "Gospel values" which are an expression of the kingdom and which help people to accept God's plan. It is true that the inchoate reality of the kingdom can also be found beyond the confines of the church among people everywhere to the extent that they live "Gospel values" and are open to the working of the Spirit (para. 20).

> The proclamation of the word of God has Christian conversion as its aim: a complete and sincere adherence to Christ and his Gospel through faith. Conversion is a gift of God. ... The church calls all people to this conversion (para. 46).

> We cannot preach conversion unless we ourselves are converted anew every day (para. 47).

Though the final statement is virtually a commonplace in missiological writings today, a little reflection will remind us that it only has force if missionaries themselves are open to personal change. And if their own conversion—our own conversion—like that of others, is commonly effected by means of radical continuity, then every person committed to mission must acknowledge that the grace of God is active through the challenge of daily encounters with the neighbors we do see, not simply through privatized and spiritualized commerce with the unseen God.

BREAD AND JOURNEYS

Increasingly for Christians the eucharist is proving problematic. For some Christian traditions eucharist is deemed to be central. Yet ministers, presiders, presbyters, priests, are in short supply. For other traditions within the Christian faith eucharist has never been at the center of life, or became marginalized. Yet those traditions are currently facing the challenge of Jesus and of the earliest common Christian tradition in relation to eucharist. For Christians from all traditions, therefore, eucharist is currently a critical issue in mission theology and practice.

There is an increasing tension—not unequivocally a bad thing—between the desire to encourage the development of meaningful local liturgies and the need to hold on to the tradition that marks us as heirs of the first generations of the people called Christians. But the Christian Gospel is not something to be accepted piecemeal by local communities, any more than liturgical forms can be created whimsically; continuity and integrity are as much a part of inculturation as change and selectivity. The problem will not go away, and the tension is probably intrinsic to a church that strives to be both universal and local.

Yet some creative forward movement must be possible to those on a journey together, and of course it is. Just because those who are impervious to the lessons of the past are doomed to repeat its mistakes does not automatically imply that Christians in the newer churches must relive the worst excesses of Western Christendom over two millennia. If the eucharist is to be situated firmly as the focal point of Christian communities of the future, then very significant forms of inculturation need to happen. If we are offered bread by Jesus, but our church makes it inaccessible or offers only "stale" or "ersatz" bread, how can our communities be sustained? The hungry must cry out; someone must respond to the cries.

If Jesus tells us to remember him and his life of sacrifice through the liturgy of the eucharist—the celebration of the body of Christ, the sacrament of the Paschal mystery—yet hungry communities await the arrival of distant eucharistic ministers and gather in strange surroundings and amid unfamiliar symbols and gestures, are they not in danger of forgetting what they should remember?

The central part of our narrative will address these questions in some detail as it considers the twin themes of bread and journeys.

DIACHRONIC AND SYNCHRONIC STUDY

The study of phenomena through time (or historically) is diachronic; a synchronic study concentrates on what is happening at a particular time and place. Since part of our concern is to remain faithful to authentic Christian tradition while looking across a range of contemporary cultures, we will need binocular vision: diachronic and synchronic.

Adaptation is not the same as inculturation. The former may well be impressive but is ultimately only cosmetic, while the latter is radical and carries profound implications. If we look at the Christian faith and its liturgical practice only superficially, we may quite easily make some adaptations from culture to culture. Unless we look below the surface and through time to discover the fundamental truths and crucial relationships on which Christianity depends, and only then attempt to translate them across cultures, we will have given people a stone when they asked for bread, a snake instead of a fish, a scorpion instead of an egg (see Lk 11:11-12).

Inculturation is successful when people have received the essential nourishment offered by Jesus, but in a way that is identifiable to and appropriated by them, linguistically, culturally, existentially. This by no means removes the challenge, nor undermines the novelty of the Gospel. But in order for inculturation to happen, both the Gospel and particular cultures need to be studied sedulously so that they disclose their deepest realities and most profound truths, for only at the deepest level can the Gospel and culture interpenetrate. Otherwise their meeting will be casual or formal, but not the basis for long-term relationships and the transformation of lives in Christ.

But if, as we will urge, mission is indeed an undertaking that knows no limits; if true missionary activity searches out the boundaries and the margins where the poor, unknown, or abandoned are to be found; and if inculturation calls for very serious adaptation and "translation" of the Gospel, then the pages of this book constitute a kind of comparative or ethnotheology, where the comparisons are both diachronic and synchronic. But this is not to make theology, or the Gospel, or truth, relative. It is simply to say that just as the incarnation came to pass with Jesus being born in a particular culture at a particular time—as a first-century Jew with all the attendant cultural roots and horizons—so the Jesus we proclaim today must be identifiable to, and then welcomed by, particular people in particular cultures with particular roots and cultural limitations of their own.

If this Jesus—the living Christ whom we also call the Second Person of the Trinity—appears as a creature from another world, people will not be able to relate to him or feel understood by him. Consequently his incarnation in myriad cultures must, in a sense, deliver him as a brother to all the people of those cultures. The kind of ethnotheology advocated here would consider how Jesus might be understood and accepted by people of different cultures and in rather different ways without betraying Jesus or repudiating culture. And in so doing, it should have something to show people of various cultures as they contemplate similarities and differences between their own Christian response and those of other times and places.

STRANGERS AND ALIENS[1]

Since the call to mission extends to each person in virtue of baptism, this book is addressed primarily to Christians and only incidentally to "Roman" or "clerical" or "religious"; those represent my own particular context and bias. Different people will appropriate it in different ways according to their own experience, context, or role; another example of the comparative nature of this kind of theologizing. My intention is not to deny differences so much as to emphasize the similarities in the calling of all those invited to respond to the missionary imperative.

Yet in actual fact this book is not for every Christian. It does not discriminate, but many will exclude themselves from its pages. It is for those who take their faith seriously, who sense that they have here no abiding city, yet who are committed to journeys and to proclamation. It is true that St. Paul says we are no longer aliens (Eph 2:12,19), but that is said of our relationship with God; in relation to "the world" we remain, and should always remain, aliens. Only to the extent that we embrace this rather marginal status can we be committed to the mission of Jesus.

A recent book called *Resident Aliens*[2] has proved very popular and somewhat controversial. In a later and richly quotable article[3] authors Stanley Hauerwas and Will Willimon argue that the church must relinquish its comfortable position as "establishment"; it must "leave behind past forms of unfaithfulness and live adventurously."[4] They say that "it is wonderful to live in a time when Christians have to discover another person is also a Christian rather than being able to assume it";[5] and making their point about the importance of the ecclesial community and its intimate connection with the plight of real people, they emphasize not the church triumphant or triumphalist, but a church that needs "resident aliens" and people in search of personal and social conversion.

> Bishops and theologians are both servants meant to direct the church's attention to the significance of the lives of the faithful. In a very strong sense, theology cannot help but be unfaithful if it is "creative."[6]

> It is time for the church to recognize that it is in a missionary situation in the very culture it helped to create. . . . The church ought to be in a missionary situation at *any* time and in *any* culture.
> . . . The very idea that Christians can be at home, indeed can create a home in this world, is a mistake. . . . There is nothing unique about [the] call for the church to recognize its status as sojourner except that the material conditions may now exist to force the church to be faithful.[7]

For the Christian committed to the mission of Jesus and the church, what this amounts to is making no compromise with a comfortably institutionalized "established" church. Our journey is to discipleship, not to social acceptability in a post-Christian world. "Resident aliens" are less encumbered and beholden than comfortable citizens clinging to their constitutional rights.

ECCENTRICITY AND REVERSAL

The missioner is not someone in the mainstream, not a person carrying in both hands well-meant gifts for others. Rather, the disciple sent to others is called to swim against the mainstream, to come openhanded or at least with one hand free to receive assistance. If it is liberating to consider ourselves "resident aliens" in a global community, it can be equally creative for us to think of ourselves as not quite at the hub or center of things: in other words, as somewhat "eccentric." If it is at the edges of our own comfortable worlds and across the borders between categories that we seek to follow Jesus, then we *are* eccentric. We march to a different drum.

This does not, of course, give us license to indulge in outrageous or egotistical behavior. Nor does it permit us to isolate ourselves and remain intransigently marginalized and passively eccentric. Active marginalization and real passion for justice are the issues here. We are challenged to accept the responsibility of being acutely sensitive to those whose voices are hushed and whose lives are not marked by hope or faith. But rather than assuming that all who do not know Jesus do not know God, or that we are cast only as givers and others only as receivers, we will respond to our missionary mandate by learning to be servants and by seeking God in other people. If this demands a radical reversal of some missionary approaches, then we will commit ourselves to such a reversal, not because it is fashionable or self-effacing, but because it is the way of the suffering servant, the way of the cross, and the way of the resurrection. This is the path to transformation of ourselves, of other people, of all things in Christ. Here again is *Redemptoris Missio*:

> In Luke, mission is presented as witness (Luke 24:48; Acts 1:8), centered especially on the resurrection (Acts 1:22). The missionary is invited to believe in the transforming power of the Gospel and to proclaim what Luke presents so well, that is, conversion to God's love and mercy, the experience of a complete liberation which goes to the root of all evil, namely sin (para. 23).

> The Acts of the Apostles records six summaries of the "missionary discourses" which were addressed to the Jews during the church's infancy (Acts 2:22-39; 3:12-26; 4:9-12; 5:29-32; 10:34-43; 13:16-41). The model speeches, delivered by Peter and by Paul, proclaim Jesus and invite those listening to "be converted," that is, to accept Jesus in faith and to let themselves be transformed in him by the Spirit (para. 24).

Given the importance of personal conversion, we will pay as much attention to it in the following pages as to the conversion of others. And given the importance of vernacular experience and language, we will pay as much attention to local culture as to the decontexualized Gospel.

The book is arranged in three sections, consistent with the title. In general terms, the first section is intended to be a personal reflection for those called to mission; section two looks at the cultural riches we should encounter; and the final section moves toward a synthesis or, in the current language of theology, toward inculturation of the Gospel.

PART I

PREPARATION

Chapter 1

Missionary Journeys

As a general rule, migratory species are less "aggressive" than sedentary ones. There is an obvious reason. . . . The migration itself, like the pilgrimage, is the hard journey, a "leveler." . . . The journey thus preempts the need for hierarchies and shows of dominance. The "dictators" of the animal kingdom are those who live in the ambience of plenty. The anarchists, as always, are the "gentlemen of the road."[1]

Faith does not transport us to a magical city, but enables us to appreciate the significance of what we find at home.[2]

We shall not cease from exploration
And the end of all our exploring
Will be to arrive where we started
And know the place for the first time.[3]

MISSION AND A WORLD OF DIFFERENCE

There was a time (or maybe we dreamed there was) when the word "missionary" was universally acceptable and referred to an admirable but virtually inimitable person touched by faith and heroism. And there was an age (perhaps in our imagination) when "the Missions" referred to faraway places where the Ladder of Perfection was laid against the Ramparts of Evil, where Virtue engaged and overcame Vice, where clear, straight paths of righteousness were laid down and trodden across trackless wastelands, and where light was carried triumphantly into strongholds of darkness. In an age of heroes and heroines and dogmatic certainties, "missionaries" received respect and affirmation from "the faithful" to whom they in turn offered inspiration and almost impossible ideals.

Yet for all their personal sacrifice and social privations, and despite a relatively wide range of tactics, missionaries of many stripes had a remarkably common strategy and a keen and clear sense of their mission. In

3

consequence, that mission may be said to have been simple or uncompli-
cated, at least in a structural sense.

Closer to our own times, the missionary "job description" certainly dif-
fered from one denomination to another, and in the less evangelical
churches, even within a particular denomination. Missionary applicants or
"vocations" were drawn from a variety of social categories and intellectual
backgrounds. Thus a range of understandings of mission and ministry was
reflected. And in spite of St. Paul's emphasis that in Christ there are no
distinctions (Gal 3:28), institutionalized Christianity clearly thought otherwise,[4] producing as it did an enormous variety of forms and functions.
Yet a missionary was always identifiable as someone selected, trained, and
sent by the church to lead or collaborate in the expansion of the Christian
community in places where it did not yet, or only recently, exist. And prac-
tically speaking, this meant that missionaries were those ministers of the
Christian churches who worked in far-flung areas among people whose
cultural traditions were unfamiliar, people who had not heard the Good
News of Jesus Christ, people perhaps deemed not even to have heard of
God.

Now, whatever may have characterized the past in its depth and diversity,
both "missionary" and "the Missions" (the realities as well as the terms)
have come under close scrutiny and, in the experience of many, worse than
that: they have been mauled, desecrated, and rejected. Today, "missionary"
may just as easily conjure up wild-eyed and incoherent fanatics, clean-cut
and offensively persistent young men on doorsteps, and many intermediate
shades of bombast, insensitivity, and dire warnings. In an age dominated
by the New World, apostles and pioneers armed with cross and bible (and
sometimes with not-so-surreptitious sword),[5] set sail in comfortless caravels
and sent back stories of battles won and souls saved; in the post-communist
age of a "New World Order," tourists and travelers armed with film stock
and dollars (and sometimes not-so-tiny chips on shoulders), sally forth in
luxurious liners (by sea or air), but bring back rather different stories.

"The Missions" are now widely exposed to charges that they are arenas
of cultural devastation, neo-colonialism, and socio-political dependence on
alien regimes. Missionaries are stereotypically perceived as joyless reac-
tionaries or rabid proselytizers. "The Missions" and the "missionary" are
no longer (if they ever truly were) uncritically accepted as respectable.

But this is not all. As a result of massive religious and social change,
especially over the past two generations, those who themselves wear the
title "missionary" and who spend their lives working in or on "the Missions"
have not escaped personal reassessment of their ministry and its execution.
For some, this has been intensely painful, and they have felt as isolated as
a deep-keeled sailboat stranded at low tide, or as self-conscious as a customer publicly accosted by a store detective. Will the tide ever refloat the
beached yacht? Will the customer be exonerated? And for others, it seems,
the implications of a thorough reexamination of the tactical approaches

employed for so long are too threatening, or redundant, or both. It is as tragic as it is unsurprising that some people become demoralized and lonely.

If one believes, or assumes, that "unreached peoples" will not be saved until and unless they explicitly profess Jesus Christ and are baptized into the visible church, the essential missionary task will remain clear, if daunting. But as soon as one canonizes the rights of the individual conscience, imagines that God could be revealed long before certain areas had been "discovered" by well-meaning Christians, or allows that the salvation of others can hardly be contingent on the timely arrival of evangelizers or convert-seekers, then the role and the justification of missionaries must be critically reappraised. The only alternative as far as missionaries themselves are concerned would seem to be what might be called the "Ostrich Solution."

The following pages will attempt to pursue some of the issues already alluded to here. They will consider, informally and descriptively, the implications of the presence of God in cultures before the arrival of the missionary. They will try to take very seriously the autonomy of conscience; that is, the notion that conscience not only *may* be followed but *must* be followed. They will ask what the word "missionary" might mean in a changing world. They will examine the shift in terminology from "the Missions" to "mission," and the implications underlying it. And they will contrast a missionary-focused Mission with a Spirit-focused Mission in order to discern areas in which the missionary may practice silence before the mystery of God's Spirit, and graciously defer the last word to the compassion and grace of God. In addressing these issues the inspiration is the Gospel itself, and the rest of scripture and tradition. The intention is to tease out some applications to contemporary mission, applications which seem unavoidable though they may have been either avoided or preemptively discussed from armchairs or offices.

FROM "THE MISSIONS" TO "MISSION"

"The Missions" was a term employed when the world was younger: when "over here" was contrasted with "over there," and when light, truth, salvation, and even God, were "over here," leaving darkness, falsity, perdition, and Godlessness "over there." "The Missions" tended to refer to those areas of the unenlightened world to which the enlightened world was in duty bound to send messengers, teachers, and, almost, "saviors." "The Missions" belongs very comfortably in a dualistic universe, a world composed of opposites, a world in which many of us have at one time lived.

"The Missions" is not a dead term by any means. Just as some people act as though the earth is the center of the universe, or uncritically imagine that English is the language of God's choice, and others assert that "truth" is a commodity like gold (expensive, scarce, and sometimes counterfeit), rather than a reality like grace (free, unlimited, and always genuine), so there are those who are firmly convinced that this really is a dualistic world, a world of opposites. They still live in a world in which "the Missions" denotes places and people very far away from "here," locations where there is (or was until very recently) only falsehood, darkness, and Godlessness.

But when we begin to think cosmically rather than parochially, globally rather than locally, ontologically rather than geographically, and theologically rather than anthropologically, it becomes clear that "the Missions" simply will not do. God's love is inclusive, God's salvation universal. The mission of God is limitless in practice, and the mission of the church is limitless in theory; only its existence in time and space, and the finiteness of its faltering expressions of Christ's love, constrain it. Mission therefore applies to every place, since no place is beyond God's love in Christ. But if we dissolve the distinction between "here" and "there," what happens to "the Missions"? And even more challenging, what happens to the "missionary"?

"Mission on Six Continents" is an increasingly familiar slogan, as clear in its message as it is questionable in its arithmetic. It refers to mission as a universal reality and enterprise, an "already" as well as a "not yet." Karl Rahner spoke of the "world church" as a phenomenon of our times, but it is a phenomenon that is, frequently, as little recognizable on the streets of Chicago as in some jungle enclaves. And if the world church is "already," what is left for the missionary? If the church is "not yet" among many of the poor and marginalized "over here" (not to mention its questionable presence among the comfortable middle classes), how can we say the missionary is one who goes "over there"?

Only when former categories have been challenged can new insights bear fruit. Not until old boundaries are destroyed can new relationships be created: "they" can become a little more like "us," exclusiveness can move toward inclusiveness, opposites can embrace, and new programs can be discovered and created. The pulling down of walls and the dismantling of ideologies are not so much an end as a beginning. Once we move from a notion of "the Missions" to one of "mission," therefore, we both shift categories and dismantle boundaries. No longer is the missionary quite the exotic creature of days gone by, or, for that matter, is mission work quite as romantic. From now on the mark of a missionary will be fidelity to the graces of baptism by which people become disciples committed to the welfare of all humankind; the arenas of missionary work will be as extensive as the world itself.

This raises another issue, and for some, another problem. If what is being said makes sense, then it would seem to follow that every Christian is in fact as well as in theory a missionary, that every self-styled missionary is thereby engaged in authentic mission, and that every place in the world is actually a place of mission. There are questions here that need careful attention.

THE CALL TO MISSION: BAPTISM AND THE CHURCH

Increasingly in recent years we have been reminded that baptism is the sign of incorporation into the Christian family and the rite which marks us as responsible and effective members of the body of Christ. But rites are external signs of interior transformation, and transformation must become a feature of the life of the Christian. Otherwise we might imagine that we could and should do nothing by way of cooperation with the grace received, and that the rite itself is all that is needed. This is simply to believe in magic! The Christian, by contrast, is one who understands that he or she has received an invitation to which a response is requested and possible. And this in turn carries a serious burden of responsibility.

So baptism is a sufficient prerequisite for mission, and every baptized person becomes part of the People of God, the church. And the church is missionary by its very nature; the People of God, though perhaps differentiated by rank and function, are unified in call and service.

There is one chosen people of God, one Lord, one faith, one baptism; there is a common dignity of members deriving from their rebirth in Christ, a common grace as children of God, a common vocation to perfection, one salvation, one hope and undivided charity. In Christ and in the Church there is, then, no inequality arising from race or nationality, social condition or sex, for there is neither Jew nor Greek, there is neither slave nor free, there is neither male nor female, for [we] are all one in Christ Jesus (*Lumen Gentium*, 32).

We have here a magnificent statement about the common missionary vocation of the baptized. A much more recent one by Pope John Paul II reminds us that "all the laity are missionaries by baptism" and that "from the very origins of Christianity the laity—as individuals, families, and entire communities—shared in spreading the faith" (*Redemptoris Missio*, 71). Regrettably, however, this by no means goes as far as it might, and a quarter of a century after the close of Vatican II the laity are in practice accorded little more than an ancillary role, and very little authority to appropriate their baptismal mission. It is not only ironic but tragic that so much remains words on a page or tokens that have been dreadfully devalued. Indeed, the chasm between some of our rhetoric and current ecclesiastical discipline and practice sometimes seems unbridgeable. Yet those committed to mission are also committed to the Spirit and to seeking God's justice; and Jesus said of those who hunger and thirst for such justice (*dikaiosunē*), that they will be not only "satisfied" but "fattened" (*kortasthesontai*). In a world of hunger, this should be very well received.

Still, only two things are necessary in order that Christians be true missionaries: that they react to their baptismal call, and that their missionary response be encouraged, acknowledged, and endorsed by the church! If the People of God were to find their missionary response thwarted by the institutional church, this would constitute a grave miscarriage of justice. But that still leaves individual Christians with the responsibility of answering their baptismal call in a certain way, otherwise they remain missionaries only potentially but not in fact. So what signs might characterize the Christian who responds specifically as a missionary?

THE RESPONSE TO MISSION: OUTREACH AND COMMUNITY

To some people there is "pastoral" work and there is "missionary" work; though the two may co-exist adjacent to each other, they are perceived very differently. From a certain perspective there are missionaries and there are non-missionaries (and it is easy to see which of these categories creates its opposite). According to a particular point of view, a missionary is as much the person who joined an identifiably "missionary" institution, was trained, and was then retained at home in obedience, as the one who, having joined and trained, was duly posted overseas. Likewise, a person retired from overseas with some active life remaining could legitimately retain the title of missionary on the strength of membership and former activity. "Once a missionary, always a missionary" was a proudly chanted slogan. Yet, though perhaps intended as a reminder, a spur, or to be couched in the optative mood, it sounded very often like a simple declarative sentence. But is it true?

To be a missionary it is no longer, if it ever was, sufficient to rest on one's oars, claiming experience, former activity, or membership of a particular group. Nor can a person simply assert that he or she is *in fact* a missionary in virtue of baptism. Perhaps we should look at a way of understanding the missionary enterprise that is neither a function of one's membership in an organization nor a matter of geographical distance from home.

"Pastoral" work has sometimes been identified as work of maintenance, or work in a familiar and relatively stable context, while the term "missionary" has been applied to pioneering work in unfamiliar places. If this perspective is adopted, a missionary overseas, working in a long-established parish with familiar parochial structures, might be thought of as not a *true* missionary (and might therefore invoke, self-defensively, the slogan "Once a missionary . . . "). Similarly, an African sister from Zimbabwe working in a college in Zimbabwe might not be considered a missionary, but if she went to Sierra Leone and did exactly the same work, she would be! Any member of a fully canonical Missionary Order working in a remote area of the Pacific might be automatically accorded the title missionary, even though he or she never attempted to learn the local language but rather became increasingly isolated and was intolerant of the people. But by what criteria could a lay missionary (with virtually no formal training in theology or evangelization, sent by a membership-led and non-canonical organization, operating in a cross-cultural situation for an intentionally brief time, and engaged in agricultural, secretarial, or developmental work) claim, or be accorded, the designation missionary?

And so on and so forth. Definitions have been created and defended, people have almost come to blows, and still we have little consensus on what constitutes a missionary or authentic missionary work, so much so that to some people the solution lies simply in rejecting the word "missionary" itself. There must be another approach.

It has been said that whenever and wherever the church lost sight of or lost commitment to its centrifugal thrust — its "outreach" — then sooner or later it withered and died. This is something for discussion, but the point is salient: the church, from Pentecost onward, is propelled, moving, sent ("co-missioned"). It follows therefore that pastoral work that totally lacks that outreach or propulsion is antithetical to true mission; likewise, what we might call *true* pastoral work is also authentically mission. Pastoral work must never become preoccupied with self, closed to the "others" of whom Jesus so often speaks.

Pastoral work in this sense should be a central feature of the missionary outreach of the church. All parishes, no matter how long-standing or well-organized, should also be truly missionary. To some mentalities this is perplexing! But pastoral work should be a preparation for mission, lead to mission, give birth to mission. There is absolutely no need for it to be polarized against mission. Perhaps if we look at Jesus, we will be able to see some light.

JESUS, MISSION, AND TRANSFORMATION

The vision of Jesus is grounded in his mission, and as he appropriates or lives out his mission, so his vision widens. He is portrayed as sent to the lost sheep of the House of Israel, but as a pastor he must search them out, encounter them, rescue them, and carry them in his arms; they will not come to him. But they do!, you will say. They come to him frequently! And this is indeed true, though partial.

It seems clear, and is currently being emphasized by scholars, that Jesus' understanding of his mission *developed* during the period of his ministry; not only did he come to extend the horizons of his mission beyond the House of Israel and to the ends of the earth but, by virtue of encounter with persons and with needs, he was changed, modified, and we might legitimately say, converted. And if this seems a rather strange notion to attribute to Jesus, perhaps it is worth an excursion by way of explanation.

Like all of us, Jesus was socialized. He was raised in a particular social, religious, and geographic context, and imbued with certain values and a sense of self. Jesus came to learn who he was, not simply as a Divine Person but as a human being. He discovered his limits (physical, emotional, even spiritual: from the desert to Gethsemane), and he was able to foresee some of his needs (for rest, food, companionship, affirmation). He knew who he was in relation to others (male, Jewish, compelling); he also knew that he was "unattached" (unmarried, having nowhere to lay his head, familiar with moving around). But crucially, Jesus had a sense of himself, his autonomy, his boundaries, his likes and dislikes. And *then* he was assailed by all, had his privacy invaded, was challenged (especially and critically, by women: the Syro-phoenician woman, the Samaritan woman at the well, the Marys), and was pulled, pushed, and invited to cross his boundaries.

It seems that we can discern exactly how and when Jesus was "missionary" as we look at the Gospel accounts. Every time he comes up against his personal boundaries, prejudices, comforts, or expectations, and transcends or penetrates those boundaries (sometimes with the help of personal resources, sometimes by virtue of the support or encouragement of others), Jesus is in mission: propelled, moved, sent, in the service of the Realm of God (Lk 4:18). His "pastoral" response causes him to reach out, to be pushed or pulled, to risk, to encounter. His "mission" is not defined by geographical criteria but by his existential response. And that response leads, both personally and in terms of his plans, to his conversion or transformation.

In chapter 8 of the Gospel of Luke we have a catalogue of examples: the Gerasene demoniac who called Jesus to a frightening encounter; Jairus, whom Jesus himself followed (an interesting reversal, this); and the woman with a hemorrhage who showed Jesus an unexpected faith and edified him greatly. But this is merely a chapter at random. The gospels are filled with examples of Jesus being stretched and called, and reaching out in response, very often in surprise and amazement at what he finds.

But equally we see Jesus leading and facilitating others in their own participation of the mission of God. In chapter 10 of the Gospel of Mark we can contrast the rich young man and Bartimaeus. In both cases they encounter Jesus. In both cases they are aware of some of their own limitations, their boundaries. But the rich young man is not able or willing to transcend, to risk, to go beyond, to follow. Jesus does indeed call, saying "Go . . . ; then come, follow me." But he goes away sad, perhaps because he wants simple rules and definitions, and Jesus offers nothing simple and does not put definitions around boundless love. Yet blind Bartimaeus, with only his cloak to hide his nakedness, jumps up, unafraid and gloriously unencumbered, and literally bounds toward Jesus in response to the call! Bartimaeus is commended for his faith, his willingness to risk, his transcending of boundaries. Jesus "co-missions" him, "go!" And immediately he follows Jesus along the road, transformed.

To go far from home, however, is not yet to be engaged in mission; to move to the margins and over the edge of one's own familiar world in the name of the Gospel and the Realm of God is. Sometimes, in going far away, we go like tortoises, taking our house and home (prejudices and blinkers) with us. But if we can identify our narrowness, our pettiness, our limitations, and our boundaries, and if we can break through them and into the world of others, we are truly on the verge of mission.

This is not easy, and rarely comes spontaneously. We are narrow-minded, insular, complacent, ethnocentric, in varying degrees and for relatively good reason. If we were not, we might not actually *have* any perceptible boundaries! But if we come to *recognize* our limits (boundaries), often with the help of other people who cause us to compare our own untested ideas of the world with their slightly or radically different ideas, then we are in principle able to negotiate those boundaries and the people we meet there. Consequently, unless we are adequately socialized in such a way that we have a fairly well-rooted idea of who and what we are as autonomous, self-reflecting persons and as interdependent, socially responsible beings — in other words, possessed of the kind of boundaries that provide us with a *person*-ality and a *social* identity — then we are not yet capable of the kind of outreach or boundary-breaking that presupposes our having real boundaries to cross![6]

Mission, then, leads us to encounters on the margins and not at the centers, in unhabituated places rather than by familiar landmarks. It is where our personal space or territory or turf is opened up to others, and where others invite us into their own world. For Jesus, it happens at the water's edge, in graveyards, in deserted places, by a well, at a bedside or a tomb, up a mountain, in a dark garden, on a cross; it is manifest in the breaking of bread, at a supper, a breakfast, with a hungry crowd, at a marriage feast, and in myriad spontaneous and surprising encounters.

For ourselves, too, mission is impossible without movement and change, but changes happen as much in our perceptions and agenda as across tracts of land or trackless oceans. Mission has a centrifugal momentum, calling us to true availability to others and genuine readiness to compromise our comfort and to modify our manner of life — calling us to transformation.

In short, mission is impossible unless it is also a careful and sensitive response to the real needs of the other. But who determines these needs in such a way as to avoid paternalism?

CHANGING MISSIONARY STYLES

Jesus, our exemplar, is pushed and pulled through boundaries and magnetized by margins. He goes where he does not particularly want to go but knows he must; he does not presume dogmatically to tell people what they need, but actually asks them; he allows his agenda to be modified according to the needs of the people. As a result, his time is not his own and he must struggle to retain his space, privacy, and energy in the face of a demanding ministry. For him, availability and a willingness to go beyond are quite compatible with nurturing his own physical and spiritual needs and knowing when he is stretched too thin (Mk 1:35-36,45; 6:31-32; 46-47; 7:24b; 8:13; and on and on).

Such readiness to take people very seriously and to acknowledge the presence of God in their lives long before our own is what characterizes "mission in reverse,"[7] a way of carrying out our missionary mandate respectfully and with mutuality. But this style is possible only when the missionary is deeply convinced that he or she does not know all the answers, has not yet arrived, and cannot exemplify the spirit of Jesus in a vacuum (that is, without reference to the local context and local understanding, which initially, at least, are unknown). It is predicated on the twin facts that the missionary must be ministered to, as Jesus was ministered to,[8] and that no one is outside the loving embrace of God.

Assuming that we move ourselves from the most central position (in terms of power, privilege, or access to truth) and situate ourselves at the margins of our own familiar world (testing familiar limits and pushing through some of our boundaries), we have still not encountered others; to do so we must be *met* by those who are to be found there. Jesus was sent to the "lost sheep," but in order to find them he had to leave the centers and discover where the lost were to be found. To encounter those who were marginalized, Jesus had to go to the margins: in fact, to become marginalized himself. If one wishes to engage those away from the centers — the "eccentric" — one must risk becoming, and indeed become, somewhat eccentric oneself!

Yet such are the pendulum swings that we can only too easily respond to one imbalance in our lives by going to the other extreme, thus creating another. Somehow we must make *appropriate* corrections, and not simply wild shifts. If we were gently to lay down our familiar role of givers, we might allow ourselves to take up that of receivers. This would be an improvement, because insistent givers lack graciousness and may come to be hated as much as they are depended upon. But true relationships are based on reciprocal giving and receiving, that is to say, on sharing. Even God's gifts are vain unless someone receives them. And the person who has absolutely nothing to give — not even gratitude, acceptance, warmth — is lacking a fundamentally human quality. Here are some suggested transformations:

• If we have tended to lord it over people, to indulge in rather grandiose behavior ("magistry": from which are derived "magisterium," "mastery," and "maxi-"), then the antithesis would be to become of no account, virtually insignificant: ("ministry" in this sense would imply the very opposite of "magistry," as "mini-" is contrasted with "maxi-"). But a truly *collaborative* missionary relationship would produce service in the spirit of Jesus. And the ministry of service includes the church's magisterium or official teaching function and is as characterized by non-judgmental healing care as by the serious exercise of authority.

• If we have set store by our authority, which may have degenerated into a rather less modest exercise of power ("authority" is sometimes defined as the legitimate and legitimated exercise of power, while "power" itself is understood as the simple ability to achieve certain ends, often by fear or force or other forms of suasion), we may have to undertake to become rather more vulnerable. Vulnerability—the ability to be wounded—implies the removal of fortifications and armor. Yet vulnerability is insufficient if it is spineless and abject; what is needed is trust, as Jesus frequently reminded people.

• If we have seized and held initiatives in mission, a simple reversal would be to yield, to become passive. This would merely be to move from an active to a reactive stance, and would fail to demonstrate the ability to engage in teamwork for the building up of the community of faith. For that, there must be a conscious move toward mutuality, which would balance the taking of initiatives with the production of responses, treating both as signs of discipleship and ministry, and learning to respect the integrity and talents of others.

• If we have seen ourselves as equipped to judge others by virtue of our moral insights, but have lately heard Jesus who says "judge not," then we might be inclined to tolerate everything, make values and virtue relative, and become uncritically indulgent. Not only would we become anything but peaceful, however, but we would also fail to produce one of the essential fruits of mission: the challenge it offers to other people and other cultures. Just as other people and other cultures issue challenges to missionaries, so must missionaries enunciate the challenge of the Gospel. To do any less is to fail to be missionary. Yet since the missionary is not personally the judge of persons or cultures, the challenge of mission is something to be discerned, both by the missionary and by local people.[9]

• If we sense that we have spoken too much, we may now fall silent. But out of context, silence is no closer to real communication than is monologue. Dialogue, born of mutual respect, mutual words, mutual listening, and mutual silences, is the fruit of "mission in reverse."

• If we have been purveyors of a religion that is doctrinaire, systematic, legalistic, and arid, we may be tempted to subvert previous efforts and offer a bland and empty fare—of generalities, opinions, and novelty—flimsily held together by what some may call respect, or even love. This may be a form of naturalism, in the sense of accepting whatever the people do and appear to have done from time immemorial as unquestionably the best thing for them. But Jesus came neither with religion nor with tepid doctrine; the church of Laodicea is condemned for lukewarmness (Rv 3:15-16). No, Jesus brought revelation that is unconstrained, open, awesome, and fertile.[10] The missionary, in the spirit of Jesus, is the propagator of that same revelation, of and from God.

• If we came with our certainties and they were abrasive and insensitive, then what good if we return with nothing but our doubts? We may feel more honest and open, but confusion as well as certainties needs to be shared, offered, discussed, and discerned. "Mission in reverse" will teach us how to be involved in mission-as-discovery; we will acknowledge that doubts and certainties co-exist, both in "us" and in "them," and are expressions of the gifts we bear and exchange.

• If, finally, we once thought of ourselves as bringing conversion to others and making them into a people of God, we may have moved to a kind of laisser faire individualism; we now expect God to take care of the niceties of other people's consciences without ourselves being committed to church growth. We may also have the wisdom now to know of our own need of conversion and of the presence of God among all people. But such knowledge is not enough because it does not betoken mutuality or community. "Mission in reverse" will lead us to a new creation: a People of God united in a community called church, but also a pilgrim people together on a journey that leads to the Realm (Kingdom) of God.

Here is a tabulation of the previous considerations, and a partial indication of a movement from thesis to antithesis to synthesis, or from action to reaction to integration, to what could yet become:

THESIS	ANTITHESIS	SYNTHESIS
(action)	(reaction)	(integration)
Central	Marginal	Eccentric
Giver	Receiver	Sharer
Magisterial	Ministerial	Serving
Powerful	Vulnerable	Trusting
Initiative	Response	Mutuality
Judgmental	Indulgent	Challenging
Monological	Silent	Dialogical
Religion	Naturalism	Revelation
Certainty	Confusion	Discovery
Converting	Individualism	Church/Realm

THEMES AND VARIATIONS

A response to the challenge of contemporary mission in the contemporary world requires a range of attitudes and tactics, and will certainly bring in its train a number of theoretical and practical problems. The philosophical axiom "whoever wills the end, wills the means to the end" tells us to accept the challenge, noting the means appropriate to the end in an orderly if not in a perfectly systematic way. The latter qualification is necessary, partly because there is no obvious "system" for something as open-ended as the missionary enterprise, and partly because there are many degrees of overlap in the areas we need to consider. Yet that should not preclude orderliness. It is quite possible to be thematic while acknowledging that the themes should dovetail and strengthen each other. For the purposes of structuring this book, there are three particular themes, on which a number of variations will be played: spirituality, eucharist, and transformation.

Spirituality

Though the word "spirituality" turns out to have had a rather checkered and ambiguous history,[11] there is a growing consensus about its meaning and importance. Notwithstanding the distaste in which the term has been held by some,[12] it appears to be a perfectly good word if certain denotations are declared and certain connotations clarified. As nominally distinct from the discipline of theology, though clearly part of it, spirituality may be understood as concerned with practice rather than theory, life rather than law, embodied faith rather than intellectual belief, and experience rather than academic knowledge. Spirituality in this sense refers to a way of responding to a message, a truth, a person, a theophany. Crucial to such spirituality is that it be sensitive to context; therefore, as contexts vary and as people move from one context to another, there may be modifications in the spirituality, in its style or expression. This has not only not been acknowledged by some people, but the implications across cultures and over time appear to have been inadequately discussed.

If spirituality is about specific, personal appropriations and understandings of the reality and relevance of God in one's life, and if it is manifest in the activity or lifestyle that this generates, then gender, sex, age, health, intelligence, education, qualifications, and many other contingent realities matter very much indeed. One's spirituality can be as unique as different people are unique, yet as identifiably Christian as myriad people are identifiably human. According to changes in personal circumstances, and as persons of different circumstances encounter each other, it should also follow that spiritualities change. If they do not, then people remain fixed; but to be fixed is to be dead, or without life. It would be as harmful not to adapt or change our spirituality — our style of being in the world with God and others — as to refuse to change or modify our clothing over a lifetime. Such intransigence would be as stunting to our spiritual growth as exposure to every breeze or wind of spiritual fashion would be ultimately destructive.

We must be concerned to ask how we Christians and missionaries can and need to create, develop, and modify our spirituality so that it becomes and remains appropriate to the movement in our lives. But it will also be important to suggest how we might avoid plowing lonely furrows and instead weave some common themes as we journey. There will be much to discuss and many issues to raise.

Eucharist

For all Christians eucharist is critical; it provokes a crisis of sorts. For some it is revered as the center and the summit of Christian life,[13] though to others these are empty and even cynical words. For others again, it is seen as so special or surpassing as to be a rarity, inaccessible to many. It is hardly a center, and if a summit it is out of contact with life in the valleys.

Some have experienced eucharist as a casualty of denominational battles, marginalized or even put in storage. But for all, without exception, the issue of the presence, availability, significance, and appropriateness of the eucharist remains alive and unsatisfactorily addressed, whether in terms of ecumenism or in terms of the needs of local communities. We must be concerned, as loyal and committed Christians, not to say hungry ones, to raise some critical questions relative to the eucharist in the life of the contemporary church throughout the world. That task will be undertaken in a central section of this book.

Transformation

Change is not only a defining characteristic of life but part of Christian theology. We, individuals and community, are in the process of becoming. We anticipate being gathered up into everlasting life. We are called to *metanoia*, to a continuous purification and conversion of heart. These are different ways of stating that transformation is and must be part of human and part of specifically *Christian* life. In the following pages we must address questions such as: What does transformation imply? How can it be undertaken? If transformation is intrinsic to our lives, how can we formulate more or less fixed plans? Who is the agent of transformation? What is the difference between change that produces transformation and change that produces flux or instability? What does Jesus show us about transformation that can nourish our spirituality and missionary approaches?

In the next chapter we will attempt to bring all three themes—spirituality, eucharist, and transformation—into a single framework before looking at them individually in subsequent chapters.

BINARY MENTALITY, CREATIVITY, AND MISSION

On a number of occasions we have alluded to a mentality that constitutes a threat both to the missionary enterprise and to the persuasiveness of the good news. This is a constraining dualism, a binary mode of thinking that confuses the way we think about things and the way things actually are. Because this is pervasive and subtle, it is worth our trying to clarify such a mentality.

Black and white, good and bad, up and down: these are undoubtedly helpful categories for our thinking. Philosophically, such "contradictories" help us separate, cluster, mark, and remember. That some things are black and others white is as true as that some are up and others down. Our problem is twofold. First, in the real world not everything is absolutely a member of one or other class: zebras are *both* black and white, while flamingoes are *neither*. Secondly, a particular perspective will have a constraining effect on the assessment one makes: to a person on the twentieth floor, the tenth floor is a long way down; to someone on the ground, it is a long way up. The problem therefore is caused by our believing that the way *we* think is a faithful reflection of the way the world actually is. Once we go into other people's worlds, the problem can become enormous.

Some people are excited by ambiguity, inclusiveness, and multiple meanings; others are appalled or threatened. To some, things that are different can nevertheless be good and beautiful. To other people, if beauty or truth or goodness is identified with a particular thing or person, then all other things or persons which are not identical are not good or beautiful or truthful. To some, there is a world of possibilities beyond themselves; to others, the world beyond must be directly challenged and, if different, changed. It is almost impossible for some of us to question the validity of our perceptions and our truth.

Such a projection from our ways of thinking onto the objective universe is what I will call a "binary mentality" operating in a "binary universe" (notwithstanding the fact that binary thinking is, of itself, a splendid heuristic device or intellectual aid). In a binary universe there is, as sure as stars and as real as rocks, right and wrong, light and darkness, truth and falsehood, wisdom and foolishness, and, of course, us and them. It is virtually impossible in such a universe to imagine that anything different from our perceptions and judgments could have much, or any, value. Add that some of "us" are specially trained, mandated, and sent to "them," and it follows that "we" will take ourselves very seriously indeed. That might in practice mean that we take "them" rather lightly. We will consider ourselves, quite understandably, as entrusted with riches, insights, and solutions; by comparison, "they" will appear, through no fault of their own, as rather impoverished, dull, and incompetent.

Such is life in a binary world! And there are many missionaries and prospective missionaries who are its citizens! But as Wilkie Au reminds us in the epigraph to this chapter: "Faith does not transport us to a magical city, but enables us to appreciate the significance of what we find at home"; unless, in faith, we make some discoveries "at home," we are unlikely to make them elsewhere. Yet even at our most open-minded we remain attached to our worldview; in our prejudice we can be imprisoned in it. We must seek to be set free so that we can wear our worldview and be attached to our ways of thinking as easily as we wear our clothing and are attached to our hair; we are not defined by them, much less can we define other people by them!

One of the ways to liberation from the prison of narrow thinking and inappropriate judging is through "mission in reverse"; this we will consider explicitly in Chapter 4. A further way is by virtue of our own conversion or transformation; this is the work of the Spirit, and with our cooperation it will take a lifetime. But we will revisit this theme fairly frequently.

LIFE AS JOURNEY

"The Pilgrim's Progress" is not only the title of one of Western Christianity's most influential tracts, but gives words to an enduring image: that of the traveler, the person on a journey, the pilgrim. The epigraphs to this chapter also suggest a special value in pilgrimages and exploration, for those who recognize the significance. The disciples on the road to Emmaus were partially unfulfilled pilgrims—until they recognized Jesus in the breaking of bread. We too are embarked on journeys of exploration, and we hope to be pilgrims. But where is the bread we break? What kind of bread is it? With whom, and at whose behest do we break it? Does it nourish? And in the breaking of the bread, do we recognize Jesus, or only our own hunger and dissatisfaction?

In keeping with the title of this book and the motif of traveler and nourishment, we will have occasion to ponder the nature of the pilgrimage the missionary undertakes, and the company he or she keeps, avoids, and seeks. And we will look at the food which sustains the missionary, asking whether it is appropriate, life-giving, God-given food. We will need to ask whence it comes and for whom it is intended, whether it is recognizably and authentically "fruit of the earth and work of human hands," scarce or abundant, shared or hoarded. We will need to know to whom it belongs, who provides it, and who may receive and share and be fed on it—and who may not.

So, as we proceed, we will attempt to gather themes together, discuss issues, and try to discern the Lord Jesus in the bread broken in our lives and on the journeys we undertake, bringing good news of peace.

QUESTIONS FOR THE ROAD

- What evidence do you have to justify a modification of the role of missionaries over time? What evidence do you have that indicates that there has been or is such a modification? Are you encouraged by the evidence?
- Do you think discipleship is subject to change? What are the implications of your response for missiology and evangelization?
- How necessary do you think missionaries are?
- Do you find it helpful to consider your own missionary response as a journey, a pilgrimage, or an exploration? How tolerant are you of the unknown, the unexpected, and things outside your control?

Chapter 2

Spirituality, Eucharist, Transformation

Spirituality is the style of a person's response to Christ, before the challenge of everyday life, in a given historical and cultural moment.[1]

The best way to understand "conversion" is to examine the practices brought to bear on a person in order to effect fundamental change. . . . Baptized Christians [said Augustine] become themselves the eucharistic bread. . . . "You are what you have received." . . . The initiate was at once food and eater, eating the body of Christ and, by eating, becoming that body.[2]

[By 300 A.D.] the identity between the gospel and the world it transformed provided one of the finest illustrations of the work of consummation wrought by Christianity, and so genuine was this transformation that it appeared as a natural extension of the life of the church.[3]

Christian expansion is serial. It produces successive transformations of culture. The cross-cultural momentum is essential to Christianity.[4]

THE CONTEMPORARY WORLD AND EVERYDAY LIFE

It may be unremarkable nowadays to claim that the challenges of everyday life determine and describe our spirituality, but it is certainly not self-evident. In other times such challenges were avoided or denied by many on the journey of discipleship. *Fuga mundi*—flight from the world—is a convincing response for dualists, those with a binary mentality, and particularly those who expect an imminent end to the world. But today at least, *engagement with the world* is a hallmark of the missioner, and the incarnate God is perceived more as one who suffers alongside others than as a triumphant king who rules over them. But still we ask: what kind of engagement? which world? And we want to know how missioners can maintain a

19

counter-cultural witness to transcendent values if they stray too close to the consuming flame. The issue of identification of and with the poor is sometimes a semantic conundrum or an intellectual exercise that produces multiple incompatible answers.

Some quote the Letter of James, which maintains that "pure, unspoilt religion is keeping oneself uncontaminated by the world" (Jas 1:27); the fourth Gospel is invoked by others, wishing to distance themselves physically as well as spiritually from the world (Jn 17:14-16). Yet there remains tension between being "in" and being "of" the world, and between the "world" created by God and the "world" that Jesus has overcome (Jn 15:19; 16:33; 17:6,15). So long as there are different people, perspectives, and emphases, texts will be invoked and will yield mutually conflicting results, justifications, or explanations for behavior.

The church used to see itself and be seen as a ship on a trackless sea rescuing all and sundry. According to such a simile, "out of" (water or world) stood in sharp contrast with "into" (ship or church); in a world of opposites and exclusiveness it was a powerful image of salvation. A shift in the simile—to church as sign, light, leaven, community—might bring with it a movement to complementarity or inclusiveness—or some uneasy tension might remain. But in a contemporary world in which many metaphors co-exist and tensions abound, it is hardly surprising that when one attempts to speak about cross-cultural mission or interreligious dialogue, the conversation is anything but relaxed. Respect for a strongly traditional reading of the Great Commission (Matt 28:19-20) sits uneasily with respect for cultures and the autonomy of conscience. And the kindness of a loving God would seem to be quite incompatible with a deity who punishes all who are not members of the church—particularly when we recall that less than one person in three, worldwide, is a Christian. Where the church, or parts of it, may move in the future depends very largely on present attitudes and viewpoints. Here are three hypothetical ecclesiastical perspectives, each with its attendant view of liturgical forms:

—A "universal" church, committed to *universalization* (mission outreach, evangelism, church building, emphasizing the maintenance of unity-by-similarity) will presumably promote *standardized liturgical forms* and judge them to have a relevance, and perhaps an appeal, which is supra-cultural and supra-local, that is, not (able to be) limited by culture or place. In practice there will be disregard for, or a de-emphasis on the particularities of local cultures or persons, including their spirituality.

—A "local" church, committed to *localization* (pastoral maintenance, catechesis, development, and perhaps church building by extension, emphasizing the maintenance of unity-by-diversity) will presumably promote *contextualized liturgical forms* and judge them to have a relevance, and surely an appeal, which is presumably intra-cultural and intra-local, that is, directly related to a given culture or place. In practice there will be regard for and an emphasis upon the particularities of local cultures and persons, including their spirituality.

—A church that claims and strives to be both "universal" *and* "local" in outreach and relevance will presumably be pulled by tensions and subject to ambiguities. This will give rise to *volatile liturgical forms* with more or less convincing claims to relevance and appeal, and equally strong counter-claims. In practice there is likely to be confusion, disagreement, and both reactionary and liberal manifestations of spirituality, worship, and ap-proaches to change or transformation.

The final example will be familiar to cross-cultural missioners, either in the place to which they go, the place from which they come, places in between, or all of the above! The familiarity is not merely bookish, but an experiential and enervating intimacy; it can sap our strength and assault our hope for the church and for the Realm of God. Yet, so powerful is the great whirlwind in the church of Jesus Christ and the community of believ-ers, that far from expecting to reduce the effect of these forces and achieve the peaceful tranquillity of a windless day, we must rather learn to under-stand turbulence and vortices, to respect and even harness some of their power.

But this is only the beginning. Since "mission" is not a spectator sport we must also be prepared to walk on the waters ourselves! (Matt 14:29). The committed missioner, more than anyone, should be engaged with the vicissitudes of life, not attempting to avoid them or imagining the elements can be tamed, but dedicated to the transformation of all things in Christ. At the same time missioners must cultivate resilience and flexibility, or else we will find survival impossible. A tall order indeed, especially for earthen vessels like ourselves, but we can take heart, as Paul did, from the fact that the "overwhelming power comes from God and not from ourselves. . . . We see no answers to our problems but never despair. . . . But as we have the same spirit of faith that is mentioned in scripture, . . . we too believe and therefore we too speak" (2 Cor 4:8,13).

THE PROBLEM OF CHANGE

Change is a delicate problem for every human institution. If a plan is good, why change it? If faulty, perhaps the institution itself is failing. For the church the tension often appears particularly painful. Fidelity to tra-dition, to Jesus, and to its own commitments would all seem to point in the direction of continuity, and of resistance to change, but responsiveness to the cries of the poor, to the open-endedness of Jesus' challenge, and to justice clearly point to the need for adaptability and change. The point is exquisitely made in the Gospel of John (Luke 5:4-10 has a rather different emphasis); having reached his lowest ebb two days after the crucifixion of his leader, Peter seems to have given up, but as if to persuade himself that there was at least one thing he could do right, he announced: "I'm going fishing" (Jn 21:2-6). Not only did the professional fisherman fail abjectly—as he seemed to have failed at everything else—but his failure was public, evident to the six others in the boat! It was the *stranger* who made the suggestion, offered the challenge, proposed a different plan; to a depressed "man's man," it must have been so difficult to be gracious, so tempting to belittle the stranger, to posture and prove himself! The reward was not only a wonderful catch but the rehabilitation of Peter and the abiding lesson to the community—that strangers are not uniformly ignorant or selfish!

Why does change have such threatening and negative connotations to people of faith? Is it because our faith is weak, because we cling to the idea of changeless truth and a changeless universe and have even made for ourselves an image of a changeless God? If our mission tactics are founded not on the rock which is Jesus but on castles of shifting sand, then however well codified our propositions and finely wrought our theological axioms, such tactics will produce nothing that will last. If we carry only the instruments and defenses associated with battles fought long ago and positions unwisely held, it will be difficult to escape being crushed by the weight of our own impedimenta, and impossible openhandedly to accept gifts and new resources; an embrace is only possible when arms are opened, or laid down.

The question of how to resolve some of these problems without reneging on the Gospel or on Jesus is as old as the church. Academic theology has no salvific power and casts no spells. What is needed is conversion, transformation of the individual. Here is a Reform theologian from Germany, writing at the dawn of the seventeenth century:

> Many think that *theology* is a mere science, or rhetoric, whereas it *is a living experience and practice*. Everyone now endeavors to be eminent and distinguished in the world, but no one is willing to *learn to be pious*. ... Everyone wishes very much to be a servant of Christ, but no one wishes to be his follower. [But] a true servant ... must be Christ's follower. [Those who] love Christ will also love the example of his holy life, his humility, meekness, patience, shame, and contempt, even if the flesh suffers pain. It is now the desire of the world to know all things, but that which is better than all knowledge, namely to know the love of Christ (Eph 3:19), no one desires to learn.[5]

Four centuries have not dulled the force of this reminder. In a cogent and inspiring description, Gustavo Gutiérrez offers a contemporary paraphrase and a positive approach to the spiritual possibilities of change. Like Arndt he asserts that many Christians are "intent on domesticating the Good News," and that a certain kind of traditional theology has failed to produce

> the categories necessary ... to respond creatively to the new demands of the Gospel. ... But theological categories are not enough. We need

a vital attitude, all-embracing and synthesizing, informing the totality as well as every detail of our lives; we need a spirituality. . . . A spirituality is a concrete manner, inspired by the Spirit, of living the Gospel. . . . It arises from an intense spiritual experience. . . . A spirituality means a reordering of the great axes of the Christian life in terms of the contemporary experience. . . . [T]his reordering brings about . . . a conver[sion] into life, prayer, commitment, and action.[6]

There is great wisdom in this message which also draws together the strands of spirituality, eucharist ("prayer"), and transformation ("conversion") for our weaving. The passage is as realistic as it is idealistic, and as with Gutiérrez' other writings, leaves us in no doubt about the pain and the cost of the conversion necessary to bring about the required change. But the point is critical, especially for those attempting to live their missionary vocation today: intellectual knowledge without personal transformation is vain. In the encyclical of John Paul II on the church's missionary activity, we also find inspirational passages, yet they sometimes gloss over or seem not to recognize the implications of what they say:

Inculturation means the intimate transformation of authentic cultural values through their integration in Christianity and the insertion of Christianity in the various human cultures. The process involves the Christian message and also the church's reflection and practice. . . . Through inculturation the church becomes a more intelligible sign of what she is, and a more effective instrument of mission. . . . Mission[ers] must move beyond their own cultural limitations. It is not a matter of renouncing their own cultural identity, but of understanding, appreciating, fostering and evangelizing the culture of the environment in which they are working, and therefore of equipping themselves to communicate effectively with it, adopting a manner of living which is a sign of Gospel witness and of solidarity with the people (*Redemptoris Missio*, 52-53).

But for all the value of such passages, and for all their acknowledgment of change, they consistently betray a bias in favor of "the church" and of "Gospel values" that effectively indicates that change must occur preeminently in local cultures and people, only somewhat in the missioner, and not at all in the church. Unintentional though this may be, it is dangerous. It is something we must confront (see Chapter 4), because it threatens true dialogue. Nor do such inspirational words give much practical indication of how inculturation can occur, while between the lines runs a thread of caution and universalism that is sometimes close to (Roman/Latin Rite) monoculturalism. Small wonder, then, if missioners "no longer know what the church expects of them" as the encyclical notes (para. 65).

CHANGE AND CONTINUITY FOR MISSIONERS

If God universally calls and invites to conversion, then the church and missioners are not exempt. And unless we ourselves are committed to the kind of dialogue that is open to changing the hearts of all parties, evangelism is no better than proselytism. Walter Hollenweger writes:

> Evangelization is *martyria*. That does not mean primarily the risking of possessions and life, but rather that the evangelist gambles, as it were, with his understanding of belief in the course of evangelizing. He, so to speak, submits his understanding of the world and of God and of his faith to the test of dialogue. He has no guarantee that his understanding of faith will emerge unaltered from that dialogue. On the contrary. How can anyone expect that the person who is listening to him should be ready in principle to change his life and way of thinking if he, the evangelist, is not notionally prepared to submit to the same discipline?[7]

This is rather different from an approach to interreligious dialogue that begins from the premise that I am right and you are wrong! The world of Jesus is far from a crude binary world; in his world dialogue leads to surprises and transformation. Surely, if we are to approach dialogue with this degree of risk, our whole spirituality must be involved. As Gutiérrez says, it

> will center on a conversion to the neighbor. Our conversion to the Lord implies this conversion to the neighbor. . . . Conversion means a radical transformation of our selves; it means thinking, feeling, living as Christ.[8]

Transformation *of* ourselves is not transformation *by* ourselves; it is not a private but a public act, not social but religious in the deepest sense. Such transformation is only possible to risk-takers, the trusting, those who— as Peter almost did—are committed to doing the impossible, walking on the water (Matt 14:22ff). "Courage!" says Jesus to the cowardly. "Do not be afraid!" he says to the fearful. "Come!" he says to the uncommitted. The transformation to which Jesus calls is a process in which we redefine and even transcend some previous limits.

For many Christians personal spirituality was formed long ago, along with knowledge of history or of how to drive an automobile, and it was expected to last a lifetime. Consequently little has changed over the years, except perhaps some unadmitted forgetfulness about aims, a certain blurring of focus as eyes grow dimmer, and a natural sluggishness of response. But spirituality is *not* like history or kinesthetic skills; nor, to shift the image, can we compare it to a comfortable pair of old shoes or a favored article of old clothing. Unless spirituality is *embodied in the actual person we are now*, and unless it constantly challenges us as Jesus challenged Peter to leave the boat, we shall either remain petrified or sink under the weight of our encumbrances.

It seems especially winsome and significant that (again in the Gospel of John, not of Luke) when Peter finally began to understand, he was again in a boat and did indeed jump into the water (Jn 21:4ff). But he still had to cover his nakedness, and he probably swam rather than walked! Yet blind Bartimaeus had no need of such false modesty; he threw off the cloak that might have impeded him and, thus free, stumbled blindly and trustingly to Jesus (Mk 10:50). Perhaps the evangelist who records this later episode also recalled the irony and shame of a moment when his own nakedness was uncovered as he ran *away from* Jesus (Mk 14:51)?

If nakedness is a helpful image for thinking about spirituality, it must be truthful and wholesome, wrinkles and all, not meretricious nudity hiding all imperfections. We might think of our spirituality as the clothes we wear to cover our nakedness, but even better perhaps is the image of spirituality as the person we are when we dare to cast off the disguises, cloaks, masks, or fripperies, and stand in broken integrity and humble pride before God. And we may recognize too that there are different times, places, and points on our life's journey and in our own conversion or transformation. Life *is* change; nothing remains the same.

If we are afraid or ashamed of our bodies, careless toward or disrespectful of them, or besotted by changing fashions, we will never experience a spirituality that will be both transformative of ourselves and a signpost to the Realm of God. Some of us continue to be inscrutable to many of the people among whom we live and work due to a certain ambivalence toward bodies and embodiment: our own and others'. It is not surprising if we do not attract people by what we say, if our body language is joyless and unnatural! As missioners we must engage the issue of an embodied spirituality (see Chapter 3).

Authors speak about God's stripping us, the better to reach and deal with us. But the metaphor seems crude and violent; this is not the approach of a loving parent, and in a world where abuse is rife it has little to recommend it. Rather, ours is a God before whom we can come to stand *as we are*: called, chosen, redeemed, yet not finished, not yet gathered up, "already" and "not yet." For many Christians, reared in a binary world and imbued with a Manichaean hatred of or ambivalence toward "the flesh,"[9] nakedness is not a helpful image for personal spirituality. But in the world of Jesus, where realities and not appearances are important (Matt 23:25-28; Mk 7:14-23), purity and epidermis are compatible, and wrinkles and respectability are friends.

EUCHARIST, TRANSFORMER OF SPIRITUALITY

If spirituality is to be suited to persons and their contexts; if it is to adapt and respond to the transforming grace of God; and if it is to sustain us on our own journey and project beyond ourselves a reflection of Christ's light as well as to provide us with strength for lifting the burdens of others, then it must be intimately connected both to Jesus and to the community of believers. Otherwise it will become privatized, self-focused, and will wither. This brings us to the images embedded in our scriptures: the vine and branches, the shepherd and sheep, the master and servants, the loving father of the prodigal son. But by far the best and most central connection for the Christian, partially developed in the scriptures but institutionalized by the living church, is the eucharist.

The memorial (*anamnesis*) of Christ's sacrifice (a gift, a meal, and a lesson about love and loyalty, justice and joyousness), the eucharistic feast has become for many a famine and a scandal. The preeminent sign of nourishment and unity for Christians and to the world, the eucharist is currently the focus of embarrassment, division, and dissension as much as it is a beacon of light and a standard-bearer of justice. Here are four simple and limited stereotypes.

— For some, the eucharist seems to have been *domesticated* in the Mass, where pious and elderly (this is a stereotype!) gather like hummingbirds around the nectar, hovering in their own space, charming and harmless, effortlessly sustained, and apparently unrelated to a wider world of hunger, homelessness, and hostilities. Unless challenged and motivated to discover an appropriate response by extending their boundaries, they will quietly die.

— For people in fragile Christian communities amid war, famine, and poverty, the eucharist is a *foreign* import, controlled by foreigners who rarely visit. When they do they bring their own bread and wine and their own words and gestures, while the people observe distantly. Unless a Christian community deemed responsible enough to receive baptism is also given the right to its own eucharistic liturgy,[10] it will neither develop as a mature community nor be able to undertake mission itself.

— For others again, the eucharist is a crossroads under fire, where a privileged, male, hierarchical church, with its munitions and *matériel* of complacency, arrogance, and power, has taken the high ground and commands a wide angle of approach. It may issue invitations to those below to come into the open, but a wounded, anguished, and somewhat disarrayed company, convinced it has been betrayed and misled, cannot avoid being self-conscious and angry. If commanders and conscripts are to achieve unity, let alone celebrate eucharist, radical transformation is required.[11]

— And there are still more situations: like that in which the eucharist, spoken of as the preeminent sign of unity and peace, is held as a prized possession by groups claiming loyalty to Jesus yet not able to share and sometimes not able to respect each other. They are united by one faith and divided by the same eucharist. Until many more Christians are prepared not to rest until the scandals associated with the eucharist are addressed and resolved, the transformation of which it is capable and which the world sorely needs will be postponed.

Before the contemporary "problem" of the eucharist can be resolved it must be recognized as such. This is where a "missionary" perspective is so helpful. As people push through their boundaries and remove the blinkers of their own ethnocentrism, they will be more able to respect, if not to empathize with, the views of others and the realities of their lives. Furthermore, they will become sensitive to rampant inequity and injustice. The following chapters will explore some such perspectives, but will start from the belief that half a millennium is long enough for a disagreement and that cultures not initially rent by schism should not have to repeat the history of those who were.

In much of the church not only is the eucharist as "summit and center of the Christian life" a scandalous misnomer, but its status and reception by the faithful are in urgent need of reexamination, especially for those who presume to bring good news of peace to an uneasy world. The professed aim of mission is, after all, to invite people to become incorporated into the one body of Christ; but, setting forth without bread of their own (Mk 6:8), they will perish unless sustained by bread for the journey. The centrality of eucharist (not simply of "the Mass") as the real and actual— not just the theoretical—focal point of the Christian life is an issue to preoccupy us.

One further concern is the relationship between our spirituality and the eucharist in our lives. Either we have a eucharistic spirituality or we do not. If not, by design or deprivation, then it would seem to be a major departure both from where Jesus asks us to be and from where the church tells us we are! But if we do, how does it direct our lives in mission and permit our continuous growth and resilience? There seems to be a reciprocity between Christian spirituality and the eucharist: if we take Jesus' words and intentions seriously, spirituality without eucharist must produce malnourishment[12]; and eucharist without spirituality would be at best formalism and at worst superstition. The key to opening up both spirituality and the eucharist is transformation.

TRANSFORMATION: A PRINCIPLE FOR CONTINUITY AND CHANGE

Transformation, in both common and technical usage, is a central thread of this book. Technically, though, it can appear intimidating, so we will approach it gradually and cumulatively. Commonly, it may be similar to change, and it certainly has very valuable theological currency. But its technical meaning is far more specific. Because I find it particularly helpful for cross-cultural ministry amid theological change and continuity, it is offered here for serious consideration.

How do we know when people's behavior—what they do, say, or tell us—makes sense? We know because we have criteria or structures against which to match it. If it fits, it makes sense; if not, it is deficient. But that assumes an appropriate set of criteria, and anyone who has been in an unfamiliar linguistic or cultural community knows that this can be a huge assumption! Sometimes our criteria are inadequate, and we are ignorant or incompetent. Sometimes, too, people's behavior or language is judged inadequate: they are wrong, ungrammatical, and so on. The important thing is to note that behavior and language are inseparable from *meaning*; and meaning is translatable.

Language is not random but governed by rules. Given the virtually infinite number of potential and actual speech[13] in a multiplicity of languages, linguistics—the science of language—must attempt to account for the fact that speakers can produce or "generate" a staggering variety of expressions. Perhaps even more intriguing, hearers can, almost instantaneously, make sense of strings of sounds never previously uttered in that form in the history of the world! There must be some criteria, some "device" that monitors the production and reception of language so that it conforms to standards of acceptability and meaning. Clearly, a speaker cannot have learned all the possible utterances in the world before speaking or making a choice; nor can a listener.[14] But both must have some grasp of rules, some creativity and interpretive skills, if communication is to be possible. The technical notion of transformation is helpful here.

The action of boiling water transforms a fresh egg from gelatinous to semisolid and then to solid. Examples of transformations are all around: of spring into summer and fall, child into adolescent and adult, life into death. They are as much about continuity as about change: each stage is recognized (if not always immediately recognizable) as deriving from and linked to a previous one.

Now consider the specifically linguistic meaning and application of transformations. "Cain killed Abel" and "Abel was killed by Cain" *mean* virtually the same thing. "I ate a hamburger" is somewhat related to "I did *not* eat a hamburger" and even to "I ate a hot dog," but clearly it is quite unrelated to "The sea is angry." How do we know this? And how can we accept "I ate a hot dog," but reject "I was eaten by a hot dog"? How might we economically change (parts of) the meaning of similar utterances without having to create completely new and unrelated ones? Linguistics shows us that with a finite and smallish number of specifiable rules of grammar we can generate an almost infinite number of acceptable and grammatical linguistic forms. Further, the rules themselves will reject, or simply not allow the production of anything that fails to meet the criteria of grammaticality or acceptability! Part of the mechanism for this is called a "transformation" or a "transformational rule."

Native speakers do not consciously apply grammatical rules, though they are systematically applied. Compare this with a non-native language learner, who must first identify rules and then apply them.

Transformational rules, applied to one particular linguistic form, transform it into another. They are not applied to actual sentences but to the "deep structures" underlying them. Thus a native speaker who wants to say "I do not like you" does not begin with "I like you" and then apply the "not" rule, thus producing the utterance! If so, conversation would be slow and tedious — as indeed it is for learners, and for that very reason! A "deep structure" is an abstraction, a representation of logical or grammatical relations of a sentence.[15] But a little reflection should assure us that if we start from the correct "deep structures" (whether we think concretely of a raw egg, a baby, or spring), then appropriate and recognizable transformations (a boiled egg, an adult, summer; but also a *poached* egg, an adult *elephant*, or *winter*) are possible. Such transformations or actualizations of deep structures are called "surface structures."

Spoken language "utters" or gives birth to ideas. Initially abstract, these may be realized in many different languages. A multilingual person may speak French to Jacques and immediately translate into German for Hans. But the translation will be a translation of *ideas*, not simply of the words that were spoken in the French — and perhaps the actual process of thinking will be in yet a different language! In order to do this, the speaker must reach below or behind the spoken word to a deeper level, that of the ideas themselves, which are a matter of relationships between things. This postulated deeper level is where "deep structures" are found.

A transformational rule then is one by means of which a speaker converts the constituent structure of one sentence into that of another. Compare [I-LIKE-TO-EAT-BANANAS] and [WE-HATE-TO-DROWN-PUPS]. Structurally they are very similar, but only at the level of their deep structure or *logical and grammatical relations*, not at the level of their surface structure, obviously! No transformational rule can convert the "banana" sentence into the "pup" sentence, because *their meaning is completely different*. But we might use a transformational rule to convert [SHE-ROSE-AND-WENT-WALKING] to [DID-SHE-RISE-AND-GO-WALKING?] (note the different shapes of the verbs), since they are obviously not unrelated in meaning. But we must avoid [ROSE-DID-AND-WALKING-GO-SHE?], since the transformation is unacceptable and meaningless.

To recapitulate some critical ideas:

— Transformational rules are not consciously applied by native speakers, but explain how certain logically and grammatically related utterances are derived by speakers.

— Deep structures are abstractions that clarify the relationships between grammatical or syntactic elements.

— All actual utterances are surface structures, and their meaning can sometimes only be clarified by reference to underlying deep structures.[16]

— Although meaning is often found in actual performance (or surface structures), translation can only occur by reference to underlying deep structures.[17] This fact, that *translation requires knowledge of underlying deep structures*, is crucial for processes of inculturation, for the effective translation of the Gospel *message*,[18] and for cross-cultural ministry generally. We can now apply this information to our theme of spirituality and eucharist.

SPIRITUALITY, EUCHARIST, AND TRANSFORMATION

There is no universal language but only particular languages, however widespread some of them may be. And given the multiple social worlds, phenomenal worlds, and worlds of meaning, there could never be a universal *natural* language, no matter how superficially attractive the idea might seem. In the real world of human speech, even within a single "tongue," there can be many "languages" or language varieties; they serve to emphasize human differences in ways of seeing the world and in speaking about what is seen.

But there *is* universal speech. People are not infants forever (*infant*: "without speech"); they "possess" language and speak and understand it. *In principle* any two people can understand each other, however painful the process or different their languages. Critical here is necessity or usefulness. But mutual intelligibility is achievable through effort, reciprocity, and the modification of both language and speakers over time, that is, through transformation.

Likewise there is no universal eucharist, but only myriad particular eucharists. This is not outrageous if we take a dynamic view; contexts and faith communities differ widely and there is no universal thanksgiving but only specific and localized giving of thanks. If the eucharist is standardized or simplified it will become artificial and superficial. If it becomes esoteric, like a dead language, it will become inaccessible to flesh-and-blood people. It is neither a private, domestic event nor a jamboree, but the paradigm for our communication as Christians with all people everywhere, even though a paradigm only imperfectly articulated in any single eucharistic liturgy. And crucially, it is the transformer of all other human, personal, and social relationships.

For whom then, is the eucharist intended? For the inarticulate: those who need to utter more clearly and more comprehensibly the praises of God. For the hungry: those who need to be transformed by the sustaining nourishment of justice and *koinonia*, community. For the weak: those who need strengthening to do the will of God. And for sinners: those who, never beyond the reach of a loving God, still need to experience loving arms and a hand pointing in the right direction and hear, with the divine efficacy of the Word, "Go, and do not miss the mark (*hamartanē*) any more" (Jn 8:11). Across cultures, nobody abstains from a meal unless excluded by or hostile toward the assembly. Yet meals are also for sharing not only with friends but even with enemies or those who want to become friends. Inasmuch as the eucharist is a meal, it cannot and must not be only for the well-fed and those who have already eaten, and to use it as a reward or bribe would be to invoke judgment (1 Cor 11:17ff; esp. 29-31).

The eucharist has power to nourish even those suffering from malnutrition or starvation and to include even outcasts. Indeed this is its strength, for it is a sign and signifier of transformation of hearts and of minds. All living things change. As Newman said, "To live fully is to change often," a maxim that we perhaps deny, a truth that we do not fully believe. Generally synonymous with change, in its religious or theological sense transformation connotes not atrophy but fulfillment or completion; linguistically it recalls deep structures and radical continuities rather than disjunction or superficiality. In short, the notion of transformation is so powerful that it can be used to build up a number of propositions or enthnological assumptions:

—The eucharist is all about transformations. Thus, we might come to see it, metaphorically, as a "transformer."

—Evangelism is a call to transformation. Thus, evangelism becomes (in the language of behavioral psychology) a "cross-cultural stimulus."

—The eucharistic community is called to transformation. Thus, the community becomes (again in the language of psychology) a "cross-cultural response."

—Cultures are not random or incomprehensible mutations of humanity but marvelous (and imperfect) transformations of what human-beings-in-social-groups are. Thus, cultures have a necessary and critical function in creating and maintaining human groups in all their versatility.

If transformation is really so helpful we should be able to apply it, to disclose underlying deep structures and to understand better the dynamics of social and religious change. But first we consider three applications: the transformation of the worshiping community, of the worshiper, and of society as a whole.

Transformation of the Worshiping Community

There is some convergence in recent ecumenical thinking. "Baptism, Eucharist, and Ministry" ("The BEM Document") says that "the eucharist brings into the present age a new reality which *transforms* Christians into the image of Christ."[19] "The BEM Document" refers several times to the theme of transformation (renewal) and says: "The Church lives through the liberating and renewing power of the Holy Spirit."[20] This is, in effect, what Ghanaian theologian Mercy Oduyoye is addressing as she reminds us that

we are seen to be a new reality, a *new manifestation* of humanity that is indeed imbued with divinity. It is the only reality that will make the world stop and consider our claims. It is that reality which will *turn* the eucharistic community *into* one which draws unto itself the whole world that Christ died to save.[21]

Again, with the word "[re]make" indicating the required transformation, liturgical theologian Arthur Vogel writes:

The Eucharistic pattern of Christian living takes us as we are in order *to [re]make us* and our world what we are not—God-like.[22]

All this is beautiful, and it is widely echoed by explicit statements from across the spectrum of Christian churches; yet one still has to ask: How? How can we *become* transformed, a new reality, a new community? And where does the newness come from? How, in actual practice, does transformation happen? The answer, at least in part, is to be sought in the workings of grace in the worshiper.

Transformation of the Worshiper

As ever, when addressing questions of discipleship, we can look first at the one who led by being a servant and who described discipleship as fidelity to the ways he did things (Matt 11:29). So what evidence is there for Jesus' own transformation? What opportunities for newness existed in his life and ministry? And how might we learn from him?

Jesus approached God directly and was in communication with God. Communication is a key to changing people. In many cultures there is understood to be a very great divide between God and humanity. Nevertheless, there are often special circumstances about which the people know: when all else fails and you are literally on your last legs, pursued by retribution or vindictiveness, you may have direct access to God through supplication, by throwing yourself on the mercy of that distant One who is more considerate than those in pursuit! Here, indeed, is an opportunity—though it is an extreme case—for transformation; all is *not* lost.

The novelty of Jesus for people in such cultures—and those closer to home—is his making the distant God accessible *in ordinary circumstances*. And it was surely Jesus' intention that the eucharist should be an ordinary rather than an extraordinary circumstance (see 1 Cor 11:26)! "The BEM Document" identifies the eucharist as a means of transformation for every single person who participates. The commentary states:

[The] gift of salvation is received through communion in Christ's body and blood under the signs of bread and wine: *every member* of the church, the body of Christ, *is renewed* by this communion in which he or she is given the assurance of the forgiveness of sins (Matt. 26:28) and the pledge of eternal life (Jn. 6:51-58).[23]

Not only is this an unequivocal statement but it implies that since the transformation or renewal of every member is a fruit of participation in the eucharist, it has not yet occurred. The eucharist is not for the perfect but for those who are being perfected. Clearly, God's availability is not limited.

When we approach God directly we are most like Jesus. To this end Jesus called people to him, in moments of belief, repentance, and mission ("Come"; "Be healed"; "Go"). Knowledge of, closeness to, healing by, and commissioning from Jesus therefore, constitute the transformation of the disciple and of ourselves. As Jesus transforms lives and expectations, so we as a eucharistic people and as the body of Christ can help transform others — and they us. But if we teach the availability and approachableness of a God who transforms, and then exclude people from a transforming eucharist, we are lying. Jesus said, "Whenever [*hosakis*: "as often as; in whatever place"] you drink it, do this as a memorial of me"; and St. Paul glosses this frequency and availability, saying, "*Until* the Lord comes, then, *every time* [*hosakis*] you eat this bread and drink this cup, you are proclaiming his death" (1 Cor 11:25-26). This is surely an invitation from Jesus, through Paul, to the worshiper; and the worshiper who accepts, can and must be transformed.

Jesus offers another kind of example. He is open to the challenge of others. Throughout the Gospel we are shown people — characteristically women, but also many other "marginal" persons — who are responsible for redirecting Jesus' plans or responses. Have we paid insufficient attention to this? As missioners we may particularly need to be reminded that to change one's mind, to "go the extra mile," is a godly thing!

Jesus is a challenge and a question to each person, but he is also an ally and an answer. He does make impossible demands, but he assists us in our response. He treats us as individuals (though not individualistically, if understood in opposition to or outside the context of a community), but social individuals, individuals-in-relationship. We are reminded that

> relationality is at the heart of all things. To speak of a theology of relation however, . . . is to insist on the deep, total sociality of all things. All things cohere in each other. Nothing living is self-contained; if there were such a thing as an unrelated individual, none of us would know it.[24]

But this is not yet enough. For society to be transformed, people must begin to know about this, must begin to respond to these realities. But how can that happen unless through their *own* media: cultural, visual, linguistic, and the rest? Aylward Shorter, speaking from wide-ranging experience, and using the language of St. Paul, puts it this way:

> A new creation is coming into being, brought about by the Spirit of God, and humanity itself is part of the process, groaning and straining toward a revelation of this new order. The material world we see, is subordinated to, and *transformed* by, the transcendental reality which it signifies.[25]

So society must be transformed from *within*. We have to discover the values of others, and as missioners in honest and respectful dialogue, call them (and be called!) in the name of Jesus to a new response: a transformation. External change alone is virtually meaningless because it does not derive from the deep structures, the underlying values or principles on which societies are built. Naively to promote external change alone, therefore, is destructive; to limit ourselves to external change is to show disrespect!

The healing rituals of the !Kung[26] of South West Africa restore a broken world and transform relationships; the two are intimately related. The eucharist should surely be able to speak to this experience if it is allowed and encouraged. But people of many other cultures address their own need for healing and reconciliation through systems of thinking and behavior as exotic — to some of us — as witchcraft and voodoo. Unless the eucharist can speak to people's life-experiences it will remain marginal at best, and the compassion of Jesus will fail to be delivered to those suffering keenly.[27]

Morality has recently been described as "hospitality to the stranger," a particularly redolent phrase but by no means a novel idea (see Rom 12:13: "You should make hospitality your special care"). The eucharist must likewise be seen to offer hospitality to strangers and to be involved in the transformation of their lives. But we should not overlook the stranger's own potential for bringing the gift of transformation. As Thomas Ogletree says:

> The stranger does not simply challenge or subvert our world of meaning. She may enrich, even transform that world. When repentance occurs ... the host/stranger dialectic gives way to solidarity in the struggle for liberation.[28]

The eucharist, bringer of transformation, has the necessary potential; it can be involved in an authentic dialogue that will result in the transformation of society generally. As Christians we profess to believe this. What does it take to move it closer to realization?

If the eucharist were really seen as a sacrament of initiation, then its power to transform might be more readily appreciated among peoples entirely familiar with the transformative function of their own rites of initiation.[29] But the responsibility lies here with ourselves as announcers of the Good News and, in turn, with our own sensitivity to the recipients of that news. There is, however, a responsibility on the part of those who espouse inculturation to ensure that the local churches have something to teach the universal church, for the eucharist can never be simply the indulgence of local custom or individual fashion but must flower to its full cosmic dimensions as in fidelity to Jesus and to the Spirit it continues to be offered for the transformation of the world.[30]

We have attempted to gather some fragments of bread for the journey: the journey of whoever goes in the name of the Lord, the journey of each and every Christian. Transformation can happen and has happened (as Sanneh reminds us in the epigraph); it must continue to happen. If Augustine is right, and we are what we have received, then as community we are the body of Christ and nourishment for each other and for the journey. Later chapters will examine this more closely.

QUESTIONS FOR THE ROAD

- Do you think there is an inevitable tension between the local and the universal aspects or claims of the church? If so, what might be the value of this tension? If not, how might it be resolved?
- "A spirituality means the reordering of the great axes of the Christian life in terms of contemporary experience" (Gutiérrez). Does this not make spirituality relative? How realistic is Gutiérrez' statement?
- Hollenweger suggests that we should gamble with our understanding of belief. What might this mean in practical terms? Are there limits to such a gamble?
- If it is naive and dangerous to promote external change alone, how might a missioner engage in processes of deep change, social and religious?

Chapter 3

The Conversion of the Missionary

If you have not learned to love yourself, I am afraid that you will cheat your neighbor as yourself.[1]

To be loved by God and to love God is to suffer.[2]

*You must be rooted in [Christ] and built on him and held firm by the faith you have been taught, and full of thanksgiving (*perisseuontes en eucharistia*).*

Colossians 2:6

Surely you have enough respect for the community of God, not to make poor people embarrassed?

1 Corinthians 11:22

Truth is not a doctrine, a teaching, a series of concepts. Truth is a force that denounces and destroys the lie. Truth is the birth of new reality. By their activity, the communities give birth to a new reality—the reality of humanity.[3]

THE MISSIONARY CHALLENGE: RESPONSE AND MUTUALITY

Mission may be thought of not simply as a "going," but specifically as a "being sent"; it is a response as much as or more than it is an initiative. But does a person undertake mission as a response to a body of "senders," or rather in response to those who ask for and receive a stranger? This is worth pondering, especially by people not chosen and sent by Mission Boards or their equivalent, or not usually sent in reply or reaction to particular requests from local churches. Inasmuch as mission is a response to a "sending," we must ask: By whom? to whom?

Mission often appears as an initiative, even unilateral, which a receiving

36

community is expected to welcome and is criticized if it does not. But mission is surely supposed to be a sign of mutuality, and this demands at least some deference toward those who are expected to be hosts. Anything less is a betrayal of simple good manners. Reception of baptism may be a theologically sufficient justification for someone to be a missionary, but, even buttressed by a reputable missionary organization it surely does not confer the right to invade another person's home or life. And theological arguments that trample on people and consciences must be spurious.

Sometimes local communities are hardly consulted, and the sending group has virtually total control of initiatives. Apart from the sheer insensitivity of such an approach there is a further apposite issue — the possibility of spiritual growth for the missionary. What is the effect of such an imbalance in the responsibilities, expectations, and rights of senders and receivers? And what does such lack of real mutuality do to the missionary, let alone the local people?

Familiar material concerning spirituality and conversion need not be repeated here. Rather, the present chapter has a threefold purpose, centering on a wholesome missionary engagement. It addresses issues relating directly to the cross-cultural dimension of missionary life: experience at the edge or beyond the edge of one's own familiar world, whether in the jungles of our cities or the remotest parts of the globe. Second, it looks at our own need for ongoing or continuing conversion, lest we who have preached to others be ourselves found deficient (cf 1 Cor 9:27). And finally, it is about the way in which those two issues combine, about how, given the particular circumstances of our lives, the uniquely different persons each of us is, the context in which ministries are played out, and the people who are our companions on the journey, we who are many might be called *existentially* to a nourishing, attractive, and pluriform spirituality.

Stephen Neill[4] notes that "missionary" ("missioner") is a theological concept unknown in the New Testament, but "call" and "response" certainly are not; the essence of a contemporary Christian response should certainly find an echo in the New Testament.[5] So, if we reexamine call and response we may be better able to understand the ministry appropriate to a missionary. The word "vocation," and surely the notion behind it, is familiar: in essence it simply means call. But some of us may have used it to create differences and maintain hierarchies rather than to underline our individual and common choice by God and God's covenant with each of us through baptism.

But the theological notion is not easily introduced into conversation; nor is it self-explanatory to many of those among whom we minister. Further, it is a relational or paired term, which can only be understood alongside its reciprocal, whether "response" or perhaps "sending." A call is not an initiative. The former is external to the subject, while the latter originates in the subject. So a call presupposes not only two subjects but a relationship or the potential for one. In the context of a putative God-given call, this is an astounding idea: creator in reciprocal relationship with creature! Where can we find indications of such a call in the New Testament, assuming we are readily familiar with the idea of covenant and call before the incarnation?

The Great Commission (Matt 28:19-20) has been the rallying call and the justification for generations of missionaries.[6] It is centrifugal, magisterial, and authoritative: centrifugal, indicated by "go!"; magisterial, understood from the word "teach"; and authoritative, implied in the notion that the nations should comply and "observe" the appropriate commands of Jesus.

But this is not the only basis for mission. Comparing other statements of Jesus, we note rather different emphases. "Come, follow me" (Mk 2:14) is centripetal, ministerial, and responsive: centripetal, since it is a call to seek Jesus as the center and focus of life; ministerial, inasmuch as "following" is an attitude of service rather than obvious leadership; responsive, since it confers no initiative but asks for humble trust.

If we Christians identify ourselves with those called to undertake the Great Commission, must we not also identify with those invited to come and follow Jesus rather less ostentatiously? Institutionally the church has claimed the mandate as expressed in or exegeted from chapter 28 of the Gospel of Matthew; as a community of those who believe in Jesus' example of ministry-as-service, missionaries are surely challenged also to a rather more humble and diffident ministry, one which would be a convincing sign of respect for and love of those who are outcast, wounded, or simply different. If so, how does such a posture of follower (in the Greek, *akolouthos*: "follower," attendant; not *apostellos*: "messenger," apostle; or *mathētēs*: "learner," disciple) affect the ministry proper to a missionary?

It is easy enough to say we want to be converted to Christ; it is not difficult to imagine that we are in the process of continuous conversion. But to put our hand to the plow and not look back, to take up our cross daily and to *follow* Jesus, this is the test of a real disciple and a true convert. It is also, humanly speaking, impossible.

Each of us is reared, socialized, in a particular way and within specific contexts; much as we might wish to transcend or break through our limitations and pursue Jesus in mission, our world of meaning is rooted in the social world in which we are grounded. People who are violently uprooted or who lack the opportunity to strike deep social roots have great difficulty in determining their own identity. Unless ours is fairly well-rooted and well-bounded it is virtually impossible to become socially responsible or mature. The commandment to love God and our neighbor as ourselves presupposes not only that we know God in some sense, but that we love *ourselves* in some way too. People who have never been rooted, or who have been deeply traumatized, may lack a stable personality or human identity; those who are unloved may be unable to love; and those who cannot love themselves cannot truly love others.

Consequently, a certain insularity or subjectivity and an element of self-love are prerequisites for commitment to mission. Yet our mission is in response to a call to an increasing globalization of our perspectives and a transcending of our self-love through the process called conversion. Here is the paradox and the challenge: we must be converted in order to make our own wisdom relative and truly love our neighbor; yet it is because we take our own wisdom seriously and have a well-rooted sense of self that we are in a position to consider the invitation to follow Jesus and be converted!

The implications of conversion are even more problematic. However easy it is for us to imagine other people being wholesomely and happily converted, it is by no means as easy to imagine ourselves undertaking a similar program of change. Subjectively viewed, it would appear as a compromise of the principles on which we have built our own lives: a social and religious deconstruction. Or, to emphasize a different perspective, changing our ways or points of reference, "converting" as a conscious choice, is rather different from responding or reacting to an external stimulus, "being converted." Is conversion for others then quite different from our own? And is a personal initiative for conversion different from a response to an unrequested stimulus?

Pursuing the first of these pathways might uncover the dynamics by which other people come to change their worldview or, in some sense, to be converted.[7] But the second issue concerns us more. As questions for each of us missionaries, it could look like this: How might we undertake continuous or ongoing conversion and come to change a worldview on which so much of who we are now seems to depend? More generally, what might conversion mean in the life of one who *already* takes commitment to Christ and the Gospel seriously? And how might our own conversion affect missionary undertakings? These are not simply questions about our best intentions; they are questions about existential possibilities.

RADICAL DISJUNCTION AND RADICAL CONTINUITY

In the context of the classical missionary outreach to unevangelized peoples, conversion has customarily been seen as an "about face" or "180 degree turn": I will label this "radical disjunction." St. Paul is the most quoted exponent, by virtue of a literal disjunction: the fall (*not* from a horse [Acts 4:9]), the turning and returning. But if one does a 180 degree turn and yet conversion is intended to be ongoing, what happens next? To proceed straight ahead is tantamount to asserting that conversion is complete and only needs to be perpetuated; but another 180 degree turn will bring one back to the original position!

Not only is this model less common than we might suppose, but St. Paul is not a particularly good example of it. He did not consider himself converted in a static, once and for all way. David Bosch expresses it well, saying that "Paul's spirituality was never a kind of permanent attribute; it was renewed again and again, from within."[8] And Orlando Costas also disagrees with a traditional evangelical view, which would see conversion as a

> static, once-for-all, private experience . . . viewed as a trans-cultural, noncontextual event, . . . the same everywhere for all believers, at all times. I would like to explore what I believe to be a more biblically, theologically, and socio-historically sound view: conversion as a dynamic, complex, ongoing experience, profoundly responsive to particular times and places and shaped by the context of those who experience it.[9]

This is a succinct, perceptive, and missiologically sound description, very much in the spirit of the present chapter. It undermines the radical discontinuity perspective as the only way to understand conversion, and it challenges us to follow its implications.

Anthropologist Victor Turner produced seminal studies about the transformative effect of initiation rites in traditional societies.[10] Helpful though they have been for illustrating the processes of socialization by radical disjunction from the past in order to facilitate future orientations, they are not without problems, especially when one attempts some comparative applications. "The past is another country," wrote L. P. Hartley. "They do things differently there." But unless there is continuity with the past, how does one move forward? Whence come the skills and wisdom?

Medievalist Carolyn Walker Bynum was the first to my knowledge to challenge Turner's thesis of radical disjunction.[11] Arguing that the experience of most women is much closer to radical continuity than to radical disjunction, she concludes that Turner was at least half wrong! Was he interpreting and generalizing from a white male perspective? And if so, then he may be more than half wrong, since there are many different cultural experiences, as well as many women.

Historian Richard Gray, looking at sub-Saharan Africa, quotes a study of the Kimbanguist Church. Founded by Simon Kimbangu in what was the Belgian Congo, it revered him as a prophet, yet asserted that it was authentically Christian (it is a member of the World Council of Churches). So what of the perception of Simon as prophet? Has it been radically extirpated? On the contrary. The Kimbangu-centric and Christo-centric perceptions

> are co-existing and "organically related" and the Kimbanguist finds it quite possible to be able to slip, as the need arises, from one perception to the other and back again.[12]

Gray concludes that conversion is not only indicated by radical disjunction, even though this may happen. But

in Black Africa conversion has drawn deeply on the springs of toler-
ation, humility, and wisdom inherent in Africans' age-old searchings
for truth and salvation. [There is] also a much more temperate, pro-
longed dialogue in which the universal church's understanding of
orthodoxy is itself modified, developed, and enriched.[13]

The insight about mutual modifications through dialogue is important
for missionaries, so what if dialogue is avoided or merely token? Bynum's
feminist hermeneutic and female perspective may have even wider application than she claims. Many people, male and female, have to continue
their lives after conversion experiences, without the practical possibility of
radical disjunction. We need only reflect on the contemporary women's
ordination movement; women may feel called to a radical conversion of life
but are nevertheless expected to know their place and stay in it. They are
prohibited, forbidden, from responding to a radical call of that particular
form.

Conversion, then, may be a cause, an effect, or both, of women's (and
some men's) isolation from and within the institutional church. Bynum's
argument about women's call to reaffirm their loyalties rather than to
change them seems entirely compatible with ongoing conversion, though
clearly no justification for the intransigence or injustice of others. She
quotes recent research suggesting that

> women are less likely to experience life-decisions as sharp ruptures
> because women, raised by women, mature into a continuous self
> whereas boys, also raised by women, *must* undergo one basic re-
> versal[14];

a point increasingly substantiated and emphasized. But it is not only
because women are raised by women; radical continuity is applicable to
those cross-cultural ministers whose religious socialization was in a community or denomination they will never leave; they—we—also need conversion, and not only by radical disjunction.

Bynum finds that women, unlike men, do not generally think of their
lives as dramatic but rather as evolving, not so much traumatic as interesting. For such women, continuity is the Ariadne's thread of their lives. This
is to say that transformations occur (in life as in linguistics) not as incomprehensible events unrelated to what preceded them, but as meaningful
precisely in terms of what preceded. And that in turn implies that the past
(or the deep structures) be not repudiated but respected, not forgotten but
remembered.

To assume that the only real conversion is by a radical break with our
history is to expect other people and ourselves to achieve reintegration only
on the ruins of personal disintegration, and to move into the future with
no sense of the past and with no compass-bearings. Small wonder if this

proves unrealistic or if syncretism or dual religious systems persist; if we cannot take some wisdom, personal or communal, from yesterday into tomorrow, then each individual and each generation are fated to start from the beginning. Where then is the value of culture? And how can grace build on nature if nothing substantial remains?

So conversion may be radical and real without repudiating all that has preceded. Bosch says conversion to "the cross" implies a radical identification with the world in which we live, the world as it actually presents itself. This would neither deny the need to remain uncontaminated by the world in its more secular manifestations, nor undermine the thesis of those who urge that missionaries engage with and challenge situations of oppression and injustice. But it would allow for a reappropriation of personal histories and social processes, giving rise to the radical continuity occasioned by conversion.

Francis Crick and James Watson, of double helix fame, recalled the infinite variety of complex structures in nature, and replicated in culture and technology. In terms of contemporary technology we might visualize all the upheaval and reorganization involved in a domestic "conversion" from gas to electricity, from a conventional oven to a microwave, or from an outdoor water pump to indoor plumbing; analogously, "religious" conversion may be no more unusual or impossible. Understood as radical continuity rather than radical disjunction (even though that too happens), it may help us to respect who we have been as well as who we are called to be.

CONVERSION AND ORDINARY EXPERIENCE

If conversion is a continuous process, then *metanoia* or "conversion of heart" must take place where we actually are and as we change within a changing world. It does not happen in a vacuum but in a rather volatile microcosm: our own life. The most obvious context for our life is our own body, but embodiment has hardly been acknowledged, much less celebrated, as a variable in spirituality. It needs to be considered in relation to mission generally and is very pertinent here. The body we have or are, and its condition or state, is not an outcome merely of personal choice or caprice. It is meaningful and comprehensible in relation to social as well as personal factors. The particularities of our embodiment are significant: the body's state of health, age, sex, and esthetic appeal. Given that conversion is a social experience and that embodiment has a social context, how is our embodiment acknowledged, redeemed, and integrated—or is it unacknowledged, bypassed, and overlooked?

However fashionable and persuasive it might once have been to disparage one's self, repress one's embodiment, and bury one's talents, current wisdom is that these attitudes are dangerously close to denying the giver of all good gifts and the one in whose image and likeness we are made.

And however strong a former tendency to assimilate a classical spirituality, a "spirituality for all seasons," a fixed set of values and attitudes presumed adequate for all eventualities, current wisdom is strongly biased against it. People were treated interchangeably in terms of spiritual training and assessment, and if not treated as angels neither were they unashamedly physical. Therefore a Christian hardly worked within real and changing parameters, much less developed a spirituality in harmony with them; one operated as if disembodied and repressed, neither of the world nor in it.

But we have come to understand more about the enormous and irreducible variety of human persons and the vast range of cultures produced by different circumstances and human responses. It should help us understand that there is no such thing as "man" or "woman," "culture" or "spirituality" in the abstract. They exist in context, in the concrete, and they change. Every person is uniquely different. This is not to deny commonalities, for we can link and group and relate people according to a variety of criteria such as race or sex or religion or occupation. And by embodiment.

We might helpfully speak of a micro-spirituality and a macro-spirituality. The former unique and private and ego-focal, the latter more public and socio-focal. Your own way of praying, the way most appropriate for you at any given moment, is a characteristic of your micro-spirituality; so is your choice of favorite biblical texts, for example. Participation in a communion service, a eucharist, or some other public devotion is a manifestation of your macro-spirituality. Each person is characterized by individual initiative and response (micro-), and by participation in the great ceremonies or rituals of a particular religious tradition (macro-). Thus people can be both differentiated and grouped.

The object is not simply to categorize people, but precisely to appreciate that they are not to be reduced to categories. They are unique; they are also similar. And given a certain number of variables we might be able, tentatively, to understand not only their similarity and uniqueness, but how these cluster in patterns. From there we might begin to understand some of the reasons for all this. This is a promising line of enquiry,[15] reminding us that human behavior need be neither random nor deviant when it differs from what is familiar to us. Further, we might be encouraged to look within and beneath some of the superficialities to the underlying values: the deep structures of spirituality and embodiment, and the things that unite and distinguish us.

Since our conversion must be realized in a particular world and through our ordinary experience, those in cross-cultural ministry might go further and correlate different cultural meanings with different cultural experiences. If this sounds opaque, here is an example: Is there perhaps a correlation between the stereotypical distrust of the body among Puritans, and a cold, damp climate in which bodies exist? Is there a "fit" between their preoccupation with covering and hiding and chastising their bodies and their notion of a God of judgment and severity? Or what of the people encountered by the crew of H.M.S. Bounty on Tahiti, people who had a "shockingly" trusting nature, were unambiguously hospitable, and who rejoiced in and gave great expression to their embodiment? Theirs was an environment conducive to a minimum of clothing, with an openness to the skies and to the transcendent. Their way-of-being-in-the-world was as congruent with the world in which they lived (warm, friendly, trustworthy, open), as the Puritans' was with theirs (cold, tentative, concerned, limited). And then again, how would we correlate our own way-of-being-in-the-world with the world in which we are? Or our manifestation of embodiment (spontaneous/controlled, extrovert/introvert, healthy/neurotic, blooming/ decaying, and so on), with our ideas of God?[16] As missionaries we have a responsibility to assess and acknowledge some of the characteristics of our own way-of-being-in-the-world and to understand and compare those of our hosts. Only then will we be open to the process of conversion: the transformation of ourselves, of others, and of all things in Christ.

José Comblin underlines personal development as growing within a social context and among reciprocal relationships:

> Human beings become real human beings when they are converted ... to accept the interpellation of the other and look at the face of the other: the victim, the poor, the widow, the orphan, in biblical terms. ... A human being must be [re]born as a person; and this birth is accomplished only in communication among persons—in the reciprocity between person and person. On the other hand, the person appears by way of a conversion of the individual, by way of a negation of oneself as an isolated subject.[17]

This issue is merely stated here, but it remains to be explored and exploited by each of us, whoever and wherever we are. And since the *who* and the *where* change all the time (both in radical continuity and sometimes in radical disjunction) our task is as long as our life. How does our existential experience invite us to undertake a journey with those around us and at a distance, challenge our developing spirituality, and call us to ongoing conversion, both individual and social?

CONVERSION AND THE EUCHARIST

Descartes not only separated body from mind but persuaded Western thinkers that their reality was seated in that nonexistent organ. Whether we have read him or not, our thinking is as affected by mentalism as it is by aspects of dualism or binary oppositions. But billions of people would never dream of saying "I *think*, therefore I am"; it is not their powers of ratiocination so much as their sheer actuality that gives them an identity. They know they are, not because they think they are but because their community authenticates them and maintains their social identity. On a personal, individual level they exist because they experience their physicality: they feel, see, and sense that they are. Not only is the mind/body dualism of Descartes alien to many contemporary cultures, it has also been dealt a mortal blow by the current feminist critique of knowledge, as well as by phenomenology.

Human celebrations are to be experienced and enjoyed by real people. The eucharist is a celebration of real people, bodies as well as spirits, imperfect as well as perfectible, social as well as individual, public as well as private. If it is to be the sacrament and liturgy it is meant to be and is capable of being, it must be celebrated as an authentic meeting of people united in community and united with Jesus. But a eucharistic liturgy that is largely an inner, private devotion or a spiritualization of religious experience will fail to reach its potential; it can hardly be claimed as bread for the journey in any helpful human sense. If we introduce such disembodied and disconnected liturgies into cultures where embodiment and connectedness are highly prized, we should not be surprised if such liturgies atrophy or are treated merely as fetishes.

The idea of embodiment might illuminate our reflections on our personal experience of eucharistic celebration and help identify areas needing further development, thus enabling eucharist and our own spirituality to encounter each other fruitfully and become mutually transforming. Unless this happens the eucharist will never become the real focal point of our lives, and our spirituality will develop, at best, in isolation from it. A worshiping community which, due to diffidence or apathy, only minimally acknowledges its constituent members gathered for eucharist, is most unlikely to recognize them to much effect outside the liturgical setting; such a community is neither "remembering" nor exemplifying the living body of Christ. The community that does not pray together does not stay together, at least not as a sign and sacrament of salvation.

How does eucharist relate to our ongoing conversion? As regards the participants, does the eucharist we celebrate serve to reflect, endorse, and redeem—or to suppress and deny—the actual person we are and the experience we bring to the assembly? Does it encounter us in the midst of creation, incomplete and somewhat harassed, or are its symbols and ceremonies more suited to a choir of angels? Do we feel the warmth and solidness of the sense of touch in our sign of peace or the welcome of the community? Do we feel that we really participate, or simply observe; does the presider "say" Mass, while we "hear" it? Or do we, as a community, celebrate? If our experiences in this regard are negative, we are not nourished in the eucharist. We lack bread for the journey.

Again, as regards our ongoing conversion, does the liturgical setting put us in a recollected mode, a slightly altered state of consciousness (familiar to many societies whose members gather in prayer)? Do we smell the aromas of incense and flowers and beeswax, redolent of the holy and the sacred and of childhood memories? Are we ourselves "Christ's incense to God" (2 Cor 2:15) and thus a help to the recollection of others? Or have we long since banished the smells as decidedly *not* the odor of sanctity, as we banished the bells as unnecessary and undesirable? Are our liturgical spaces busy and noisy? Do we raise our eyes and exalt in our hearts as we worship in the splendor of soaring cathedrals, built in an "Age of Faith" and smelling of centuries of devotion, lavishly decorated with supernumerary carvings, statuary, and catechetical murals? Or do we lower our eyes and discipline our hearts as we worship in the simplicity of functional spaces, erected in an "Age of Reform" and smelling of generations of separation, simply accoutered with necessary tables and pews, antiseptic and stark? The possibilities are endless. Is our worship offered under the clear, warm skies, or in Baroque exaggeration? Do we have one voice or many? Are we united or dispersed in our togetherness? And what does it matter?

The heart of the issue is whether we acknowledge and rejoice in the real world through our liturgies or deny it or shut it out. Do we encourage a dialogue between the liturgical setting and the broader social context? Or do we worship in splendid isolation from the world and from each other and even from ourselves? Creating a liturgical context in the midst of the world demands energy, but a liturgy orchestrated without reference to the world is jejune, for how can the eucharist call us to justice unless we are in touch with an unfinished and bleeding world?[18] True, we need to be recollected for our liturgies, but recollected in our engagement with the world, not in abstraction from it. Each of the myriad possible settings for our celebration of eucharist has something to offer by way of an integration of liturgy and life. Unless we rearrange our liturgy out of respect for our lives, it will remain unfocused and tragically empty.

Finally, relative to the radicality of our conversion, what about variety? What do variations actually do to the liturgy and to ourselves? How does a shift from one to another teach us of God and of community? Are we often summoned to conversion by liturgies that challenge and inspire and urge us to justice? Or are our responses as mechanical as our liturgies are predictable? Do our eucharists acknowledge us as people who dance and sing and respond bodily to music, as the New World Shakers and many "Utopian" communities,[19] and a multitude of non-Western peoples[20] have done for centuries?[21] Or is there a painful and unnecessary disjunction where there should be radical continuity between the ways we are embodied in "ordinary" life and ways deemed appropriate to the liturgy? What is the effect of local culture on the liturgy, and vice versa? Could a liturgy remembered from Timbuctoo pass for the one we celebrated in Toronto, or a celebration in Denver be mistaken for one in Delhi? If so, liturgies are not yet inculturated and spirituality is not being adequately fed. If people are to be converted in the breaking of the bread, then the way they gather, the table around which they gather, and the ritual expression of the breaking will themselves first have to be "converted." Only when each and all of us can find the means for conversion wherever we are and as an expression of the genius of the place will our spiritual repertoire be adequate.

THE BODY OF CHRIST: OTHER PEOPLE'S BODIES

How can the body of Christ not vary if communities vary; how adaptable is our liturgy to people of various cultures, times, ages, and states of health? The two questions are intimately related. "We do not so much live in a universe, as a universe lives in us."[22] Yet not only do individuals experience their bodies in different ways through the course of a lifetime, but societies vary widely in what we might call "body tolerance," a matter of considerable importance when we consider liturgical appropriateness and adaptation. Some peoples enjoy and decorate and flaunt themselves with great naturalness, while others conceal or neglect or treat their bodies as shameful. If liturgy should reflect and celebrate life, what varieties of eucharistic celebration might we expect and promote across the globe, not as novelties but as intrinsic to ongoing conversion and developing spirituality? If eucharist is to stand at the center of our Christian lives and be appropriately set at the center of all lives, then it needs a variety of manifestations.

This is by no means to promote uncritical or whimsical adaptation but to call for the kind of adaptation that would challenge every eucharistic community to conversion, to transformation, and to an earnest commitment to the Christian journey, which is also the way of the cross. In every human community there are distortions of what it is to be human. If the first-world image (body beautiful; the cult of youth; and wrinkle-free, plastic-surgical, cosmetized and deodorized individualism) is widespread, it nevertheless barely conceals our neuroses, violence, and self-destructiveness. Likewise, the third-world image, far from reflecting the garden of Eden, is often a projection (in the bodies of the mutilated, the crippled, and the dying) of the horrendous effects of war, starvation, and sickness. The eucharist must try to speak to all these experiences, the fantasies as well as the real, or remain irrelevant. Indeed, when societies are infatuated with their own attractiveness (narcissistic), or helpless in the face of grinding reality (fatalistic), it is much more likely that the eucharist has no place in them, a matter to give us pause for serious thought and response.

People's way-of-being-in-the-world is the only way along which they can be approached. If the eucharist does not engage with and challenge real people, *as they are*, in their concreteness and through their own experience of reality, then it will be meaningless. If their reality is voodoo or spirit possession or witchcraft, drugs or other addictions, sickness or starvation, self-indulgence or consumerism, then the eucharistic community needs to learn some new languages or fall mute and unconnected. It is difficult to undertake what must be undertaken, so sometimes we fail to do so. But the daily experience of Jesus is our model and guide; he came into contact with just such a world and just such people. And he nevertheless wanted to build eucharistic communities. Can we persuade ourselves that we are being converted if we do not do likewise?

Critical to true inculturation, then, is its relationship to embodiment. Unless the life-giving Word can speak to people in the sheer actuality of their physical existence, it will have scant power to transform them spiritually.

THE BODY OF CHRIST: OUR BODIES

If the eucharist can be understood, at least partially, as the self-offering of Jesus in order to encounter and transform our way-of-being-in-the-world, then we in turn must accept responsibility for perpetuating the offering and the transformation. Beverly Harrison forcefully argues that we cannot be disciples except by acknowledging and employing our bodiliness, which means admitting our potential for ill yet actively choosing good:

> We may wish—like children—that we did not have such awesome power for good or evil. But the fact is we do. The power to receive and give love, or to withhold it—that is, to withhold the gift of life— is less dramatic, but every bit as awesome, as our technological power. It is a tender power. And—as women we are never likely to forget— the exercise of that power begins, and is rooted, in our bodies, ourselves. If we begin with "our bodies, ourselves," we recognize that all our knowledge, including our moral knowledge, is body mediated. . . . Failure to live deeply in "our bodies, ourselves," destroys the possibility of moral relations between us.[23]

In a brilliant examination of bodiliness and knowledge, anthropologist Michael Jackson describes the difference between intellectual and embodied knowledge. Speaking of his study of female initiation rites and its attendant frustrations for a male ethnographer, he says:

> To stand aside from the action, take up a point of view, and ask endless questions as I did . . . led only to a spurious understanding and *increased* the phenomenological problem of how I could know the experience of the other. By contrast, to participate bodily in everyday practical tasks was a creative technique which often helped me grasp the *sense* of an activity by using my body as others did. This technique also helped me break my habit of seeking truth at the level of disembodied concepts and decontextualized sayings. To recognize the embodiment of our being-in-the-world is to discover a common ground where self and other are one.[24]

This speaks eloquently to us as missionaries who need to "connect" with others, and as individuals who sometimes feel unappreciated. But it also challenges us to approach "participant observation" in unfamiliar contexts, not just as a way to knowledge but specifically as the *only* way to true conversion in a given situation with particular people. Arthur Vogel states that

> we can be incorporated into Christ's body only in our bodies, for only in them can the type of structure which is Christ's body find its kind of being in us. . . . [There will be] additional meaning in the eucharist if we follow up in still more detail the parallel between our Christian lives in the body of Christ, and our lives in our bodies.[25]

Only by an experiential understanding of some of the many ways in which people are embodied, incarnated, incorporated in the world, and the ways in which they relish or struggle against their embodiment, can cross-cultural missionaries contribute to building up the body of Christ. Then we might be able to relate body-tolerance or body-fear to certain social attitudes. Perhaps we will be more able to understand the social shape of acceptance or hostility, inclusion or exclusion, welcome or rejection, as well as inward-looking or outward-looking peoples, excitable or restrained temperaments, joyous or joyless individuals. And at that point we might consider the eucharist as a possible forum both for the acceptance and for the trans-formation of the bodily experiences of believers, and as a ritual of incor-poration into the life of the community, rather than as an empty ceremony destined to remain peripheral to it.

One thing is certain, perhaps two: unless we develop fitting attitudes not only to our own embodiment or way-of-being-in-the-world but to that of others as well, we will fail to discover an integrated spirituality and appro-priate liturgical forms; and unless the eucharist of the Roman Rite (or indeed any local form in any Christian community) is itself transformed as it encounters other cultures, it will be incapable of transforming the believ-ing communities.

EUCHARISTIC FEAST – OR FAMINE?

The happy mean in life seems much more elusive than the unhappy extreme; a natural human and indeed social tendency would seem to be to correct one kind of behavior by swinging in the opposite direction. Through-out the history of movements in spirituality or of eucharistic practice (see Chapter 8), we can see this. Thus, a reaction to an ascetical movement like the early Quakers of Charles James Fox is found with the "Shaking Quak-ers" or Shakers of Mother Ann Lee, forced out of her native England for her impertinence and crypto-feminism! Likewise, clerical, hierarchical, male-dominated Western medieval Christianity found its counterparts in movements like the Beguines, founded by women and for women, and loosely organized as a leaderless, unaffiliated, informal model of communal Christianity (and of course hounded by "orthodoxy").

In eucharistic practice too we can discern major shifts of emphasis: from eucharist in the context of a full meal to the sharing of sacred food in a purely ritual context; from the intimacy and amity of a house-church to the anonymity and enormity of a basilica or cathedral; from a common sharing in the eucharistic food to a withdrawal of communion from the laity; from oral, physical communion under both species to only ocular, spiritual communion for the laity; from an understanding of the whole community as the body of Christ to a crude realism that identified the body of Christ only with the consecrated species. There are other movements and shifts of emphasis, notably and subtly the movement from eucharist as a haven for sinners to eucharist as a gathering-point of the respectable.

In terms of the radicality of our conversion, we somehow have to blend continuity with the past with adaptation to current needs in various cultural and regional contexts. A church that claims to be "one" must not underwrite major discrepancies in the eucharistic practice of its parts while still claiming fidelity to tradition; and a church that prides itself on reforms (under Pius X and particularly since Vatican II) intended to make eucharist readily available to all, must not perpetuate untruth and injustice in the face of mounting evidence.

It is appropriate to examine the place of eucharist in the church universal and local, for that was a concern of Jesus and because there is currently a virtual starvation in many eucharistic communities. This has profound effects on the spirituality of the missionary, which is our present concern. To many Christians today (for reasons related to the choice and availability of presiders or ordinary ministers of the eucharist) it makes no sense to claim—as does *Mediator Dei* (1947)—that the eucharist is the "summit" and "center of the Christian religion." That is sheer nostalgia or wishful thinking. In many communities, and this is familiar to many missionaries, a living eucharistic liturgy is no more a reality than is the pot at the end of the rainbow.

Consecrated bread "reserved" for and "preserved" by the People of God, or carried on bicycles from one distant village to the next does not (even when accompanied by candles or processions) constitute the living eucharist of Christian tradition, much less does it nourish radical conversion. Sometimes, if not sacrilegious, such arrangements are embarrassingly inappropriate and a travesty of the *anamnesis* of Jesus' sacrifice. When proposed as the only legitimate form, to communities with reputable leaders and faith-filled members, they are unconvincing, contrived, and insulting. Hungry communities deprived of eucharist are discovering that it is not, in fact, the summit or the center of their religion (and certainly not of their lives). They will look elsewhere unless it is once again made available to them; or starving people may seek and find food, and feed themselves.

If the eucharist is central to Christian tradition, it must not be allowed to become a fading memory or a rarity for any community. If some communities in some places have a captive priest and an easily available eucharist, while others are regularly deprived and forbidden to confect their own, this would look very like rank injustice, a preferential option for the privileged, and a bad and unworkable law. More honest to say that eucharist is the spiritual or symbolic center and summit than to perpetuate this untruth.

This chapter is about the conversion and transformation of missionaries; the eucharist has a place precisely because its position in the life of Christians has recently become unclear. If it is central to ongoing conversion and an intrinsic part of missionary spirituality, then eucharist must be incorporated as such into life. If it is becoming less obviously central then we need to examine our spirituality and conversion, or the eucharist itself in its current shape, and assess the effects of the shift. There is an urgent need to encourage major discussions and much thought about the theological and social status of the eucharist, especially in the lives of those working cross-culturally, where it is an endangered species.

Eucharist was never intended as a meal of satiety but as a symbolic (but not a token) meal "for the road" or "for the journey": for people united as community. St. Paul insisted that normal meals should be eaten at home and that eucharist must not be abused by gluttony, selfishness, factionalism, or hierarchies (1 Cor 11:20-22). Does it not follow that eucharist is intended to sensitize us to the needs of others, to justice, and therefore that communities which do not experience some neediness and personal poverty as they gather for eucharist risk becoming complacent and inward-looking, the antithesis of a missionary perspective? Far from arguing for eucharistic deprivation or artificial hunger, this is to urge that eucharist is inseparable from and an expression of the hunger for justice constitutive of our own pilgrimage to conversion.

We could challenge our spirituality and conversion even more directly, for "the formation of a religious self around passionate attachment to the sacrament of the eucharist [in isolation] can result in obliviousness to the world's problems, [and] an escape from engagement."[26] Woe to us if this should happen! But if our understanding of eucharist is limited to the formal sacrament, we risk "domesticating" our Savior and privatizing his presence among us. But as participation in, and as the very body of Christ, eucharist is not limited to the formal sacrament. Unless we can find eucharist in the broader sense among those excluded or absent from the formal sacrament, we fail as a eucharistic people to be transformed and to be instrumental in the transformation of others. Eucharist that is so cozy as to make us impervious to the world's problems is a major scandal! (1 Cor 11:27-34).

The transformation of the missionary, as of the host people, occurs in the real world. It is not a kind of fairy tale; the starting point is the existential situation. And the real world is, sadly, populated by the estranged, the alienated, and the disenfranchised, "outcast" and "sinner." It is useless for us to expect them and others to come to us unless we undertake to engage with them. The journey on which we are embarked as Christians is a journey we make *together* with all men and women, "gentiles" and "pagans" alike; and it starts from here.

Surely it is still possible for us to be a eucharistic people, and for the eucharist to be at the center of our lives, but not yet, and not before some fundamental reorientations in our spirituality and our commitment to justice for all people. That is the measure of our conversion. That will be the measure of the transformation of all things in Christ. Ours should be a eucharistic spirituality, and together we should be a eucharistic people. There is a long way to go, and if we are to find bread for the journey, we must seriously modify our habits. "Mission in reverse" might help reorient us, and then we can look again at the cross-cultural implications of eucharist.

QUESTIONS FOR THE ROAD

- What justification for mission can you invoke, apart from Matthew 28:19-20? Do you find other scriptural passages equally compelling?
- Is radical continuity a new idea for you? Do you expect that the normal course of conversion—your own and other people's—is through a radical break with the past, or by a radical reengagement and recommitment? What is the significance of culture and experience in the work of conversion?
- Do you accept the notion of embodied spirituality and embodied knowledge? What is the effect on personal spirituality of aging, of states of health, and of other variables? Has sufficient attention been paid to these variables?
- "We are the body of Christ." What does this mean to you in terms of eucharist? What does it mean to you in terms of the particular community with which you identify?

PART II

BREAD

Chapter 4

Mission in Reverse

The Good News . . . is not a human message, . . . it is something I learned only through a revelation.

Galatians 1:12-13

Careful reflection [is required], especially on the part of missionaries themselves, who may be led, as a result of changes occurring within the missionary field, no longer to understand the meaning of their vocation and no longer to know exactly what the church expects of them today.

Redemptoris Missio, 65

All language about God is self-committing language. It has to change us, bring us to the point of conversion.[1]

Christians are not distinguished from the rest of people either in locality or in speech or in customs. . . . They dwell in their own countries but only as sojourners. . . . And they endure all hardships as strangers.[2]

A NEW "OLD" WAY OF MISSION

We may identify and sympathize with the sentiments expressed by Pope John Paul II in the 1990 letter quoted above. Yet the reflection for which he calls must be supported by adequate knowledge, since the changes of which he speaks are by no means confined to "the mission field" in the classical sense of the term. Furthermore, "exactly what the church expects" is no simple matter to pin down, especially if we consider the church's own need to be converted.

As we pursue our Christian missionary journey, aware of our need for sustaining food, we are immediately faced with a choice: we may prepare and take our own bread with us, or we may, in the spirit of Jesus, take no bread for the journey (Mk 6:8). Or perhaps, prudently acknowledging that we do indeed hold a treasure we wish to share, we may choose both options. But unless we believe that those to whom we go have some bread themselves, and unless we trust that they will share their bread with us, our journey will be a travesty of the Christian mission. The so-called *Epistle to Diognetus,* from the second century, captures well the spirit of the Christian in relation to others; as missioners we too need the same kind of simplicity and respect.

Already in the early 1970s the term "mission in reverse" was employed; twenty years later, though almost in common use, it is sometimes ambiguous. It is worth noting the history and original meaning. Claude-Marie Barbour, a Presbyterian minister working at the time in Gary, Indiana, gave this formal title to a way of living out the Christian mission in the existential situation. With some of her colleagues and associates in Shalom Ministries,[3] she has written about its meaning and implications:

> The mission-in-reverse approach teaches that the minister can and should learn from the people ministered to — including, and perhaps especially, from the poor and marginalized people. By taking these people seriously, by listening to them ... personal relationships are developed, and the dignity of the people is enhanced. Such presence to people is seen as necessarily allowing them to be the leaders in the relationship.[4]

Though we will have more to say about "mission in reverse," it is important to note here that others have used the phrase in a number of different senses. It has been employed to mean the sending of missionary personnel from the South to the North, or from the so-called Third World to the First World (yet this has sometimes also been called "reverse mission"). It has been used to refer to the contributions that erstwhile overseas missioners can make when they return home. And it has been used in the sense originally intended by Dr. Barbour, but renamed "reverse mission"! There is thus confusion, overlap, and ambiguity. But we will use it in its pristine sense, referring to "both a spirituality and a method of approach to mission and ministry."[5]

We noted in concluding Chapter 3, that the transformation of the missioner occurs in the real world, in the existential situation. Here is how mission in reverse has been characterized:

> It is incarnational because it attempts to imitate Christ's own entrance into our world and his total identification with a particular culture — an identification so complete that he was not recognized as God. It is dialogic because dialogue seems to be the best way in our day to describe how we can enter the world of others, at least when dialogue is seen primarily as an attitude and not simply as a technique.[6]

"An attitude and not simply a technique." Techniques may change without necessarily affecting human relationships, but attitudes are a very different matter; the attitude a missioner brings characterizes the very nature of his or her evangelism. This being so, we shall in the current chapter consider mission in reverse as an attitudinal approach to mission and examine some of its implications. We will emphasize some instances of urgent pastoral need and call for all who identify with the missionary challenge of Jesus to strive for justice in the communities in which we work.

We will also, throughout this central section, be sensitive to the theme of the bread for the journey: the bread we bring, the bread we receive, the bread we break together, and the broken bread of our lives, whose fragments must be gathered up respectfully (Matt 14:20). And we will consequently be on the lookout for signs and types of eucharist in our midst.

THE PROBLEM OF MISSION IN REVERSE

Our opening chapter introduced the notion of binary thinking and of a binary universe. In such a world (by contrast with the existential world and the world of Jesus) good and bad, truth and falsehood, and other contrastive pairs tend to be absolutized, polarized, made concrete, and readily identified with persons or things. But this leaves little room for shades or gradations, no place for partial good or partial truth. What is not immediately identified as truth or goodness becomes associated with its opposite and is judged or condemned as falsehood or evil.

Such an attitude may be very good for those who wish to keep accounts or to be impartial, but it signally fails to show understanding or compassion, or indeed the kind of partiality Jesus consistently showed to those who were oppressed. Jesus was particularly encouraging of people struggling in less than perfect circumstances. He was able to affirm good will, to condemn sin without annihilating the sinner, to lift up the brokenhearted and not crush the fragile reed, to show love and not to worship legalism.

But, given a certain judgmental attitude, it will be difficult for us to escape the binary way of thinking and acting, and virtually impossible to minimize the importance that we attach to our own rightness, truth, and wisdom. Worse still, in our prejudice we may be imprisoned within the boundaries of our judgments, neither a good place nor an impressive attitude for authentic discipleship and evangelism!

Now mission in reverse may sound fairly straightforward, if radically novel, particularly to people steeped in binary thinking. But precisely because it demands a certain attitude, yet attitudes are deeply rooted, it is by no means a simple undertaking for many of us, especially those of a certain age and trained in dogmatic theology and a world of absolutes. Mission in reverse would be a reversal, not only of many assumptions about who holds the initiative in mission work, but a reversal too of the direction in which mission is sometimes assumed to occur, namely from "us" to "them." If we are locked within a binary mentality then "we" have the truth and wisdom, while "they" do not; in such a universe mission in reverse is clearly impossible. For it to happen, therefore, we must discover a different kind of world and be converted from a particular mentality.

In the world of Jesus (not the physical, geographical world but the world of faith and experience), "what do you want me to do for you?" (Mk 10:51) is an elementary and crucial question; much of the agenda of mission will be determined according to the reply. But you can only ask other people to state their needs if you trust them and are prepared to risk. If you think they are fundamentally wrong or selfish, you won't allow them to say what they need; either you will not believe them or you will not trust them because you "know better." And yet you cannot even ask such a question unless you already have some credibility. Those who are certain they know what is best for others are incapable of dialogue; those who offer only what they themselves want to give simply patronize. Many people give second-hand goods or unneeded cast-offs; few people give really new things, and fewer give their full and undivided attention. But Jesus encouraged Barti-maeus to name his own need; and Bartimaeus received *new* sight. More than that, he received vision; that was what enabled him to follow Jesus in mission, to Jerusalem (Mk 10:51). Our need, too, is for vision.

In the world of Jesus the unsophisticated are allowed to raise embar-rassing issues: "Even the dogs under the table eat the children's leftovers," says the putatively insignificant Syro-phoenician woman (Mk 7:28). In the world of Jesus the unexpected responses from the most unlikely people become occasions for Jesus to marvel at the workings of grace and to acknowledge that God-given faith brings about the working of miracles above and beyond his own doing (Matt 9:22; 15:28; Mk 10:51). In the world of Jesus, the faith of others is a support for his own (Lk 7:9). As individuals and as church, perhaps we have failed to learn these lessons and to ask about human needs, so busy are we with giving what we have brought, with fulfilling our agendas, and with meeting our own expectations.

Mission in reverse, though a comparatively recent phrase, draws atten-tion to a set of age-old issues: how to follow the command to go and preach the Good News, yet at the same time be sensitive to the presence of the Spirit of God who arrived before us; how to respect the integrity of the people to whom we go, yet at the same time announce the news that really is new; how to minister by being ministered to, yet also bring healing and hope. It thus demands a radical modification of some attitudes that are as easy to slip into as they are difficult to shift. St. Paul expressed this con-version quite well in the Letter to the Romans (1:11-12): "I am longing to see you, either to strengthen you by sharing a spiritual gift with you, or what is better, to find encouragement among you from our common faith." My assumption is that the "common faith" of which he speaks is, for us too, as much something in the process of discovery and discernment as it is a matter of empirical fact.

Yet it would certainly not be accurate or fair for us to think of mission in reverse as a crude reversal of all that has been done according to a classical style of mission. Neither justice nor Jesus would be served if we were to repudiate the notion that the missioner is a necessary component of the church. But it is important for us to recall that the primary agents of mission are the Spirit of God and the local people; Jesus, not the missioner, is savior! And it is equally important to inject a little subtlety into the process of evangelism. Consequently, were we simply and merely to reverse certain attitudes, then, to use the language of the dialectic, we would still only have moved from thesis to antithesis, when what we need is authentic synthesis.

A further point concerns the irreducibility of experience. Different cultures and experiences actually shape people in different ways; that is, these differences are such as to produce people who, notwithstanding fundamental similarities, are different from each other. The implications of this need to be more explicitly addressed today in the context of inculturation. It was always bad psychology and bad theology to treat people as blank slates, "tabulae rasae," on which a missioner could presume to write comprehensibly. It was always poor anthropology and poor spirituality to undertake a "clean sweep" policy, attempting to eradicate people's culture and values in order to replace them with "the truth." Not only did these not work, they assumed only one kind of truth or wisdom—that which was fully incarnated in the missioner.

Mission in reverse, however, is both a more effective and a more respectful approach, though also more risky and more demanding of the evangelist. Reducing or standardizing everyone to a single model Christian type, or belittling people's formative experiences and cultural values through selective literacy campaigns, monocultural imperialism, or culturally biased applications of biblical interpretation are not only unjustified methods, but stifle the unconstrained Spirit of God. Mission in reverse explicitly embraces the fact that salvation occurs in the midst of human history, which means that God can and does reach people where they are, not where someone might like them to be. In our final chapter we will look at examples of actual situations and discern in them the workings of grace and the call to ongoing conversion; for the moment we will continue to open up the notion of mission in reverse.

MISSION IN REVERSE AND CONVERSION

The phrase "mission in reverse" itself suggests an approach to mission that is, we may say, counter-intuitive or in some way different from classical forms of mission. Not that it is new; far from it. But though Jesus himself exemplifies such an approach, it has not always characterized more recent evangelistic attitudes. Yet if it is to be a hallmark of authentic mission, it will need to be worked into our own attitudes; without it our conversion is impossible.

Describing the missionary mandate given by Jesus, the synoptic accounts show some variations: the Gospel of Matthew notes that authority over unclean spirits is given, that of Mark talks of preaching repentance, and the Gospel of Luke adds the mission to proclaim the Realm of God. But all three (Matt 10:1; Mk 6:13; Lk 9:1) speak about the gift of healing power, and all three use the verb *therapeuo* (*ein*) rather than *iaomai*. The latter verb is in common usage and translates simply as "to remedy, heal, correct"; the former is much more interesting to those committed to mission in reverse, for the infinitive means "to attend, to wait on, to serve." It is much more a verb of relationship, of reciprocity, of responsiveness. And it is commonly used in the Greek New Testament as the verb we translate as "to minister."

If we are to minister and to be ministers in the name and spirit of Jesus, this is what is entailed: attending, waiting on, serving. This kind of attention to the needs of others is, as is clear from the story of Bartimaeus, certainly a reflection of the way in which Jesus approached his own task. And like the character in Molière who "discovered" that he had actually been speaking prose all his life, so we, as we examine some characteristics and effects of mission in reverse, may discover the extent to which we may in fact have been practicing it ourselves.

Limitations and Boundaries

We can distinguish the former as the absolute extent beyond which we are virtually unable to go, and the latter as the actual perimeters through which we do not in fact go. In practice, however, they are often synonymous. But one's actual boundaries are rarely insurmountable; it is amazing what people are capable of. And one's imagined limitations are frequently transcended, given an appropriate incentive. We should therefore be aware that our capacities are not infinite and that some boundaries are necessary; then we can seek judicious ways to overcome, break through, surpass, be transformed and converted.

But since conversion starts from where we actually are and operates on who we actually are, we also need to be assured that it is fitting that we have actual limits and boundaries. And we need to know what, for us, is excessive, alien, intolerable, as well as what is distasteful, unfamiliar, or threatening. Then, if conversion should imply a radical continuity rather than a radical disjunction, we will have to extend and modify those boundaries that are relative, while strengthening those that are absolute. But the choice is not a whimsical one, and it can only be made through discernment and trust. We must hold fast, as some translations of St. Paul say: "Hold to the outline of sound teaching which you heard from me" (2 Tim 1:13); or as the Letter to the Hebrews has it: "Let us hold unswervingly to our profession which gives us hope" (Heb 10:23). Such fidelity is also part of conversion.

A way of life that accepts the existence of boundaries as well as the necessity to test and transcend them will produce a spirituality of risk, or trust.[7] Sometimes we will not know whether an action undertaken in good faith is in fact the most appropriate. But different contexts and circumstances may call forth different responses. Trial and error may be an unfamiliar and indeed an unacceptable theological maxim, but if we trust in the guiding Spirit of God and the basic integrity of people, a spirituality of risk will be touched by the virtue of prudence and will not degenerate into an attitude of stupidity or fecklessness (we will pursue this point in Chapter 9). Only if we stay within the fastnesses of our microcosms, refusing to change, to dare, or to be challenged, will we be like those who buried their talents in the earth, where they produced nothing (Lk 19:11-26). But unless we learn to trust in the Spirit of God and in the people, we are effectively asserting that our plans and our initiatives are the embodiment of all wisdom. To do this is to fail to work within our real limitations and to fail to be partners with Christ in the work of our redemption.

Conscientization and Mission

Conscientization, the process by which our boundaries are shaken and our sensibilities shocked, is catalytic for further change within ourselves. It is therefore a potential step to conversion. Conscientization is the softening up of our hardened perceptions or philosophical positions; it is the breaking down of obsolete and unnecessary defenses. It will result from the interaction between what we may label the "normal self" and an unfamiliar situation, such that the latter has a significant effect on the former. Clearly, if we avoid all such interaction, then conscientization will have no part in our lives.

But if we believe in centrifugal mission, we believe in interaction. Conscientization in this perspective must, and will, lead to radical conversion on at least two levels: the intellectual and the spiritual. Intellectual conversion is objectified once a person is inspired to undertake an active reeducation that deepens the initial conscientization and assures of its continuing impact. Spiritual conversion is occurring when conscientization has suffused a person's way-of-being-in-the-world to the point that such a person not only thinks differently but acts and reacts, judges and interprets according to different criteria. Here is the attitudinal change that we diagnosed as constitutive of mission in reverse.

Ministry and Dialogue

Such a conversion will of course exercise a profound effect on our life; it will truly transform it. Some of our most fundamental paradigms will be permanently modified, because we will not only have listened to people's stories but we will have lived them, and sharing stories in honest and true dialogue is where theological reflection begins. Then the fruits of this process of conversion will fall into other people's gardens as our branches, as strong as our roots, extend in attentive ministry and healing service.

"Are you here for/of yourself or are you here for us?" the people would say almost *ad nauseam*. One would have thought it was obvious: why else go to West Africa, much less stay there? But they knew very well how to identify monologue dressed as dialogue. And in the course of time they indicated just how much missioners' conversation was really monologue. We carry a crushing burden if we try to transport Truth singlehandedly. "Come to me all you who are heavy burdened," said Jesus (Matt 11:28). But those who have both hands wrapped around their burden find it difficult to embrace others. Mission in reverse is absolutely impossible unless one dares to change posture and at least lay down the burden for a moment. Then perhaps others will help lift it; perhaps, too, some of its contents will be found readily available in the locality. But dialogue is only possible for those who know they are not self-sufficient, and for some people this is very difficult to acknowledge.

Perhaps the best way to discern the value of mission in reverse is simply to keep looking at Jesus. "What do you want me to do for you?" "Give me a drink." "Which of these proved a neighbor?" "Take this cup away from me." These are not the words and actions of one who lords it over others. Nor do they point to one who undertakes so-called dialogue from a position of strength, unwilling to modify or react to the other person. These are the words—and the whole life of Jesus bears them out—of one who came looking for faith, who was moved by the faith he found, and was surprised by some of the persons and places where he found it.

Jesus is the model for a ministry of risk and trust, an example of the mutually liberating effects of dialogue. And mission in reverse is nothing if not mission undertaken in the spirit of Jesus. It is predicated on true mutuality. Jesus was constantly criticized for this palpable mutuality, for eating and consorting with "sinners": prostitutes, lepers, unclean people, outcasts, tax-collectors, and the rest. But he did not simply patronize them, much less "use" them; they *were* his mission and ministry. They contributed to his transformation in mission, as he encouraged and marveled at theirs. They set the agenda as much as he did. The more outspoken of them, like the Syro-phoenician woman (Mk 7:24-30) or the woman at Bethany (Matt 26:6-13; Mk 14:39), were more direct than others, but the crowds in general, the sick and the lame, the lepers and the bereaved, also had their say and were heard.

A person committed to mission in reverse is not lacking in faith or uncommitted to seeking the truth, but in Hollenweger's word, he or she "gambles" with a personal, limited, current understanding of faith, trusting that this is no less than Jesus asks. "Why are you afraid?" "Fear is useless:

only have faith." "Where is your faith?" Those who believe in transformation know that grace can abound where there was sin, that hope may arise from hopeless situations, and that heroism does emerge from the most unlikely places. Those who believe in transformation understand that they will find bread for their journeys (Mk 6:8), and remembering the feeding of the five thousand, they know too that the little they bring in faith will be multiplied in the communities they encounter (Mk 6:35ff).

An End to Mission?

A feature of bounded thinking within bounded universes is that things have a beginning and an end. But though mission may take place in time, it is as unbounded as the love of God. Indeed, mission *is* the love of God; that is what we mean when we talk about the *Missio Dei*, God's mission to love and save all humankind. It is a complex notion, especially when we look at the injustice and suffering in the world. Indeed, God's saving love is not always easy to discern. But it may be precisely this unbounded, unlimited dimension of mission that makes mission in reverse so challenging. We are unable to pin it down, define it, draw up agendas, set goals, draw things to tidy conclusions; there is no end to the ministry, to the attention and care we are called to offer in Jesus' name.

Executives may order and control, form strategies and assess, but followers of Jesus can only trust, wait, commit, respond, risk. This is what Jesus himself did—to the shedding of blood and the offering of life, to martyrdom. And if slowly, haltingly, partially, we learn to entrust our lives, in the spirit of Jesus, to those beloved of God whom we meet at the margins to which we journey in faith, then our lives will move to a different rhythm, and time will no longer be a scarce commodity. The poor do not run out of time; they may teach us how to use it.

If José Comblin is right in asserting baldly that "the task of liberating the world has been entrusted to the poor,"[8] then, far from worrying about the time, we need to be concerned about discovering more about this liberation. In part, it is offered to those who have no abiding city (Heb 13:14), the *anawim*, the poor of Yahweh. One of the undoubted realities of our time it that the people best able to survive intense privations are not the educated, the rich, or the presently healthy; such people have few of the necessary resources. The real "survivors" are those on the margins: the outcasts, the abandoned, those sometimes seen as and labeled "sinners." They have been likened to the other probable survivors of a nuclear holocaust: cockroaches. This reality of course gives us absolutely no license to neglect such people further, but it does require that we recognize their resourcefulness.

There are oppressed people with authentic missionary zeal that far outstrips that of many missioners, and with the kind of indomitable faith that some Christians only dream about. So if the poor are so central to the missionary enterprise, how will the richer among us manage? Only, it would seem, by learning a lesson that eluded Dives, the rich one (Lk 16:19-31); only by discovering a relationship of hospitality to the Lazarus on the margins. No, there is no end in sight for mission, and God's love is being mediated by people with much to teach professional missioners. Mission in reverse, then, is not only about changing attitudes within ourselves, but about some of the surprising ways in which God may exalt the lowly.

CONVERTING THE MISSIONER

Having considered the conversion of the missioner in terms of a personal orientation and response, we are now more concerned with the people among whom he or she lives and works. True mutuality in mission demands that missioners be recipients as well as givers, and not just symbolically. Missioners are required not only to risk, but to entrust their well-being to their hosts. To do any less would be exploitative and superficial, not the basis on which to build a Christian community.

There is a rather fine line to be drawn between making unfair demands on one's hosts and becoming too independent of them. Missioners have certainly been accused of failure in both these areas, but whatever may be said about the former, they have often tried to make a virtue of the latter. How often have missioners defended their selfless generosity, the offering of their entire lives, their fidelity to giving rather than receiving? St. Paul specifically claims that Jesus said "there is more happiness in giving than in receiving" (Acts 20:35). Yet interestingly, nowhere in the Gospels is this recorded as a saying of Jesus! This is rather surprising, given the apparent weight of the statement, the fact that Paul cannot have heard it from Jesus himself, and the rather comprehensive corpus of sayings attributed to Jesus and recorded in writing.

But as any visitor to another family or culture should know, an ability graciously to receive is every bit as important as the act of giving or the ability to give. Without the former there is no mutuality; without mutual indebtedness there is no relationship. Well has it been said that "charity wounds [the one] who receives, and our whole moral effort is directed toward suppressing the unconscious harmful patronage of a rich almoner."[9] One-sided relationships are not relationships at all, and a person forced to receive from an almoner or almsgiver and unable or forbidden to reciprocate in any way can quickly come to hate the powerful and patronizing donor. Real mutuality is just that: healthy interdependence, which expresses itself as much in simple gratitude as in expansive generosity. And if our missionary pilgrimage of grace is to be a truly communal journey, then there must be real mutuality, comprised of receiving and giving, and acknowledging both the vulnerability and strength, the sanctity and the sinfulness of true "companions"—those who break and share their bread.

But there is another insidious kind of independence, well exemplified in a novel about religious sisters working among poor people.[10] The very cleanliness of the sisters (perceived and cultivated as a virtue) is alienating to people who do not have access to adequate clean water or clean clothes. Such cleanliness, it can be argued, is actually contrary not only to an authentic spirit of poverty, but to friendship itself; to cling to it is to resist the call to conversion.

Now, it is all very well to say this kind of thing in reference to certain behavioral modifications, but in what sense can we maintain that our hosts have anything truly spiritual or really significant to offer to the missioner? There has been woven into the fabric of mission history a long thread (not the only thread, to be sure, yet a noticeable one), an unself-critical missionary approach, which assumed that missioners had virtually nothing to learn from others, at least, not anything very, much less vitally, important. It takes theological insight and the mentality of Jesus to accept that non-evangelized or recently evangelized peoples may be channels of grace to us; that the Spirit of God is working in them; and that God's glory may be revealed in them whether or not they explicitly know Jesus as Savior. But unless the missioner is equipped with such insight, dialogue will become diatribe and evangelism will become evangelicalism of the crudest kind.

Assumptions about the poverty or unimportance of culture have been used in justification of some cavalier attitudes toward local languages and anthropology, and indeed of the very meaning of evangelism. Notwithstanding the many missioners deeply respectful of their hosts and committed to understanding people and making sense of cultures as an intrinsic part of authentic mission, phrases like "native customs" encountered in mission journals and magisterial documents have frequently carried heavily condescending connotations (as if "customs" are not to be confused with "values"). It is therefore apposite, while affirming those who are more sensitive than this, to note recent trenchant statements that neither romanticize the work of missioners nor minimize the importance of the study of culture:

> [Missioners] ... must *immerse themselves* in the cultural milieu of those to whom they are sent, moving beyond their own cultural limitations. Hence *they must learn the language* ... become familiar with the most important expressions of the local culture, and *discover its values through direct experience.* ... It is not of course a matter of mission[ers] renouncing their own cultural identity, but of understanding, appreciating, fostering and evangelizing the culture of the environment in which they are working, and therefore of equipping themselves to communicate effectively with it, adopting *a manner of living which is a sign of Gospel witness and of solidarity with the people* (*Redemptoris Missio*, 53, my emphasis).

The conversion of the missioner partially depends on the acceptance of the general insight that local people are channels of grace. But there is a specific refinement of this insight: "the poor," "the marginalized," or simply "the other," have particular perspectives that furnish them with views, opinions, and wisdom that no one else can afford to ignore, least of all missioners. And since the specific derives from the general, it might be helpful to be more explicit here.

People's ideas of God must not be demeaned or dismissed as superstition and wrongheadedness; they are the foundations for worlds-of-meaning and the basis upon which the fullness of Christ's revelation will build. Conversion, as we have emphasized, starts from the existential situation, and missioners need to take all necessary steps to understand people's theologies and epistemologies, however exotic they appear. But more than this, particularity and ethnocentrism are perfectly capable of reflecting some shafts of clear light, which vary as local groups vary, giving an excellent insight into the way people think, and thus into the variety of possible ways of thinking. Without this knowledge, missioners will be building their evangelism on sand. And just as St. Paul was subtle enough to use the Athenian statue to the Unknown God as a catechetical tool (Acts 17:23), so contemporary missioners are well-advised to discover where God has gone before and engage the people at that point.

More specifically, without idealizing people, and especially poor and outcast people, a moment's reflection will remind us that such people have firsthand experience of, and opinions about, justice and kindness (and injustice and unkindness), as well as of exploitation and poverty. They are more than able to interpret and apply the parables and to unmask hypocrisy in biblical characters or in missioners. Unless we who claim the latter role listen actively to their cries, attend to their perspectives, and understand the basis of their judgments (including those on ourselves and our ilk), we will effectively remain at best do-gooders and at worst no different from the lawyers condemned by Jesus (Lk 11:45-46).

It is appropriate here not simply to emphasize the necessity of the conversion of the missioner (we did that in Chapter 3), but to suggest a way in which we can be drawn into that journey. Mission in reverse has the potential for calling all parties to conversion, and as active agents. The way described here is a form of what is called "participant observation," but with a twist; the outcome is, in cooperation with the grace of God, conversion which is truly mutual and communitarian, conversion which builds up the People of God.

"PARTICIPANT OBSERVATION" AND MUTUAL EVANGELISM

Mission in reverse describes in new words a very old reality: authentic ministry in the spirit of Jesus. But in the social sciences there exists an approach that creates some not-so-faint echoes. On the understanding that missioners need some of the insights of the social sciences, and that there exists wisdom beyond what we possess already, we may perhaps try weaving together various strands in order to make a stronger and more tensile Ariadne's thread.

An Anthropological Approach

Participant observation is a research method beloved of cultural anthropologists. While it has sometimes been used as a blunt instrument rather than as a delicate tool, nevertheless, with appropriate care, it can produce a very satisfying outcome. It is essentially an approach to learning in which the enquirer becomes involved in the process being studied. And it implies some degree of mutual modification.

First, to identify a danger, some practitioners, committed to participant observation yet initially naive and incompetent, have used their local "informants" less than honorably. The word "informant" is already faintly demeaning, but such persons have at times been used as objects through which to extrude as much information as possible rather than as subjects. And there have been anthropologists who have paid scant attention to the interpretations or explanations of their informants but presumed to offer to their readers more "coherent" explanations of what these people "really mean." When this happens it indicates that the interpreter (anthropologist) believes there is only one "true" or "real" explanation, that the anthropologist is in possession of such an explanation, and that the raw information must be repackaged in such a way as to be comprehensible and acceptable to others who share the wisdom and thought processes of the anthropologist. It also, and effectively, dismisses the informant as worthless.

Now the process of translation, whether cultural or linguistic, is always a delicate one, but if approached with arrogance and from a dogmatic and partisan perspective, it is bound to be a travesty. Translation must be a two-way process, which includes reciprocity and careful testing; otherwise what seems to one party to be a satisfactory rendering may be judged by the other an unacceptable formulation or rank nonsense. Unless one's informants are treated with respect, translation will be betrayal, and one will never succeed in understanding more than a caricature of another point of view.

So much for the danger. There is, however, equally great potential in the approach, but the progeny is born of risk and of sharing: risk, because one chooses not to predetermine the agenda; and sharing, since if one attempts to see things from another's point of view one needs to take the other very seriously indeed. If anthropologists can rise to the challenge, surely it is not in principle too much for missioners? In practice, of course, attitude is everything; some missioners may be as limited as some anthropologists, with the consequent skewing of information and translation.

A Pastoral Approach

Missioners, like anthropologists, are not immune from danger; we can easily become convinced that the truth we carry can only be borne in the vessels in which we bring it and that all other vessels are impure or inefficient. Consequently we may be disposed to undervalue both messages and messengers from cultures other than our own and thus to overrate our personal credibility and style. The antidote to this is simply a more authentic and rigorous form of participant observation.

In the Gospel accounts, those considered to be actively involved in the mission given to the Twelve (Lk 9; Matt 10; Mk 6) or to the seventy-two (Lk 10) are committed to following Jesus: women and men of faith, instruments of mission. But since the initiative in mission is God's, and since people everywhere are called by an impulse of God's grace and shown a glimpse of God's revelation, Christian evangelists and the people they encounter must together discover and share their understanding of God: the God of creation who is the God of Jesus Christ. It is not only the evangelist who observes others, nor is the missioner the only one who participates in other people's lives. Local people too observe keenly and participate to a greater or less extent in the lives of those who ostensibly come in the name of the Lord in collaboration and service. Participant observation cannot therefore be a unilateral initiative of missioners. The notion that people may reduce other people's struggle and pain to the categories of their own theological tradition or personal experience is totally unacceptable.

A pastorally sensitive participant observer, then, is committed to learning sometimes to participate when observation would be more comfortable, and conversely, to learning respectfully to observe when perhaps bursting to participate. The initiative, after all, is not entirely the visitor's, and hosts tend not to take too kindly to egregious strangers. Without respectful mutuality, participant observation will degenerate into disrespectful interference. With such mutuality, however, the pastorally sensitive follower of Jesus will not only discern if and when participation is inappropriate, but respectfully avoid observing whatever might be private. St. Paul seems to acknowledge that though things might be lawful they might not thereby be judicious (1 Cor 6:12; 10:23), and the truly respectful participant observer will trust the hosts' judgment before rushing to interpret privacy as deceit or silence as duplicity.

It is thus by no means easy to strike a pastorally appropriate balance between participation and observation, or between challenge and acquiescence, especially if one is filled with enthusiasm or zeal. But if missioners insist on retaining all the initiatives and are unwilling or unable to trust other people with discernment and with their own share of responsibility for *metanoia*, then evangelism becomes proselytization and mutuality is merely a sham.

People truly committed to evangelism in the spirit of Jesus will be concerned with looking for and nurturing the faith that is already present, with searching out the wisdom of other cultural traditions, and with studying the workings of grace in cross-cultural relationships. Even in those depressed and difficult areas at the very edges of society or in the gaps—the twilight worlds of addiction and alienation—there is grace. Whoever truly goes forth in the spirit of Jesus will be empowered to develop into a participant observer without a loss of integrity, and with the assurance of becoming a recipient and not merely a dispenser of grace. Cultural and personal sensitivity should not be a monopoly of anthropologists, but a prerequisite of every apostle and disciple, for how can we preach a credible Gospel if we are offensive and indiscreet?

CLASSICAL APPROACHES, MISSION IN REVERSE, AND THE FUTURE

It is not the intention here to polarize a certain way of undertaking mission (classical mission) against what is advocated here (mission in reverse), as if the past were represented by the one and the future is to be redeemed by the other. By any other name, as we have emphasized, mission in reverse would be the same: mission in the true spirit of Jesus. And unquestionably such spirit has existed as long as there has been a mission outreach from the churches. Yet it is only honest to declare that, given a certain kind of theology and ecclesiology, there will be an inevitable drift away from mission in the spirit of Jesus toward a legalistic, fossilized institutionalization of mission and of the church to which it gives birth.

As soon as the disciple begins to take unwarranted responsibility for the conversion of others (not the same as evangelism, which is the appropriate announcement of the Good News), there is a tendency to make demands that are not according to the spirit of Jesus. "Do not judge" can be forgotten by those who feel personally responsible not only for evangelism but for controlling the way it is received, and the response produced. "Neither do I condemn you; go now and sin no more" can so easily turn into swingeing condemnations and even "automatic" excommunications. Acquaintance with the history of mission will leave us with little cause for complacency.

To undertake mission in reverse, as here described, is impossible for the doctrinaire missioner, for it requires that one forbear to judge, that one have patience with the response of the other, and above all that one allow for the possibility that people must make mistakes in the course of their movement to maturity (as we will see in Chapter 8). Those who think of themselves as God-appointed judges, those who have little patience with themselves, and those who are persuaded that they must be perfect *now*, will not be temperamentally suited to the demands of mission in reverse in spite of good intentions. Not only does such an attitudinal approach demand that we constantly try to adopt the perspective of Jesus (notoriously difficult as well as presumptuous!), but it requires that we really commit ourselves to trusting those among whom we minister.

Yet whoever announces the Good News does not operate as an individual but as an emissary, a missioner, one sent by a church. And churches, whether different denominations or simply different communities, have different expectations of their missioners, different traditions, and different understandings of tradition. And there's the rub. Mission in reverse calls us first and foremost to more faithful discipleship; it calls us to conversion to Jesus. In the process it challenges us to examine our patterns of behavior and the assumptions underlying them on pragmatic and pastoral grounds. It will make us feel the pain, as "discipline" rubs against "common sense," "rules" chafe on "pastoral need," "Tradition" clashes with "tradition," and "the old" presses on "the new." But rather than shelving issues it will urge us to engage them, even though in meeting one set of criteria it will inevitably fall foul of another. Yet still it will persevere, in faith in God and hope in the community, in loyalty to the most cherished of ancient and common tradition and in obedience to pastoral need. It will court censure and silencing; many in our day have already experienced this. But the will of God is the ultimate victor, as Gamaliel's advice reminds us (Acts 5:34- 39). Mission of this kind is indeed *martyria*, and to suffer at the hands of one's own is said to be the most painful of suffering.

Such a "hands on" approach (recalling in part Jesus' admonition in Luke 9:62: "Once the hand is laid on the plow, no one who looks back is fit for the kingdom of God") appears to be demanded by the state of the world today and by the missioner call to every Christian. It also makes good pastoral sense in the short term and helps form future agenda. This means that gradually, as the implications become better understood, those willing to follow Jesus to the boundaries and the margins will understand the pastoral value of such a tentative, respectful, and determined approach.

Believers, inspired by the challenge and the vision of Isaiah and of Jesus, recounted in the Gospel of Luke (4:18), to

> bring the good news to the poor,
> to proclaim liberty to captives,
> and to the blind new sight,
> to set the downtrodden free,
> to proclaim the Lord's year of favor,

will generously undertake to be vulnerable rather than impervious, uncertain rather than omniscient, and loving rather than legalistic. In the course of time they will learn the virtues of being a stranger rather than trying to dominate and subdue all around. The stranger has no right to claim the highest places at table, and the guest has no business to dictate rules of hospitality to the host. To think and to act otherwise is to be unmasked as arrogant, supercilious, and untrustworthy. Jesus is not only concerned that we be respectful of the strangers around us; that, after all, puts us in a "one-up" position relative to them. No, Jesus pointedly identified himself *as* a stranger (Matt 25:25), putting himself in a "one-down" position relative to those who would receive him. And as such he knew what was expected of him, as well as what he could expect.[11]

Given time and encouragement, the people among whom we walk as strangers will grace us by unmasking our intellectual and theological pretensions and by calling us to a more person-focused, risk-laden, integrity-filled form of mission and, by disabusing us of our savior complexes, will give us the keys to our freedom as children of God. As we slowly come to hear and assimilate their experience of God, church, and self-styled Christians, we will realize how unjust it would be to devalue such experience or to fail to respond to it. They will thus be the instruments of our conversion, as we may hope to be of theirs.

QUESTIONS FOR THE ROAD

- Do you find the notion of mission in reverse persuasive? What are some of its strengths? Do you see particular dangers inherent in this approach?
- What might be some of the implications for our own conversion if we undertake mission in reverse?
- Comblin declares that "the task of liberating the world has been entrusted to the poor." This is rather different from the classical understanding of mission as something undertaken by those specially gifted with a vocation. What do you think Comblin is trying to say?
- Participant observation and mission in reverse do not give us the license to act insensitively or to intrude on people's legitimate boundaries. In practical terms, can you say where there might be some tension between the agendas of the missioner and the local people in this respect? How would you go about addressing these tensions?

Chapter 5

Eucharist: Exchange and Transformation

How may one, how dare one refuse one's sisters and brothers in Christ, the Bread of Christ?[1]

Revelation is what God wants us to know and to do; religion is what we make of revelation. Revelation destabilizes and disturbs us; religion stabilizes and reassures us. The Roman Rite Mass is religion; the church as chosen race, royal priesthood, consecrated nation and people of God, is revelation; the church divided into clergy and lay people is religion.[2]

[We need] mutuality between lex orandi *and* lex credendi *rather than strict dependency of one upon the other; worship and doctrine must correspond.*[3]

The rift between the Gospel and culture is undoubtedly an unhappy circumstance of our times. . . . Accordingly we must devote all our resources and all our efforts to the sedulous evangelization of . . . the various cultures.

Evangelii Nuntiandi 20

"GIVE THEM SOMETHING TO EAT YOURSELVES" (MATT 14:16)

We approach the heart of the missionary undertaking: the gathering of the community of faith as the body of Christ to celebrate and be nourished. And immediately we encounter problems: what is eucharist? who is invited? how is it celebrated? The theoretical issues are complex, yet, paradoxically, fairly simple compared to the practical problems of really "celebrating" the liturgy that Vatican II, paraphrasing *Mediator Dei*, speaks of as "the summit toward which the activity of the church is dedicated, [and] the fount from which all the church's power flows."[4]

It is not only cynics who have great misgivings about the current state and status of the eucharist. As the number of clergy dwindles, as the availability of the Mass[5] becomes scarcer, as the challenge of inculturation and the pastoral need of people increases, so we must ask what, in reality and in prospect, is the place of eucharist in the contemporary world church. How can people be challenged to conversion and transformation, to faith and justice, while this dearth and impoverishment continues? For as long as it continues there is for many neither growth nor participation in the breathless hope that Jesus brought.

The way forward, it would seem, is through the door of change, with all the uncertainty and even fear that implies. Yet in virtue of discipleship we are called to change and committed to transformation.

This chapter is not addressed primarily to bishops or liturgical theologians; they have their responsibilities and agendas, rather specific and particularly related to the availability and the liturgical form of the Mass in a hungry world. Rather, it is for missionaries, the rank and file attempting to implement the challenges and potentialities of the Good News. We missionaries experience the problem. We are called, by Jesus and by the church, to be a eucharistic people. But, as far as Mass is concerned, it is beyond our authority to promote radical adaptation,[6] and the appropriate authorities have not yet been able to produce widely applicable or thoroughgoing examples of liturgical inculturation.[7]

There remains a variety of eucharistic devotions that are culturally and historically contextualized. As such they are not absolutely fixed nor universally applicable. Nor will they apply widely without losing their relevance or force. But such devotions might be *locally* applicable and relevant. Therefore, such hope as there is for eucharistic inculturation rests, in the short term, with so-called "eucharistic devotion outside Mass."

It is indeed foreseen that "changes in the liturgy may, and sometimes must, be introduced also by the minister. . . . The law itself authorizes the minister to make necessary adaptations . . . temporary adjustments in the course of the liturgical celebrations for the purpose of fostering full, active, and intelligent participation."[8] But we are concerned not simply with cosmetic changes nor only with adjustments made spontaneously in the course of the celebration; the shaping of liturgical actions as responses to the demands of inculturation is our focus. Adaptations should be "concerned with the furtherance of the full, conscious, and active participation of the faithful."[9] Indeed they should! And in the course of our evangelizing we ourselves are aware of numerous cases of dire necessity. In the circumstances it is ironic to read that "the golden rule is that the minister should have . . . a keen perception of the pastoral situation or, in other words, a sound practical judgment"[10] when so often hands are tied. But as Pope Pius II (Piccolomini) said half a millennium ago: "Necessity is the mother of law."

So rather than catalogue the problems, which are legion, this chapter will attempt to be positive, to concentrate on the possible rather than on long-term *desiderata*. It will try to promote dialogue between liturgy and cultures rather than indulge in either a liturgical or a cultural monologue. If we start by looking synoptically (Matt 14; Mk 6; Lk 9) at an acute pastoral problem, a group of hungry people "like sheep without a shepherd," this is what we hear:

> [Disciples]   "Send them away, so that they can go . . . and buy them-selves something to eat."
>
> [Jesus]   "Give them something to eat yourselves."
>
> [Disciples]   "All we have is five loaves and two fish."
>
> [Jesus]   "Bring them here to me."

A series of actions follows:
- Jesus took; blessed; broke; gave.
- He handed food to his disciples to distribute among the people.
- They all ate as much as they wanted.
- They collected the scraps, twelve baskets full.

Of course this event is not to be confused with the church's eucharistic liturgies. It is not a prototype of the Mass, but that does not mean we cannot discern something "eucharistic" in the events. And we certainly have here an example of a specific solution to a problem. To summarize:

response + *resources* + *transformation* = *solution*:

- *response*: the social responsibility people have for each other;
- *resources*: whatever is locally available and appropriate, however par-tial;
- *transformation*: the power and grace of God;
- *solution*: whatever meets the need in the most pastorally appropriate way.

If the inculturation of the eucharist in local churches worldwide were only as simple! If our only consideration were to apply lessons derived from the miracle of the loaves then, given the attitudinal approach referred to as mission in reverse, it would be relatively simple: we would gather people around a common table as a means of bringing theology in line with faith; we would ensure the welcome of all who hunger for the bread of life, leaving judgment to God and offering bread for the journey; we would assert that any community responsible enough to be baptized is ipso facto a eucharistic community and thus has the absolute right to eucharist; and we would produce a liturgy that would allow all this to happen. Mission in reverse would, if given rein, cause pastoral problems to be brought to a head rather than deferred or denied, create challenge and perhaps confrontation, cry out loudly for justice, and provide sleepless nights for those trying to be loyal both to an institutional church and a hungry people of God!

But of course life is more complex. People committed to mission in reverse, though seeking the Realm of God and struggling to be loyal to the church, would not fit comfortably into a church that stifled initiatives and engaged in monologue. Nor would they be happy with statements that sounded patronizing, were exceedingly imprecise, and failed to acknowledge the gap between the church as a community of sinners and the church as the body of Christ. Such a statement as this might qualify:

> Through inculturation the church ... introduces peoples, together with their cultures, into her own community. She transmits to them her own values, at the same time taking the good elements that already exist in them and renewing them from within (*Redemptoris Missio*, 13).

At issue is not simply the credibility of a sinful church but of its exercise of legitimate authority to guard and transmit the authentic Christian tradition. If missionaries and local people were more involved in determining cases of inculturation, then many tricky issues might receive ad hoc pastoral solutions rather as Jesus himself operated; but before the eucharist can be inculturated in people's lives, we need to know more about what it really is, as well as how people may best receive it.

Not much can be said here, in practical terms, about a thoroughgoing inculturation of the Mass, except that it is a most urgent pastoral requirement, and that episcopal conferences need to be encouraged and permitted to take prudent risks. The proposal in this chapter is modest and practical: that we enquire about the broadest meaning of the term "eucharist" and then suggest ways in which local churches may be offered some eucharistic hope that is within their capacity to accept, absorb, and inculturate.

At this critical juncture in the lives of young churches, the worst thing we can do as missionaries and brothers and sisters, is nothing; even interim suggestions may assuage the current eucharistic famine, providing always that the church is pledged to systemic solutions in the longer term.

THE MEANING OF EUCHARIST

The eucharistic devotions outside Mass, promoted by the church, range from viaticum to processions, and from Benediction to Exposition of the Blessed Sacrament; "eucharist," therefore, has a significantly wider currency than "Mass." So, in principle, even where the formal celebration of Mass[11] is unavailable, communities of the faithful can still learn to become a eucharistic people. Scarcity and suffering can sometimes bring great discoveries and blessings.

This is by no means to acquiesce in the unavailability of full eucharistic liturgies, especially in the maintenance of an artificial shortage. Nor is it to deny that some local responses to the shortage are very close to formalism and even superstition. The memorial of the Paschal mystery is intended to be the "basic theological content of every liturgical celebration; ... at bottom every liturgical rite contains, signifies, and celebrates the paschal mystery: ... sacraments [and] sacramentals ... converge here."[12] If this is so,

then the present state of the eucharistic life of myriad communities is a
scandal, and it is pastorally indefensible to deprive such communities of
honest celebrations of the Paschal mystery.

Having said that, a range of new liturgical celebrations and ways of being
a eucharistic community await discovery and endorsement, both in domestic
Christian communities and across cultures. The reasons are not far to seek:
different groups have different cultural gifts, and different periods of history illuminate different facets of the Paschal mystery (exemplified in Chapter 8). Furthermore, in every age those who truly hunger and thirst for
God's justice will discover appropriate ways of integrating their daily lives
with the Paschal mystery. The eucharist must never be allowed to fossilize.
The liturgy must be an expression of justice.[13] And the church, whether in
the persons of bishops, theologians, or other missionaries, has an obligation
to foster creative eucharistic responses as a feature of continuous inculturation.

So what are creative eucharistic responses? As to the history and development of the term "eucharist": the word itself, *eucharistia*, was first applied
to "the prayer-pattern or 'grace' used by Jews before eating or drinking
anything, in which they blessed and thanked God, remembering, confessing,
and proclaiming what [God] had done for the people."[14] For the earliest
Christians it became a complete meal, shared by the whole local community,
and done "in remembrance of Christ and in thanksgiving for what God had
done through him."[15]

St. Paul, talking about the preaching he undertakes (he describes it with
the verb *lalein*, "to babble," "prattle"), says: "You see, all this is for your
benefit, so that the more grace (*charis*) is multiplied among people, the
more thanksgiving (*eu-charis-tian*) there will be, to the glory of God" (2 Cor
4:15). He seems to imply that such talk or chatter helps forge relationships
between people and calls them to acknowledge God as the source and
sustainer of such relationships. This would certainly be to see "eucharist"
or "community thanksgiving to God" as broader than "Mass," even though
epitomized by it. We ourselves should not be forced to polarize the one
against the other. But if we broaden our eucharistic perspectives, rather as
St. Paul did, we might discover ways for Christian communities to be truly
eucharistic people even in the face of the scarcity of the Mass; we might
underline ways in which the Mass itself could be more deeply contextualized or inculturated in communities. As Karl Rahner once said:

> We can only achieve a genuine enactment of [liturgy] if we draw our
> strength from the liturgy of the world, from the liturgy of faith as
> expressed in concrete, "this-worldly" terms.[16]

From the earliest days of the church such a process was operating; transformations were in the air, aided and abetted by those ubiquitous twins,
"pastoral need" and "local circumstances." By the mid-second century in

Rome Justin Martyr describes eucharist in very different terms (on the surface at least; the deep structure, where meaning is located, remained). It is now "separated from a meal. It is an early morning service instead of a Sunday evening assembly and has been prefixed with a synagogue-style liturgy of the word and prayers."[17]

In the following centuries the traditional emphasis on the active participation of the whole community was maintained[18], but now the focus shifted from the "meal-event" as the means by which Christ's presence was experienced to the bread and wine themselves as the *locus* of this presence. As the church grew and spread, episcopal legislation underlined the need for catechesis and a proper disposition as prerequisites for participation. This actually served to drive people away, and by the end of the first millennium the reception of communion was becoming increasingly rare for most people. Again, theology belatedly articulated what was already the experience of the faithful, endorsing a proliferation of devotions outside Mass, and justifying the common lack of participation as a sign of appropriately distant and respectful worship rather than the earlier and more casual style of close and familiar contact.

In time, the emphasis shifted totally from bread as physically nourishing to communion as spiritually sustaining, and the community could hardly be said to have gathered to share common food for a common journey. Rather, communion was withheld and the community stratified, divided, and dispersed. It was the sixteenth-century Reformers who were unanimous about the authentic celebration of eucharist depending on a substantial number of the faithful receiving communion; the Roman church later defended the validity of Masses at which few if any apart from the celebrant communicated.[19]

We should also be aware of the divergence between the East and West. The theology of the Eastern church, from very early on, was developing in a cultural milieu different from the West. The East emphasized respectful distance, while the West was always moving to greater intimacy, and thus proximity to the eucharist. The Eastern Screen or Iconostasis is a barrier through which only the celebrant may pass; the Western altar, by contrast, can be seen by all, and liturgical gestures make the consecrated bread particularly visible.[20] Further, in the Eastern church, the assent of faith was in and to the liturgy itself (*orthopraxis*, correct performance or activity), thus emphasizing the proper celebration of the sacred mysteries. But in the West, assent to formulations of doctrine (*orthodoxis*, correct teaching) determined one's membership in the church. So while the East gave special importance to the *lex orandi*, the regulation of prayer-worship, the West was underlining the *lex credendi*, the formal confessional, creedal statements. Again we see different forms of inculturation, different surface structures as transformations of the same underlying deep structures.

In our own times we have come full circle, responding, as it were, both to the Eastern emphasis on the participation of all, and the reformers' caveats about private Masses.[21] This raises an important question of application: If "assent" is directed to the liturgy itself through active participation, yet people are excluded, or the liturgy is unavailable, what is the pastoral response to be?

A great irony today, and particularly painful to those within the Roman Catholic tradition, is that as the contemporary liturgical movement has tried to "restore the eucharist to the place which it had in early Christian practice," the church finds itself beleaguered and sometimes embarrassed by hungry communities, which look up and are not fed. Yet quite apart from the critical issue of a "eucharistic famine" — the dependency of communities on outside ministers, and Roman intransigence about commissioning ("ordaining") people from within the communities as *ordinary* ministers of the eucharist unless male, celibate, and expensively trained over long years of formal theology — there is another perspective that might offer a way forward.

TRADITION AND THE DEVELOPMENT OF DOCTRINE

Christian tradition is not always formulated explicitly and does not appear fully fledged, yet is not in conflict with scripture[22] and is most often rooted in the liturgy itself. *Lex orandi lex credendi* ("the prayer or worship of the church is the belief or faith of the church in action"). But where exactly do we find the church at prayer? And what are we to make of the multiplication of churches with their individual differences? In brief, what must be discerned is continuity with the "teaching and practice [that] has been carried on continuously from the beginning,"[23] sometimes called the "rule of faith," the *"sensus fidei,"* by Fathers of the second and third centuries. Yet this continuity is dynamic, and no slavish repetition over the years; it includes what Newman called the "development of doctrine," which means the legitimate *transformation* in expression, over time, of the perennial teaching and practice of the church.

Tradition, as the church understands it, does not stand independently of scripture, yet plays a significant role in its interpretation. Acknowledgment of this has allowed the ecumenical movement to flourish, accepting common scriptures, but also "the sense of sharing a common tradition deriving from the period of an undivided church."[24] Thus bonded in a single tradition and "one Spirit" (deep structure), there can be many expressions of variety, just as there are many gifts (surface structure). This is where cultural expressions can have their place. They are "translations" of common themes, neither unrelated to Christian tradition nor alien to local modes of understanding, and certainly not imposed imperiously by one culture on another. Here, briefly, is an example.

Around the end of the first millennium of Christianity, in response to an increasingly diverse membership and in phase with the development of scientific explanations, there grew a set of eucharistic devotions and an attendant rationale. Nathan Mitchell has lucidly chronicled the development of eucharistic theology and practice quite separable from the Mass itself.[25] Despite the close theological argumentation that explained all such devotions *in terms of* or *in relation to* the Mass, nevertheless for many centuries and for multitudes of people they were cultivated *instead of* the Mass, which for various reasons was commonly unavailable. Hunger will find ways of assuagement; sustenance by whatever name is nourishment.

The first line of the Introduction in the newly revised book of Rites reads: "The celebration of the eucharist is the center of the entire Christian life, both for the church universal and for the local congregations of the church."[26] This can only have meaning in the world of contemporary experience if "eucharist" is understood to mean something other than "Mass," or even the reception of holy communion. For Vatican II's call for fuller eucharistic participation by the faithful and the consequent undermining or subordination of devotions outside Mass converged with a new eucharistic scarcity in many of the young churches and not a few of the older ones. When people, bidden to be more actively involved, are also deprived of ordinary ministers of the eucharist, the devotions of another age are virtually the only means of access to eucharist for multitudes of people.

"Give them something yourselves," said Jesus, and out of the little available, abundance was created. In our own times the hunger should not need to become full-blown famine, if only we will give something, share something, from the barns and storehouses of Christian tradition and contemporary culture. If we cannot make Mass available, and if we feel unable to invite the invited guests to partake universally of the banquet, then at least we can do something—we *must* do something.

We can examine again the meaning of eucharist and see how we have narrowed it; we can acknowledge that exclusiveness and legalism are threatening to constrain the bounty of God; we can challenge very seriously indeed the statements of the church indicating that whatever is good in local cultures will not be disregarded. For there are vehicles for Gospel values in all cultures. There are social institutions, which ensure exchange, reciprocity, sharing, and responsibility, and indeed explicit gratitude to a beneficent Creator—and anyone committed to mission in reverse has experienced the value and necessity of discovering and sharing whatever shadowy images of "eucharist" are to be found there. Until such time as people are gathered around the table of the Lord to celebrate the Paschal mystery as one community, we who accept moral responsibility in relation to other people must take what bread is to be found, and offer, break, share, and eat, in faith.

"EXCHANGE" AS A CARRIER OF GOSPEL VALUES

The church borrows from cultures in order to survive. This is how the message is normally translated.[27] It implies that, at its best, a culture is perfectly able to articulate the Christian faith in a vernacular form, both linguistic and cultural. Chupungco states that "liturgical inculturation does not inflict violence on culture."[28] This is not to say that Christianity accommodates itself without a struggle, much less that it betrays itself. Nor is it to deny that at times violence has been inflicted in the name of Christianity; but that is not true inculturation. But the statement does indeed imply that Christianity seeks to communicate; that it is incomplete in any single specific form; that it can always find new ways of expressing itself; and that there are no inferior cultures in principle. This latter point simply indicates that every culture has the capacity to express whatever needs to be expressed, just as every language does.

That cultures can become corrupt is a commonplace. But that "Christendom" itself could exemplify the corruptibility of cultures was, until recently, unthinkable. Nevertheless, the rabid individualism, acquisitive self-interest, violence, and the rest, of what until recently was referred to as Christendom, are not commendable traits for export to young Christian communities. Without "exoticizing" and romanticizing cultures, it is at least reasonable to acknowledge that they often contain some strong Gospel values long before the proclamation of the Good News.

Many of life's important threads can be traced in terms of the rules and the dynamic of reciprocity: the exchange of food, shelter, protection, respect, rights, friendship, sexual access, and so on. No one is entirely self-sufficient, and humanity is a social breed. Reciprocity can operate for poor as well as rich, pagan as well as Christian, sinner as well as saint, "them" as well as "us." Perhaps at this level, eucharist-as-communal-thanksgiving and reciprocity-as-human-sociality are speaking much the same language, if only we could understand it and learn to communicate with it.

Thanksgiving and exchange are indeed very close, for to offer thanks is to reciprocate, to make a symbolic return in response to another's initiative. Mutual thanksgiving is mutual exchange, mutual extension of relationship. And just as we can trace the broadest historical base for the notion of thanksgiving or *eucharistia*, and then refine it in order to identify the specificity of our liturgical eucharistic forms, so we can do likewise with the notion of exchange; that is, we can trace it across cultures and through history as a creator of relationships, and we can refine it in order to identify the specificity of our liturgical eucharistic forms.

> Before entering into the area of inculturation it is necessary to make a preliminary comparative study between the Christian liturgical forms and the corresponding cultural elements . . . to discover points of convergence on which interaction between liturgy and culture can operate. . . . Liturgical inculturation [is] the process whereby the texts and rites used in worship by the local church are so inserted in the framework of culture, that they absorb its thought, language, and ritual patterns.[29]

To a people of the Covenant, the possibility of a relationship with God is central; to a people of the New Covenant in the blood of Christ, the eucharist is obviously a key expression of this relationship. The idea that eucharist might be understood as an example of "exchange" is not new; the phrase *"admirable commercium,"* sometimes translated as "admirable (or happy) exchange," goes back to Gregory Nazianzen.[30] Augustine in several places refers to eucharist as *"commercium."*[31] And Martin Luther's "happy exchange" in reference to the Atonement appears to employ the same thought. What is perhaps new, however, is the knowledge that the institutionalization of exchange has taken place universally, that every human society has practiced some form of exchange of *prestations.*[32] So universal does this behavior appear that we may suggest that such exchange qualifies as a deep structure of human behavior, something constitutive of human sociality. If this is the case then we can expect to be able to understand a wide range of cultural manifestations of exchange as variations on a theme, surface structures that can be identified as transformations of the underlying deep structure.

Now, if authentic inculturation must build on the foundations provided by each culture (notwithstanding some structural realignment), then we may start from theology, or from culture, or possibly from both, but certainly we have to maintain communication, dialogue. If we start by examining the theological criteria underpinning eucharist, we may be able to specify a fairly limited number.[33] If we start with culture, then given the variety of cultures, we will have to acknowledge an enormous range of potential expressions of eucharist cross-culturally. But perhaps we could keep a core set of theological criteria in mind, and also discover a similar core of cultural deep structures as potential carriers of eucharist. Then the dialogue between theology and culture will determine what inculturated forms of eucharist actually look like.

Recall that a finite number of grammatical rules will produce a quasi-infinite amount of acceptable speech (potential and actual), and we have a precedent. The linguistic model remains the analogy for our discussion.

To simplify, we consider exchange, reciprocity, thanksgiving, as a cultural deep structure, and we suggest that exchange is already a deep structure within eucharist. So it becomes relatively easy to encourage the development of inculturated eucharistic liturgical forms across cultures based on existing forms of "exchange" behavior.[34]

CROSS-CULTURAL GIFT-EXCHANGE

Marcel Mauss[35] noted that "gift-exchange"[36] essentially involves the "spiritual essence" of the donor. This is what urges people to give: a desire to extend themselves, to communicate existentially, ontologically. Likewise this reality constrains a recipient to make a gift in return, for the donor (that is, the donor's spirit) is now literally in the hands of the recipient.

Gift-exchange of this sort is constitutive of social life, so much so that by examining how and when the system breaks down, we understand social pathology itself.

Mauss discovered that the peoples—contemporary or ancient—whom he studied frequently did not separate, and tended to unite, gift and giver; that in consequence an enduring bond was created between donor and recipient; and that gift-exchange created and sustained the standard human relationships of mutuality and interdependence. Unsurprisingly in the circumstances, gift-exchange was no random arrangement between private individuals but a compelling social institution, which operated according to three strikingly simple, unformalized, yet strict, "rules."

The Obligation to Give

The act of giving initiates relationships and even friendship. Not to give is not to be in relationship. To refuse a gift may sometimes be seen as a hostile act. People are not free, in an absolute sense, because they have serious social obligations. However much one might like to think of the spontaneity of gift-giving, the activity referred to here cannot be divorced from obligation and reciprocity. Such giving (more correctly termed "exchange," as we shall see) is *patterned* activity and must certainly not be confused with purely economic transactions. The receiver, in the act of receiving, is forging a spiritual bond with the donor. Gifts are an extension of oneself. A huge proportion of goods and services in such a social context may be seen as "things-to-be-given-away-and-received-and-repaid," rather alien to a "Western" understanding of goods and services as "things-to-be-acquired-and-retained-and-increased." But if people want to be accepted as human, "in relationship," then they have no choice but to choose to give.

If we were to apply this to the eucharist as we know it, we would say something like the following (perhaps a little "forced" to those schooled in Scholastic categories and a post-Enlightenment world, but sounding rather more obvious to people whose understanding of freedom is not divorced from social responsibility): God *must* give if there is to be any relationship and spiritual bonding. Furthermore, we must be able to give; otherwise there would be no relationship, because no reciprocity, no exchange.

The Obligation to Receive

Hospitality, marriages, bartering—all social relationships—are built upon exchange, reciprocity. Without a receiver and a complementary act of reception there is no relationship. Refusal to receive, therefore, is refusal of relationship or the breakdown of amity. The *right* to receive may be conferred by extreme need, so that the indigent or destitute become "receivers" par excellence. But unless they are empowered or facilitated—listened to and given initiative and respect—they will not be able to perpetuate any kind of mutuality and may remain enslaved by their need. And if they are unable to act as free agents, then they will be treated as virtually nonhuman.

The act of receiving is the reciprocal of the act of giving. But though the medium is gift-exchange, the message is mutual indebtedness. In other words, the very purpose of gift-exchange is precisely the creation of ties; this is perceived as a social value, something which enhances people rather than demeans them. People are linked and bonded by expectations and obligations; the purpose of gift-exchange is therefore—and crucially—a moral one.

What can we apply to eucharist here? First, surely, that the truly needy have the right to receive. Second, that our own careful cultivation of the assumed virtue of not-receiving[37], not-taking, not-being-tied-or-indebted, is compatible neither with the spirit of mission in reverse nor with the Jesus who requests things, receives things and persons, cultivates mutuality, and gives his life itself to sustain and nourish one and all. Sharing, interdependence, and reciprocity (mutual indebtedness and not servile dependency) are essentially human characteristics. Jesus was profoundly influenced by such attitudes and values, and the Gospel abounds with examples of his willingness to receive: food and wine, water, friendship, hospitality, ointment, gold, frankincense, myrrh, a traitor's kiss, and a sponge of hyssop.

The Obligation to Return

If the donor is in the hands of the recipient, then the obligation to return becomes quite serious. But it by no means concludes the exchange, since the object is not to terminate but rather to extend the relationship, and what is returned is not the same as repayment in full, which characterizes and concludes economic transactions. Giving and receiving, then, commit the participants to partnership—unequal though that may be—through ongoing exchange, which is often perpetual.[38] It would not be right to grasp or hold onto a gift, since it is the spirit of the donor. Gifts, as extensions of persons, must be in circulation, in relationship; they are not static but reciprocated. In fact, if one covets or hoards, one might become ill, or even die, for holding onto or seizing the spirit of another person.[39]

But simply because the appropriate return of a gift may be demanding and even dangerous, one should not repudiate a gift; after all, it does carry the spirit of the donor. Somehow one must respectfully cherish it while at the same time releasing it as a life-giving spirit into the community. Respectful return of a gift is the essence of circulation. And recirculation operates on the understanding that the thing exchanged contains a power or spirit that, as it were, "forces" it to circulate. So it is appropriate, even essential, for gifts to exist dynamically.

The obvious initial implication here is that we who perceive ourselves to be in relationship with God must be able, enabled, to offer some legitimate albeit unequal form of return for what we have received. But it also follows that God too must be seen to reciprocate our own small offerings. Let us broaden our discussion of the implications of the institution of gift-exchange for an authentic inculturation of eucharist.

WIDER EUCHARISTIC APPLICATIONS

Looking at each of the obligations, we can determine specific applications to eucharist, but it is also possible to make some more general applications. We noted St. Paul's warning to the Corinthians, that is, when they gather they are not eating the Lord's Supper if they are selfish and riven by dissension. He says, "For this cause many are weak and sickly among you, and many sleep" (1 Cor 11:30, *KJV*), or "that is why many of you are weak and ill, and some of you have died" (1 Cor 11:30, *JB*). He seems to be emphasizing the fact that the eucharist, while being "carried" on the metaphor or social institution of a meal, is not primarily about feeding oneself but about the sharing of God and with God and with each other.[40] This, the true meaning and the deep structure, is what has to be uncovered if it is to be translated across cultures.

Second, we may think of the eucharist as a "perpetual alliance" (Jesus says, "Take and eat; as often as you do this, do it in memory of me") without implying that we are equal to God. But God, looking on humanity, did find us "very good." And Jesus loved us till death and beyond. In his own relationship with God, Jesus "did not cling to his equality, but emptied himself . . . and became as we are" (Phil 2:6-7). So it is entirely possible to be in an intimate and real, though unequal, reciprocal relationship with God, as with human partners. There is great scope here for a convergence of eucharistic inculturation and gift-exchange; a reexamination of Western liturgies, current and obsolete, would convince us of the riches already to hand.

Third, from the early third century onward, the time of the liturgy of Hippolytus (215 A.D.), it was expected that everyone who came to the eucharistic liturgy should bring gifts of bread and wine, from the emperor to the most recently baptized neophyte. The famous mosaics of Ravenna clearly show people bringing their own wine and pouring it into an enormous two-handled cup. If the participation of the faithful today is less than active, there is no reason to encourage such passivity; and in cultures in which the whole community is habitually involved in celebrations, there is no justification for refusing their participation.

Fourth, the "fragments" of bread—or the little hosts familiar to us today—may symbolize precisely the *insufficiency* of eucharist for permanently staunching hunger. And that should remind us of the importance of sharing and of the need for frequent celebration, that is, of continuous and long-term commitment. The disciples wondered aloud how so many people could be fed with such meager supplies, and then reciprocity and transformation led to superabundance. Similarly hunger and thirst—for food, and justice, and love—should continue indefinitely. God does not intend to fill us and be done with us, or to make us sated and indolent. The bread, frequently renewed, is for journeys and for sharing, but the journey takes a lifetime. The eucharist, considered as a single celebration, may thus be said paradoxically to provide us with a lack or insufficiency,[41] while as a continuous reality in our lives it gives promise of plenty. It certainly invites us to increasing levels of cooperation and sharing.

Finally, we might ask ourselves how often we, who are members of Christian communities, receive but do not make return gifts? The eucharist is then reduced to a routine instead of being a dynamic celebration of the *koinonia*, the community of faith. Yet the continuity of relationships through reciprocity was clearly part of Jesus' concern, as we see in his attitude to Martha, Mary, and Lazarus, or the Twelve, or in the vignettes of Zacchaeus or Simon the Leper, the woman at the well, or the good thief. It is simply not true that we can do nothing "in return" to the God who gives so much. We cannot, strictly speaking, repay, but repayment is essentially an economic transaction; a return is an acknowledgment that relationship is more important than contract and that reciprocity is not the same as tit for tat. And so our grateful reception of and respect for what we receive from God is a sign of reciprocity, which is enhanced by our promotion of justice and good works, themselves a form of proof of our gratitude.[42] Further, our God is anxious and able to receive from us, and that, signified by God's good graces to us, reminds us that our relationship continues.

Much more remains to be gleaned from a study of gift-exchange, specifically as a vehicle for inculturated forms of eucharistic liturgies. Points that would provide cultural grounds for further theological consideration, with a view to pastoral action, would include the following:

• you may not eat with your enemy; but you *do* and *must* eat if you wish to be friends;
• you do not hoard, but offer, share, circulate;
• you cannot separate gifts from honor; therefore gift-exchange is not undertaken lightly or cynically;
• you do not exclude people or refuse their offerings;
• gift-exchange *can* be dangerous, for it makes demands;
• risk may be necessary for long-term relationships;
• you must trust others in order to be trusted.

INFERENCES AND IMPLICATIONS

As we try to move toward eucharistic inculturation, we need some guiding operating principles as well as pastoral sensitivity, common sense, and loyalty to the church as the People of God. Based on what we have seen, here are some considerations—not recommendations, but concerns.

First, to elaborate an earlier point, can we not assume that whatever Jesus wishes to give (eucharist), we in turn are able to receive, since anything else would be a travesty of a gift?[43] There must be ways for communities of faith to celebrate eucharist in whatever circumstances they find themselves.

Second, if God has both a covenantal relationship with us as a people and a personal relationship with each of us, then our relationship to God must be "subversive" of other relationships; that is, it must have priority. Since God calls us to conversion and transformation, this has to be the overriding imperative in our lives. The eucharist is central to our response as a Christian community.

Whenever communities are actively engaged in relationships of mutuality and responsibility, then God is part of those relationships. So, when such communities engage in "thanksgiving" to the creator and celebration of their moral unity, does it not follow that a type of "eucharist" is present? And if a community were later to become Christian, then even if Mass were unavailable, would it not be a "eucharistic community"? If so, how should this be celebrated in an explicitly Christian way?[44]

If a community accepts baptism en masse, how can there *not* be shared eucharist in anticipation of their continuing and improving relationships in the Lord? But if there is no ordained minister available, and no airplanes with special deliveries, how are the people to identify and encourage a eucharistic presence if not by "canonizing" some of their cultural behavior and "celebrating" the faith they have embraced?

Fifth, if God has established a covenantal relationship with communities of faith, must not those communities be enabled to maintain the relationship without reliance on outsiders? Outsiders are valuable in many ways, but a dependent community will fail to be a mature community in the faith. We have wide experience of such dependent communities. Must we not then either defer baptism if eucharist is not made available to people, or ensure that eucharist becomes available as a normal part of the context of every Christian community?

Finally, if God is in relationship with communities, then as new communities discover the call to a covenantal relationship they must likewise discover new ways of expressing that relationship, with God and with each other. New expressions of relationship will give rise to appropriate ministries in a community. As God's call is heard in new ways, the newly developing forms of ministry, while expressing the church's tradition, will also be culture-specific and not foreign imports. Ministries need not be standardized, because social and cultural responses are adaptive to survival. In fact, there may be compelling reasons to look for new ministries and new ways to celebrate eucharist, so long as they are based on the deep structure of the Christian tradition and can be related to the cultural deep structures of the communities in which they occur.

THE DEEP STRUCTURE OF EUCHARIST

Though few of us can effect changes in the Mass, as members of communities of faith and especially as evangelizers we have a responsibility for building up a eucharistic people. We may not argue that there is nothing we can do; there is always something we can do to ensure that grace is multiplied among people, and that thanksgiving ("eucharist") abounds, to the glory of God (see 2 Cor 4:15).

"The Last Supper of the Lord with His disciples," says Gregory Dix in his consummate study, "is the source of the liturgical eucharist, but not the model for its performance."[45] This is echoed in a recent work, which reminds us that "the memorial (*anamnesis*) of the paschal mystery is the basic theological content of every liturgical celebration. . . . But this same mystery is experienced in different ways and under different forms according to the meaning and purpose of each liturgical rite."[46] If we are very careful here, we should find enough creative space for a variety of inculturated eucharistic forms.

The reason for the distinction that the authors make is that, as recounted in the Last Supper, Jesus performed with bread and then with wine a "seven-action scheme," but our current Mass is "a somewhat drastic modification of it. *With absolute unanimity* the liturgical tradition reproduces these seven actions as four: (1) The Offertory: bread and wine are 'taken' and placed on the table together; (2) The prayer: the president gives thanks to God over bread and wine together; (3) The fraction: the bread is broken; (4) The communion: the bread and wine are distributed together."[47]

If this characterizes the unanimous Christian tradition throughout two millennia, then we surely have here the stuff of the deep structure of the Mass. With that, we should be in a position to authenticate all inculturated forms of the Mass across cultures! This is precisely the task for the appropriate experts.

But the development of eucharistic liturgy and devotion does not stop there. Far from it. There have been numerous changes or transformations of surface structure. We recall the movement from the actual "Last Supper" to "eucharist" itself; from "holy food" to "sacred meal"; from Upper Room to house-church and thence to basilica, cathedral, parish church, catacomb, and open-air community; from celebration on the Lord's Day to celebration on any and every day; from "oral" to "ocular" to "spiritual" communion[48]; from spontaneity to fixity of liturgical form; and many others.

As form has changed, so inevitably meaning has been affected: differences of emphases,[49] different explanatory models, different applications to life, differences in access or prohibition. All these have been experienced. Eucharist has been interpreted as the celebration of a single, unitary community; as an exchange of gifts; as a sacrifice; as the real presence of Jesus; as communal dining; as ritual "communion"; as inclusive banquet; as exclusive meal. And that is not all! Two thousand years have seen changes from table-as-altar to tomb-as-altar (with further variations over time, including the use of a "table" form but with "tomb-relics" embedded in it). In addition, the ritual has shifted from symbolic to allegorical,[50] the focus has moved from the priest to the gathered community, the language from vernacular to "cultic" and back, and the communion itself from wide-spread to scarce to widespread, and back again to scarce!

And this is just to look at the variation within Mass, and to say nothing of the proliferation of devotional and doctrinal differences within and across ethnic and denominational lines. Clearly there has been scarcely a moment in two thousand years when the eucharist was static, which only goes to show that a constant deep structure is compatible with changing surface structures; content is constant, while form may change.[51] Yet Christians want to identify and be faithful to tradition, and there has to be a way to exclude potentially unacceptable surface structures. So can we identify content and form, theme and variation? Can there be authentic variations on eucharistic themes, for the future and for different cultures?

The practical question for ourselves is limited to the possible inculturation of forms that we label devotional. Our starting point is the life of Jesus, and we try to identify the eucharistic themes in his life, taking as our *model* the relationship between the Last Supper and the Mass, with the latter deriving from the former yet not being identical with it. Examining that life more closely, do we not find that in its totality it *is* eucharist precisely in the sense of thanksgiving? How then can Jesus be remembered by far-flung communities that either lack a fully inculturated Mass or find themselves deprived of it for much of their lives and much of the year? If the liturgical year is to be marked and celebrated, and if communities are to be nourished, how can this happen without some authentic expressions of eucharist?

So what do we find in the life of Jesus? The center point of the Last Supper account in the Gospel of John is not bread and wine but foot washing, with the clear injunction "if I, then, the Lord and Master, have washed your feet, you should wash each other's feet. I have given you an example so that you may copy what I have done to you" (Jn 13:13-14). How reminiscent of "do this in memory of me"! One hundred ten contemporary Christian groups in the United States alone[52] have remained faithful to this as the expression of their service and communion with Jesus. Nor should its status as an example of gift-exchange need to be belabored; it is a prima facie case of a eucharistic liturgy that could easily be inculturated quite widely.

But as we know, eucharistic worship over the centuries developed from a concentration on the synoptic accounts of the Last Supper and the Pauline development. And though the Paschal mystery can of course be summarized in the *anamnesis* of the Last Supper, the pastoral potential for eucharistic catechesis has been severely limited. Leaving aside the rich potential of foot washing,[53] there are other meals in Jesus' life associated with reconciliation, forgiveness, feasting, nourishment, love, affirmation, and so on. There is also the motif of food, particularly the story of the Canaanite woman (Matt 15:21ff) who raises the precise question of who is eligible to eat from the table! There are numerous eucharistic moments in the life of Jesus; looking beyond Mass itself, they surely have relevance to the lives of eucharistic people across cultures today. Or consider other great moments: the feeding of the great crowds; the special moments at Emmaus, Cana, Bethany, or by the shore; and so on.

All these familiar occasions are part of common human experience; they could be focal points for contemporary communities to reflect, to gather for prayer and celebration, to share food and faith, to integrate sacred time and ordinary time, and to make ordinary space sacred. Jesus instructed that certain things be done in his memory; he also reminded people that certain things would be remembered wherever the Good News is proclaimed (Matt 26:13). Could we not pursue these reminders and take them more seriously in order to produce liturgical forms to sustain local communities in a way that would neither depart from the scriptural theme of eucharist nor be incomprehensible or irrelevant?

There is a wonderful story in the Book of Exodus, that is an inspiration for those concerned with the current eucharistic famine. It tells of the people of Israel wandering in the wilderness and complaining about lack of leadership and food. Moses and Aaron are instructed by God that food will indeed be given, and they transmit this message to the people (incidentally exonerating themselves and claiming that God has taken the people's complaints personally and will provide a solution!). Yet when the nourishment is all around (under the appearance of manna) the people complain to one another: "What is that?" It is pointed out that this unlikely substance "is the bread Yahweh gives you to eat" (Ex 16:1-16). Moses explains that there is and there will be sufficient to sustain the people, and that they are to share with each other. Everyone finds that there is enough. They are warned not to hoard or store, because the manna would no longer be fresh or sustaining. So they gather on a daily basis, and there is enough for their needs (vv. 16-21). If this were a parable, how might we understand it and apply it in some of the Christian communities today!

There are many different ways of sharing and celebrating, and many different forms of prayer. In this time of promise of and challenge to global inculturation, there is an urgent need for us to attempt to make the life and lessons of Jesus converge with the lives of peoples of many cultures in ways that are ever old and ever new. The developments we will consider in Chapter 8 arose in response to social and theological demands. Many such imperatives today would indicate the need for similar responses. Rather than trying to reduce eucharist to a single form, which tries to say all that can be said, and rather than trying to standardize it, inculturation should show us where eucharistic variety can be both orthodox and imaginative, strong in root and strong in branch. Jesuit Pedro Arrupe once said that great pluralism is the best sign of unity.[54]

The quartet of gestures used by Jesus (taking, thanking, breaking, sharing) was not only used once, at the Last Supper, but several times in several contexts. Even as the irreducible bedrock on which every eucharistic liturgy should be built, still it gives scope for new developments. And whenever Christian communities gather with the intention of fulfilling Jesus' command and doing likewise, what shall we call that?

FOSSILIZATION AND FORMALISM

The declining years of the century find us at a critical point in the story of evangelization. Specifically, it is the *aftermath* to the announcement of the Good News that is at a critical juncture, for the Good News has to be received and applied to the life of communities. If the church reiterates that the eucharist is the focal point of Christian life, then there must be ways of ensuring the "delivery" of eucharist to local communities. Here are some true stories to indicate how eucharist is experienced by some communities today. They are told in a constructive spirit and should be self-explanatory. They could very easily be multiplied.

"Deus ex machina"

One of the many dioceses in which the shortage of priests is judged to be critical is very extensive, and parts are isolated. So, at a Sunday liturgy in a central parish, extra hosts or wafers are consecrated and reserved. . . . Some time later in a far-away, "priestless" part of the same diocese, the parish associate (a sister), accompanied by two reverent acolytes, approaches the small airplane arriving in the blizzard. The pilot, who is also the mailman, hands over a registered package marked "BY AIR MAIL" and "FRAGILE" and "THIS WAY UP." It is reverently accepted by the sister and accompanied in procession by the acolytes. The consecrated bread has arrived on time this week; there can be communion this Sunday for the community, which patiently, and rather passively, waits . . .

Body of Christ

The cathedral is packed for the main Sunday liturgy. It is communion time, and people are approaching the altar. They are well-dressed and well-behaved. A woman—clearly a street woman, a "bag lady"—is in line. Insalubrious and of advancing years but retreating mental clarity, she is refused the bread! Apparently disoriented, she returns to her seat.

While people avoid eye-contact or turn away, she takes out a package of broken bread intended for the birds. Deliberately she breaks a piece and offers it to the person next to her, saying, "body of Christ." She begins to share her bread as widely as she can. Some people try to ignore her. Some simply cannot refuse. And while some of those around are deeply offended, others are deeply touched.

Blessed Are Those Who Hunger and Thirst

There is a large crowd of people in the little church down South. When the time comes for communion, the priest realizes that there is only a single, large, consecrated bread, insufficient for the whole congregation. It is not customary to share the wine. Some of the people are aware of the impending shortage and rush to the altar. Some receive, but many do not. The slow and elderly are jostled. A lot of people go away hungry, and angry.

As I Have Done, So Must You Do

A group of Christians united in faith but divided by laws of intercommunion gathers in prayer and discernment. The members are trying to be sensitive, loyal, obedient — and relevant. They know how difficult it is! They are gathered in the open air on a rise above the ocean. After the proclamation of the Gospel of John, which tells of the Last Supper and Jesus washing the feet of his friends, they rise and silently walk down to the water. They stand a moment in prayer and then begin their return. The tide has ebbed, and the shore is muddy and sandy. As they reach the large bowls of clean water to rinse their feet, they know that it is not just a formality — they need to remove drying mud, and sand, and debris.

While the Gospel story is repeated, very slowly, they minister to each other by washing and drying each other's feet, including those of a small, brave, disabled child. Finally, all have returned and sat down, and they continue their prayer. Afterward they are excitedly vocal and unanimous in speaking of the profundity of this eucharistic moment.

Sinners Need Not Apply

Preaching at the Sunday Mass this week is a woman who talks about her work with women trying to escape a life of addictions and prostitution. She is passionate and eloquent as she recalls the early church's ministry among similar women and the apparent unconcern or distaste in the Christian community today.

The parishioners are strangers to the speaker, but in the front sits a phalanx of overdressed and self-conscious women who have come to "support" their champion. After Mass, when the congregation has departed, preacher and prostitutes discuss the experience. She says how touched she was by their support. She thanks them for their courage in coming and innocently asks why they did not receive communion. "We can't receive," they say. "We are sinners." "I'm a sinner too," she replies. "That's why I receive."

So long as communities have to wait for Jesus to arrive in a machine; so long as insalubrious people are refused the bread of life; so long as the insufficiency of communion leaves people hurt and upset; so long as the lack of ministers creates dependent and bewildered communities, then what has happened to the promise of a life-giving eucharist? If a sister can (only) carry consecrated bread from the airplane to the chapel; if hungry Christians can (only) wash each other's feet; if sinners can (only) gather at the table but not eat there, then what is to sustain people? But if bag-ladies can bring new dimensions to the breaking of bread; if artificial shortages can serve to underline the impoverishment of current eucharistic practice; if in the washing of feet ecumenical groups can be united with each other and with the one who says "as I have done, so you must do"; if the fearful self-exclusion of "sinners" can underline the ease with which "the just" can domesticate the eucharist and take it for themselves; then new perspectives can indeed serve to bring us back to a more vital appreciation of the euchar-ist. If it is not to become fossilized and formalized, then transformation is urgently required, transformation of our practice and of our attitudes.

INCULTURATION AND TRANSFORMATION

If Christianity is not to be a foreign import of minimal relevance to people, or a scandal, it must assiduously and creatively attempt to use elements of local culture and experience as vehicles on which to carry the universal message into the heartlands. People in unlikely places know a great deal about reciprocity, companionship, and community building, sometimes much more than those at the centers. The convergence between cultural institutionalizations of so-called Gospel values and the Christian tradition is necessary if the Christian message is to be perceived as credible.

We may wait a long time for a fully fledged inculturated Mass, Lord's Supper, or Holy Communion to be available to every community, but unless local forms of sharing and bonding and mutuality are recognized as an acceptable base on which to build relationships of eucharistic communities, we will be caught flat-footed and without plans when official attitudes do mellow.

Inculturation is not about easy domesticity or a paraphrased Gospel, much less about making God in our own image. But it is inextricable from the process of real, true, authentic translation whereby the Gospel, in mov-ing across cultures, is received according to the genius of the recipient community. All translation involves transformation. But sometimes, per-haps, in undertaking evangelization, we have been so concerned to protect the seeds we wish to transplant (with the soil of tradition and orthodoxy) that we have been less concerned about the way in which we have (at least unwittingly) trampled and flattened the local environment, which then becomes less able to produce abundant fruit. Transformation is one thing, but if the end result is quite unrecognizable, then what has happened is not transformation but something closer to transmogrification — a bizarre or grotesque change with no apparent relationship to the original form.

It must be the conviction of missionaries that God does not wish people to receive the Good News only to die of famine in the desert. "Give them something yourselves" sounds like an invitation to combine our resources and to have them transformed by grace. But we do have to bring those resources; we cannot petulantly cry out for a miracle.

This chapter attempts to describe some of the resources available within the Christian tradition and local cultures. Without attempting to wrestle appropriate authority from the magisterium, it suggests that even if the banquet is delayed, there is food for the journey. The journey must continue. The food is adequate for today. But every day we, fellow pilgrims, must be committed to closing the rift between the Gospel and culture,[55] which bedevils inculturation, and encouraging the dialogue between liturgy and life.[56]

QUESTIONS FOR THE ROAD

- Do you find it pastorally helpful to separate the Mass from other eucharistic devotions as a way to approach inculturation?
- Is the model of gift-exchange helpful as a way of bringing cultural behavior closer to the deep structure of the eucharist?
- Does the foot washing in the Gospel of John, or any other New Testament incident, give you hope for possible ways to celebrate eucharistic moments?
- Do you think that missionaries should be involved in liturgical modifications? Are you content with the way things are? Do you have any problems with baptizing adults whom you know to be unlikely to be permitted to celebrate regular eucharistic liturgy?

Chapter 6

Playing with Food and Praying with Food

If an unbeliever invites you, go; and eat what is put before you without asking questions just to satisfy conscience. . . . Why should I be blamed for food for which I thank (eucharisto) God? Whatever you eat, whatever you drink, whatever you do at all, do it for the glory of God.

1 Corinthians 10: 27; 30; 31

Yahweh says this: they will eat and have some left over.

2 Kings 4:44

Only your love will enable the poor to forgive you the bread you break to them.[1]

Prayers, daily work, relaxation of mind and body, if they are accomplished in the Spirit . . . all these become spiritual sacrifices. In the celebration of the eucharist they may most fittingly be offered to the Father along with the body of the Lord. And so, worshipping everywhere by their holy action, the laity consecrate the world itself to God.

Lumen Gentium, 34

THE MISSION OF TRANSFORMATION

To venture into foreign fields is to know insecurity and to experience the conventional nature of meaning-in-culture. Constantly trying to interpret and make sense of life, we may feel self-consciously naive at our lack of cultural fluency. We attempt to adapt our behavior and to translate that of others into more familiar terms. That we frequently fail only underscores the complexity of the process; adequate translation, paradoxically, is only really possible if we know *both* languages or cultural systems. So the process of acculturation, of becoming acclimatized within a different culture, is a

94

challenge to ingenuity, attention, commitment, and even faith.

Yet strangers and hosts do think translation possible, and we missioners believe ourselves capable of some personal modifications or transformations that will facilitate our evangelism. Transformations, like musical variations, are the same and yet different, new and yet old, unfamiliar yet familiar, very often tricky and demanding. So we continue to ponder their demands and possibilities in the context of the Christian mission.

There are of course those who, faced with the fairly daunting demands of this kind of change, busy themselves with other things. Some, with the dogmatic arrogance of the zealot, see no reason for personal transformation. They perceive themselves essentially as catalysts for change in others, perhaps because they think of mission as a technique or skill, rather than a process involving time and tribulations. But even if the task is simply to announce or proclaim (*evangelein*), it is by no means a simple task. To be done responsibly it entails translation; the meaning of what is announced must be negotiated, lest, like the children's game of whispers, what is received and relayed become a travesty of the original message. The translation process therefore demands human relationships and mutual, reciprocal modification.

Though linguistic deep structures are extremely helpful postulates for understanding meaning and relationship, we should not assume that nothing actually makes sense unless we dig very deeply beneath it. That would be the fruit of a binary mentality again, of operating in exclusive or dichotomous terms, as if a thing must make sense *either* in terms of deep *or* of surface structure. But meaning is discovered in the application of *both* criteria. Sometimes it is found in the uniqueness and spontaneity of performance, like a poem by Gerard Manley Hopkins. At other times it can only be attributed by reference to deep structural relationships, as in the case of some dramatic or musical performances. Meaning does not always have to be translated into words, or even be translatable, any more than it needs explicitly to be related to underlying structures. But it does need to be appropriated, to be received. This entails transformation of the message through the media and via the senses. Furthermore, meaning is embedded in performance and (cultural and communicative) context, and is neither universally self-evident nor whimsical.

We look now at performance, "belief-in-action," as we pursue some implications of meaning and relate performances to underlying structures. Not that enjoyment of performances depends on explicit knowledge of structure, but whoever wants to translate the meaning must do more than repeat the performance in another context and expect it to make sense. The importance of this for inculturation should now be obvious.

Two elements in the process of inculturation have been emphasized: First, the text (the Christian tradition, with the scriptures) must be scoured for underlying themes that need to be carried across cultures because central to the Gospel message. Second, the particular culture in which the

Gospel is to be inculturated must be tapped so as to uncover underlying structures or themes that may allow the Gospel message to be transfused into its very heart.

Our concern is eucharist as bread (food) for the journey. We will refine the general theme of gift-exchange and look at food as a particular expression of the theme. It is not, of course, the only expression; nor could we claim that food can be only or exhaustively understood in terms of gift-exchange. All that is attempted here is the outline of a process; its application is another matter, and needs collaboration between local people and ministers of the Gospel as well as careful and continuous study of text and context. If we can illustrate the meaning of food-related behavior in cultures, then perhaps we can find a fit between the eucharist and specific cultural contexts. Having already stated the importance of knowledge of and fidelity to the Christian tradition, we now start from the other end: the importance of people's worlds-of-meaning for the reception of the Gospel.

PLAYING AND PRAYING: FOOD AND EUCHARIST

To many ears, the words "playing" and "praying" are indistinguishable, and the behavior associated with each may also be rather similar. We missioners are trying to discover how behavior is the basis for inculturation, but sometimes we may think that only "religious" behavior can legitimately carry Gospel values. Perhaps we need yet again to dissolve some apparent binary oppositions such as religious and secular, or sacred and profane. Ordinary behavior can also be holy behavior; playing can also be a legitimate form of praying.

Three procedural points may be in order: First, "playing" is used here as a form of shorthand for general behavior or *social relationships*; it refers to the way people interact. "Praying" is also a shorthand term, referring more obviously to what might qualify as *religious behavior*. Yet behavior must not be forced into a single explanatory pigeonhole; we would not want to preempt the discussion by speaking of a holy trinity of "eucharist," "praying," and "religious behavior," and an unholy trinity of "food," "playing," and "social behavior."

Second, since we are considering food in relation to eucharist, we will use terminology like "ingredients" and "raw materials," drawing on the contrast between "cooked" and "raw" in order to help make points.

Third, we will undertake a round-the-world tour, stopping briefly at a number of places but aware that there are many more. The trip should help sensitize us to the great diversity of food *behavior* and food *language* across cultures, lest we too simplistically assume that the inculturation of the eucharist is an easy matter. Far from it! And there is no substitute for the study of local practices, such as of Tradition and traditions, before authentic inculturation can occur.

The Raw Materials of Eucharist

If we were to itemize the constituents of eucharist in a specific and a more general sense, we would have to include food, meal-setting, table-fellowship, gift-exchange, sharing, companionship, commensality (as well as a host of others such as ministry, sacrifice, tradition, and worship). When these "raw materials" are mixed together, "cooked," and "served" in a particular form, we produce a recognizable liturgical act such as the Roman Mass. But there are, theoretically, very many more ways of preparing the ingredients beyond the denominational and ethnic varieties already available and those that have fallen into disuse.

There are times in the life of Jesus when ministry, service, and feeding are concentrated around teaching or announcing the Good News. Often food and meals were vehicles for extremely important teaching. And there are other occasions, associated with a meal-setting, in which service and teaching are combined. Two are particularly dramatic: 1) the washing of Jesus' feet by Mary in the house of Simon the Leper, and the promise that "wherever in all the world this Good News is proclaimed, what she has done will be told in remembrance of her" (Matt 26:13); and 2) the washing of the disciples' feet at the Last Supper (Jn 13).

When we look at cultures we see variations on the theme of meal or food-sharing. So perhaps by looking again at some of the raw materials, and at the way these are transformed in different cultures, we will be able to undertake what Eugene Uzukwu speaks of as "mutual dialogue and criticism between [the various] traditions,"[2] surely a prerequisite to real inculturation of the eucharist.

The Raw Materials of Meals

We may talk about food or eucharist in the abstract, but we eat actual food and we gather at particular eucharists. So, when speaking of real meals and real liturgy, we need to be very specific. Rather like deep structures or root metaphors, food and eucharist do not actually exist in the abstract but only in specific realizations, surface structures: meals and eucharists.[3] When we look at a real meal, therefore, we see, not the raw materials, but something that has already been handled, treated, domesticated, cooked, transformed in order to meet people's real needs, personal and social. This transformation involves choice, selection, preparation, and presentation; every society uses these four elements, unless in *absolute want* (starvation), when anything will do, for when human groups are faced with starvation they may be reduced to behaving less like human persons and more like animals.

But so long as people are in relative control of their environment, they will behave as social, specifically human, beings. There is a social dimension to eating that differentiates it from a biological necessity, invests it with meaning and relevance, and serves to distinguish one group from another, thus providing them with boundaries and a means of mutual identification. As Mary Douglas says:

> If biology were the basis for the selection of human foods, diets around the world would be quite similar. In fact no human activity more puzzlingly crosses the divide between nature and culture, than the selection of food. It is part of the nurture of the body, but it is also very much a social matter.[4]

The implications of this for our current discussion cannot be overemphasized; insofar as the eucharist is a cultic meal, it needs cultural variation and adaptation.

FOOD AND CULTURE, FOOD IN CULTURE

Remarkably, though a child in its first two years will "eat" (or put into the mouth) almost anything, within the next couple of years it develops a very strong sense of discrimination and what we might call disgust. Such distaste is *cultural*; it is learned, and it varies from culture to culture. It indicates that food now *means* something, while previously it did not. From this point on in life the discrimination and disgust will not easily dissolve, and those people who cross-cultural and gastronomic divides will have to resist or override their cultural instincts strongly when they engage in companionship or commensality.

It is a sobering thought that other people may react with distaste to the eucharist that we cherish and respect so much! Yet this should not take us totally by surprise if we appreciate the strength of cultural imprinting. Here is a menu perhaps not to everyone's taste:

> Brochette of dog liver, roast leg of dog, saddle of cat, horse broth with millet, ragout of rat, and plum pudding made from horse marrow.[5]

This is probably extremely distasteful to many of us, and though the nutritional value of the dinner is perfectly adequate, we are not impressed. Even the recitation of the menu can make us queasy, so strong are the cultural connotations, the sense of "disgust." What happens if we are given the actual context for that meal: the siege of Paris by the Germans in 1870, when the people were reduced to scrabbling purely for physical survival and when the social aspects of eating were completely neglected? What do we then feel? Ambivalence? Confusion?

Our socialization or growing up not only programs our distaste but also creates a kind of "culinary triangle" from the following constituents: self, food, others. Eating with people from other societies will challenge our respective culinary triangles, and a guest may be pushed to the limits of esthetic or digestive tolerance. Similarly, if we want to get to know a society, then the discovery of what, where, how, when, and with whom people eat will provide an excellent perspective.[6] Worldwide, human behavior is a dialectic between eating patterns and social institutions ("standardized modes of coactivity") such as kinship, politics, economics, and religion. Therefore, to understand social institutions adequately, we must also interpret various forms of eating behavior and the metaphors they carry:

> Eating is symbolically associated with the most deeply felt human experiences, and thus expresses things that are sometimes difficult to articulate in everyday language. Nowhere are the metaphors of eating stronger than in the taboos that societies around the world place upon certain foods.[7]

Not only that, but since food only exists in the concrete, its social function can hardly be determined in the abstract. As concrete situations vary, so may the meaning of food. Whatever food may signify to a well-nourished group of people, if they are starving food will take on very different connotations or meanings, as during the siege of Paris.

We want to understand the eucharist and to celebrate it appropriately both among people who are well-fed and among those who are hungry. But if we are to be able to translate its strongest metaphors into cultures where food and drink are *already* dominant cultural (meaning-bearing) metaphors, and whose taboos may be focused precisely upon flesh and blood, then we really must look beneath the surface and disclose the deep structures, both as an aid to a discovery of the meaning of eucharist as Jesus intended it and as the only way adequately and authentically to translate that deep meaning across cultural boundaries. If eucharist is to become inculturated, it will have to acknowledge and respond[8] to cultural definitions of taboo, disgust, and acceptability; we simply cannot trample upon or ignore people's sensibilities in matters as serious as this.

When Jesus took bread and wine, that *already had some meaning*, for himself and for those with him. Today, those involved in the process of inculturation (even if rather informally or unofficially) need to look for and ascertain that meaning. Then we must ask what the action means today in various cultures, and whether the *original* meaning is lost if the cultural metaphors are changed. This is important because one sometimes has the intuitive sense that the message the eucharist transmits and the message that people receive in different cultures and settings vary widely, by no means conforming with the criteria of theological orthodoxy.[9] This must be determined according to context, but one does need to continue to ask how the meaning intended by Jesus can be transmitted or impeded in contemporary settings, since otherwise confusion or incoherence may be abetted rather than communication and inculturation. Yet this caveat should not undermine the principle that since eucharist is a many-sided, polysemic reality, standardization would only impoverish it.

The Social Significance of Food

We might consider explicitly just how important is the specifically social meaning of food-related behavior and how poorly it travels across cultures. Then, if we could discover which aspects of Jesus' "eucharistic" behavior were culture-bound and which were culture-free (that is, what has meaning only within a very narrow context and what has a much more general significance), we would have made a giant step toward inculturation. But the converse is also critical. Unless we discriminate between the culture-bound and the culture-free (what carries meaning and what loses it in transit, the deep and the surface structure), the process of inculturation is not likely to be significantly furthered.

The following is a case in point. A study of the dietary system of the English working class (blue collar) demonstrated that it is based on two staple carbohydrates: potatoes and cereal. But nourishment is by no means the only issue in diet; there is always *social meaning* ("importance"). This operates on the "raw materials" but is a transformation of them. "Importance" as a food criterion for the English working class is gauged by quantity, complexity (determined by utensils, crockery, settings), and additions. Nutritionists tried to encourage raw vegetables and fruit, but with little success, since the patterning or *social* meaning is resistant. Raw vegetables and fruit might conceivably be added to, but cannot replace, basic cereals. In practice, the additions could only be at "special" meals, which by definition the working class can rarely afford.

This brief description raises a number of important points. Food in any culture has both a functional or nutritional value, and also a social or ceremonial meaning or importance. The social need for special meals, even though they be quite rare, may partially account for the pre-Pius X rule of infrequent communion and the relative slowness with which the "relaxation" of the eucharistic rules was greeted in working-class Roman Catholic households (in Britain). But in the present century the ritual aspect of food-sharing has been rapidly undermined by fast-food cultures (which are also affluent cultures where special dining has become culturally routinized). Such factors are important in any discussion of inculturation of eucharist in the so-called First World; and if account must be taken of social change in the North and West, it certainly cannot be ignored in the East and South.

Wherever the ceremonial significance of food cannot be minimally sustained, society itself may be at risk. In Tikopia in the South Pacific a famine once led *directly* to the stoppage of ceremonies; people felt it was quite simply *impossible* to do real funerals or weddings without food.[10] What a contrast to the way we sometimes artificially prop up or sustain our eucharist in situations of famine! If there is a famine of presbyters, we "reserve" the eucharist, sometimes for months; if there is a famine of "worthy" communicants, we make our supposedly public eucharistic meal private and take communion in isolation from the community; and with a touching irony we often create a rather artificial famine and deprive ourselves of "companionship" with other Christians by fasting at the celebration!

The Cultural Significance of Food

So much for food; what of culture? The inculturation of eucharist, as of other aspects of Christian faith and practice, must both respect and challenge cultures. This demands serious attention by those engaged in mission outreach (*Redemptoris Missio*, 53; 65; 83), but an even better starting point is Jesus himself. Jesus naturally enough found himself within a food culture. There was a food context and a food language. Studying his behavior helps us learn the rules of that particular language; it will also show us where he observed and obeyed, or challenged, broke, or flouted the rules. So we should look carefully not only at how, when, where, and with whom Jesus eats, and at what he eats, but at the reactions of others to his behavior.

Jesus joins or welcomes prostitutes, tax-collectors, and other categories of "sinners," singly, in groups, and in crowds of thousands. He not only eats but feasts, shares, takes, declines, and refuses. He is alternately host, guest, giver, and receiver. In his eating and drinking Jesus shows both social relationships (can we sometimes call this "playing"?) and religious behavior (a form of "praying"?). Through his actions he communicates, and though his communication is sometimes acceptable and understood, at other times it is unacceptable and even incomprehensible. What does Jesus say to us now in the contexts of our various lives? How much are we able to accept and understand, and how much remains incomprehensible? Assuming we can penetrate the meaning of Jesus, how might that be translated, transformed by and for people with different food cultures and food languages?

Specific solutions cannot be attempted here, because contexts and possibilities vary so widely. But we can certainly emphasize the critical need for the inculturation of the Gospel; we can also suggest a basis for the kind of discussion that is crucial for everyone involved in evangelism. Fidelity to the tradition of the church is essential if the *koinonia* is to be maintained and fragmentation avoided, but unless our liturgies are orchestrated in such a way as to be comprehensible to the people for whom they are intended, they will be unhelpful and perhaps positively detrimental.

The eucharist can alternately observe and challenge local cultural rules; it can also introduce the kind of processes that will in turn rewrite some of the rules. But meaning, whether in language or in culture, is always many-stranded, otherwise we would have no need for idioms, metaphors, and other decorative figures of speech or varieties of behavior. And without variety there would only be literalness and repetition. But polysemy or multiple meaning is not ambiguity or confusion and should contribute to the enhancement and clarification of meaning rather than constraining and clouding it. Transformations such as we have discussed do not destroy; but they do introduce radical renewal (cf Matt 5:17). As we pursue our commitment to the inculturation of the Gospel, each of us will discover personal and external limitations and boundaries. But the discussion must proceed, and the pastoral needs, not to say the fundamental rights of people, must be championed. If not by us, by whom? If not now, when? If not here, then where?

FROM FOOD TO MEAL: THE MEANING OF EATING

It is simply not true that by observation and intuition we can understand what food means in various cultures; nor does personal experience prove an unmitigated blessing, particularly if we try to generalize from it. We have no business to assume that once we understand Jesus' actions and intentions relative to his friends and disciples, all we have to do is universalize them and then allow each culture to absorb what we have decided is meaningful. Inculturation is not about "us" expatriates or missioners rediscovering an agenda and then foisting it on "them"; it is about the guidance of the Holy Spirit directing both the challenge of the Gospel and the response of the local people.

A meal is a special arrangement of food, not only a cooking but a culturing. Compared to a snack or a bite, which is usually informal and perhaps private, a meal has elements both of formality and of sociality; it is an expression of community. So, in order to understand the meaning-in-context of eating, we need to look not only at food-in-society but at meal-in-society. This is particularly necessary if a *dialogue* is to be encouraged between the eucharist and cultures, since we are proposing to integrate it with societies and into people's lives and not simply offload it at various places around the world. That would be no better than an authoritarian prescription by representatives of current Western eucharistic practice; it would not be an authentic expression either of the living tradition or of the pastoral role or magisterium of the church, even though it may represent the actual situation that regrettably exists in many places today.

So, who eats, what, when, where, and with whom? And how can we understand these interactions? We must recall that the rules are "context-sensitive,"[11] that there is no *universal* commensality but only *specific* meals and feasts, but also that food language *is* universal in some sense. The burden of learning particular food languages rests with whoever wants to make sense of the system, but such language learning is possible, and rewarding! Here are some examples of food languages, with partial translations where required:

The giving and sharing of food is the *prototypic relationship* in Chinese society, as if the word were literally made flesh. Only a Chinese living alone and in abject poverty would sit down to a solitary meal. It is normal to eat with one's family and kin; when these are unavailable, people eat in teashops or at work, rather than alone.[12]

In contrast, the Melanesian Trobrianders do indeed eat alone,

retiring to their own hearths with their portions, turning their backs on one another, and eating rapidly for fear of being observed.[13]

This seems comparable to some behavior in Zambia, where

the highest compliment that the Bemba can pay to a man is *not to have him as an invited guest*, but rather to send a gift [food and beer] to be eaten privately in his hut. The least hospitable thing would be to invite a guest to share one's own meal. . . . To ask a man to share a meal would be to treat him like a dependent.[14]

And the Bemba behavior seems not entirely different from another aspect of Trobriand custom, for whereas

premarital sexual relations are an accepted feature of Trobriand [Melanesian] social life, *couples are prohibited from eating together before marriage*. People in Western societies sometimes object when an unmarried couple share a bed; the *Trobrianders* object just as strongly when they share a meal.[15]

But how can we be *sure* that Trobriand behavior relative to food prohibitions, and the isolation of a guest from the host, *means* the same thing as Bemba behavior? The answer is that without more information we cannot, and it would be very irresponsible of us to jump to conclusions. But these examples show just how risky it would be to try to inculturate the eucharist in a particular way without reference to the cultural meaning-system. The theme of interrelatedness or of the inappropriateness of dependency, raised among the Bemba, is echoed among certain Eskimos whom

you must not thank for your meat; it is your right to get parts. . . . Nobody wishes to be dependent on others. Therefore there is nobody who gives or gets gifts, for thereby you become dependent.[16]

We are getting into deep waters now as we move across cultures and find a bewilderment of social behavior related not only to food but to the institution of gift-giving with which we are now somewhat familiar. We have to stay with the present theme a little longer, however, since it cannot be entirely separated from food behavior in general.

Among the Salish Indians [of the Northwest coast of North America], there are two categories of possessions: "prestige" possessions — canoes, shells, ornaments, etc, which can be bought, sold, and exchanged; and *"holy things"* — all kinds of *food*, which *cannot be exchanged or sold, but should be given.*[17]

And in some Melanesian societies

the same food will be given and regiven in a round of gifts so many times over that it becomes decayed or bruised. . . . What does matter is that it continues to circulate, and is always accepted graciously. *Giving and regiving of inedible food* stands for friendly social relations.[18]

What might be interpreted as, and indeed mean, a flawed and insulting gift in one culture, is highly prized where its meaning it quite different, where "used" or "bruised" means permanent or respected rather than worthless or insulting.

This is not to suggest that cultural behavior is inviolate or that misreading or breaking cultural rules is always a sacrilege. Clearly, behavior and rules change, and those who inadvertently break the rules may be treated very indulgently. Our hosts are often a great deal more tolerant of us than we are of them. But a highhanded attitude on our part will not promote creative and mutual relations; nor will it encourage local cultures to commit themselves to social change or religious transformation. And since naivete is no virtue, the catalogue of *diverse* food behaviors and meanings is intended to show just how challenging is the inculturation of eucharist.

Picking up the Pieces

What then can be said by way of generalization? Almost universally the major life-stages in the biological and social development of the individual are celebrated with food and drink. But we also have to take note of taboos or proscriptions, such as in the Trobriand case, as particular transformations of the celebration of critical life-stages. We also must pay attention to the kind or quality of food involved in social relations.

Could we suggest a kind of deep structure underlying food practices? Heuristically this might be helpful; more than that would be difficult to justify. Yet we have uncovered some themes. Rules in specific societies dictate that abundance or scarcity, freshness or staleness, prescription or proscription are carriers of meaning. So food behavior is at least analogous to language-in-use and can likewise be interpreted only according to context — as contexts differ so do meanings attached to food and sharing. It is enough to have shown that the meaning of food and meals is neither self-evident nor universal, and that care and expertise are needed if eucharist (insofar as it is a meal) is to be properly inculturated. There is also a corollary: a variety of inculturated eucharistic forms might be acceptable according to different pastoral and cultural circumstances.

We have already made some qualifications to the last statement. Modified forms of eucharist cannot simply conceal a widespread and artificial scarcity of full celebrations of Mass, yet warmly welcomed expressions of the eucharistic community other than Mass could have a particular appropriateness, just as popular devotions[19] have always found and will always find a place in Christian life. But an inculturated eucharist should produce some new rites reflecting the range of eucharists or thanksgivings in the life of Jesus and the contemporary responses of cultures to a developing theology and social circumstances.[20] New liturgical forms might be seen as mirroring some cross-cultural institutionalizations of food sharing, and thus demonstrating the relevance of eucharist in the daily lives of people who both play and pray with food. As for ourselves, we might, when working to inculturate the eucharist, adopt the principle that behavior (in this case religious behavior) without adaptive value will not survive. Without careful attention to cultural meanings, contexts, and needs, there will actually be no true inculturation.

FROM CULTURE TO CULT: TOWARD INCULTURATION

To illustrate the *terminus a quo*, the place from which inculturation must start, we may consider two rich and complex institutions. If the *terminus ad quem*, the point at which inculturation aims, is to be something both new and capable of expressing the values of the realm of God, then the missioner needs a considerable amount of local knowledge like this. These are meaning-bearing patterns of behavior, which inculturation must attempt to harness and transform, not to ridicule and undermine. But these are not crypto-eucharists, though they do indicate that the *idea* of eucharist may be successfully rooted in native soils, given appropriate care and nurture. It will be important to look out for Gospel values[21] as well as impressive signs of cultural sophistication in these accounts, but we will also encounter some very real stumbling blocks.

Slametan is a Javanese communal feast. Its function is to maintain unity among the participants. At this level, at least, it is rather similar to the eucharist:

> The community is said to be joined by dead ancestors and supernatural beings. The occasion can be almost any event the giver wishes to honor or sanctify: pregnancy, birth, circumcision, marriage, illness, death, moving into a new dwelling. ... The emphasis is slightly different for each occasion, and special kinds of food are usually provided at each. Once all have arrived and formed a circle around the platters of food, the host briefly states the reason for celebrating a

slametan and calls upon the spirits to join them; a prayer is offered
in Arabic, which few are likely to understand. Each participant
(except the host, who does not eat) is given a stiff banana leaf for
samples of the special meat and fowl, along with rice colored and
molded in various shapes and patterns for each occasion. The host
then bids guests and spirits to eat. Food, rather than prayer, is the
heart of the *slametan*. The spirits feed on the aroma of the food,
leaving its substance for the human diners. After briefly sampling the
food, the guests leave, taking with them the uneaten food, which they
will share with their families.[22]

The parallels with eucharist are striking: a gathering of the whole community, living and dead; various occasions for celebrating; a little-under-
stood ritual language; a *performance* rather than a *statement*; the integration
of playing and praying; a distinction between the aroma and the substance
of the food; and the "viaticum" or food for the journey. Yet there are also
intriguing and challenging differences: *slametan* are given at the initiative
of the host; the host does not eat; and evidently, this is not explicitly Christian.

But we have here, surely, a contextualization of many of those things
that eucharist addresses and a rich array of Gospel values, virtues entirely
compatible with those propounded by Jesus. Inculturation in such a context
ought to be able to build on *slametan*, just as the eucharist as we know it
built upon other cultural forms while remaining faithful both to the Christian tradition and to the configuration of meanings within local cultures.
But the idea that the eucharist might be inculturated without reference to
slametan is surely outrageous! The actual work is delicate and demanding,
but to these people in Java the *notion* of eucharist need by no means be
alien, while the institutionalization, given ecclesial flexibility and encouragement, should prove challenging and rewarding. We must pray for the
day and prepare for it.

The second example comes from the Massim of Goodenough Island,
Melanesia, and the *Modawa/Fakili* Festival Cycle. We will examine it in a
little more detail. It is somewhat reminiscent of the Easter Vigil ceremonies.

Characterized by regular food exchanges and nightly entertainments
over a period of many months, it is climaxed by a large pig and food
distribution at which debts are paid and others created,[23] thereby
linking it to other festivals of the same and other cycles. The *Modawa/
Fakili* festival cycle is the most spectacular institutional complex that
Goodenough Islanders possess. Festival cycles are based on single
village communities. Not only have the indigenous forms of festival
been stimulated into a vigorous florescence since pacification, but they
have also been supplemented and diversified by the adoption from

Ferguson Island of memorial feasts, mortuary exchanges, and other practices associated with death. Occasions for sponsoring festivals have thus been multiplied, and there are many modes available today for the leader wishing to "make big his name." By combining numerous different elements, some imported, some indigenous, he can create "new" and hitherto untried sequences of feasts, exchanges, and festivals.[24]

At first sight this is much more problematic than *slametan*. It is focused on "big men" and the creation of debts. It is about death, and it uses pigs. Yet for us, indebtedness is a form of covenant, death is a preamble to resurrection, and pigs, like lambs, may be useful metonymics or images. There are strongly positive resonances too: a ceremony so extended over time that it might almost be a way of life; mutual indebtedness that binds a community; interlinkage of villages like communities or church (*koinonia, ekklesia*); a ceremony that really does stand as a "center and summit" of social life; adaptation of new forms that are truly life-giving; and the example of "making big one's name" by virtual self-impoverishment. Each of these has a splendid catechetical lesson to teach.

In the festival proper there are three main phases: the inauguration of the ceremony, called "lighting the fire"; the lengthy middle phase of regular entertainments and feasting called "singing and dancing"; and the grand finale, characterized by large-scale distribution of pigs and vegetables, known as the "cutting of the festival."

Lighting the fire: A few nights after an announcement, the festival is inaugurated by the ceremonial lighting of a fire. Each night after its relighting, entertainment follows, symbolizing hospitality, warm relationships, and shared pleasures. For a few nights the general community watches; then all, including visitors, are invited to leave their disagreements and "bad things" (sorcery) behind and come in a spirit of joy.

Singing and dancing: This phase is marked by an exchange of cooked food contributed by the whole community. The leader redistributes it so that everything is shared by all. Pots are ostentatiously bestowed on "enemies," who must accept the gift with as good grace as possible. During the festival people must avoid any conduct that would reflect unfavorably on them; enemies try to outdo each other in generosity and graciousness. All quarrels are avoided. A festival is successful if the host attracts fairly large numbers of people and manages to feed and entertain them.

Cutting of the festival: Everyone comes from miles around, a matter of pride to the whole community. All are brightly attired, with faces painted and bodies oiled. The leader states the hope that ill-feelings have been left at home with spears, for this is a joyous thing, not to be spoiled with malice. People who have come for war and not for food and fellowship should go home. Finally the distribution is made. First, all outstanding debts are paid, and then "presents" are made to create debts of friendship. There are two kinds of "presents": those specifically made to "enemies" to shame them, and token gifts to friends. Everyone knows the difference; a gift to an enemy cannot be refused without loss of dignity and reputation.

The leader is not permanent; the behavior is standardized: leaders can be of either sex and assorted ages; and over a period of time anyone, theoretically, can be a leader. But in practice, certain qualities are sought:

• *at the individual level* a leader models the industrious person, the concerned host, the generous benefactor;

• *at the sectional level* (that of competitiveness) a leader models group strength, wealth, moral superiority, and the prestige of the giver. Leaders are not hierarchical figures, but show self-restraint, concern, and peaceful relations;

• *at the highest level* a leader must manifest and maintain service and equality and avoid dominance. The social value of food is the dominant symbol and organizing referent of the whole festival. Each festival creates community out of social fragmentation, maintaining it through food exchange and mutual indebtedness, turning enemies into friends.

Again, the ingredients for discussion are abundant. Many Gospel values are apparent, some problems are clear, and a number of challenges to well-tried ways of doing things are issued to all committed to inculturation.

CHRISTIAN TRADITION AND LOCAL CULTURES

Unless the eucharist is inculturated it will never realize its full potential in people's lives. But this necessitates an encounter and dialogue between the Christian tradition (the "text": Gospel, creeds, theology, and history as delivered or handed down from Christ and taken up or received by the church) and real people (the "culture": local social institutions, worlds of meaning, value systems, oral traditions). There is neither a naked Gospel nor a naked culture to be clothed with the mantle of inculturation. What does exist, however, is living tradition and living communities; it is the embrace of each by the other that will give birth to inculturation of the Gospel.

If foot washing presents possibilities, what about Jesus' meals with fish rather than bread and wine? And if the deep structure of Jesus' actions actually concerns justice and service, then what other transformations might not be possible, producing liturgical acts that rather specifically address justice and service in today's world?

Once we look at transformations, why not look directly to cultural institutions like the *slametan* or the Modawa/Fakili Festival, and the many other worthy social institutions in so many cultures? Why not festival or fiesta or carnival or other forms of popular religion as possible vehicles for inculturating the eucharist? Where might not all that lead? It seems that we must pursue this kind of thinking, if only to discount some possibilities. But that may well leave others as potential carriers of Christian devotion, if not worship.

Theologians, pastors, anthropologists, catechists, and believers have a responsibility to continue to examine such issues, as together we seek to apply the principles of inculturation. Something has already been done, of course, but progress tends to be slow and the experimentation is not uniformly encouraged. It would be as stiflingly inappropriate universally to impose the cultural dress of Western liturgical forms as it would be irresponsible not to care about the growing pains associated with the development of local churches. There is a fine line sometimes between license and laxity, as between concern and control. But moral leadership is not incompatible with trust, nor genuine care with tolerance. Grace, after all, so it is said, builds on nature. Vatican II (1962-65) and *Evangelii Nuntiandi* (1975) did open gates, which have never subsequently been locked, though one might imagine the sound of rattling keys ...

• Already in 1973 the bishop of Pala in Chad, Africa, celebrated eucharist with millet bread and millet beer; for this he was (reputedly) relieved of his authority by Rome.

• In 1978 an African theologian suggested that what Africans eat becomes *thereby* proximate matter for eucharist, and that staple foods should become the "species" for African eucharists.[25] Given the admirable intentions here, one might nevertheless suggest that social contexts and shared meanings should be examined and made explicit in relation to specific communities before generalizing about "Africa."

• In 1980 (and again a decade later), Eugene Uzukwu, a Nigerian and an Igbo, examined African staple diets and drinks[26] much more systematically. He noted *their role in African life and experience*, and he considered grape wine in the Jewish-Christian tradition. He raised the possibility of celebrating eucharist in Africa with African "elements." In other words, looking at how Jesus transformed his own tradition, Uzukwu tried to apply his insights to current situations. Finally, in a rather careful conclusion, he suggested millet and palm wine as the best, most accessible, and most acceptable elements for an African eucharist.

This brave and timely effort needs to be accompanied by many more such studies to generate the discussion necessary for fruitful developments. For example, though Africa is a single, enormous land mass, of itself this is surely an insufficient reason to treat all its people uniformly, even though one needs to search out some eucharistic symbolism that would have universal relevance. Uzukwu offers a general overview, which might be refined in the application to more specific contexts. There may be many points of convergence in the social behavior on the African continent, but there are also hundreds of languages and a vast range of customs and social institutions relating to food. No outsider can understand meaning without knowledge of context, while insiders rarely have explicit formulations; meaning is embodied in use rather than in formulae. One simply does not know how an Africanized eucharist might be received in many African contexts if local staples were approved for use, or if millet and palm wine were given general authorization.

FOOD FOR THOUGHT

Though Jesus pushed back boundaries, moved out to others, and included the excluded, he also belonged to a culture. He acted within a context and responded to others in terms of theirs and his own. Does this not suggest that he did not presume to say the last word or fix the eucharist in a monolithic way? Some of his ways of expressing justice and service were culture-bound. Social conditions change, as do particular responses. Might the demands of inculturation take us far from where we are now, and continue the restructuring undertaken not only by Jesus but by the early communities and their descendants?

Increasingly, local churches beyond the Mediterranean region and the Western European tradition are calling for greater flexibility in the liturgy, according to the spirit of Jesus. Jean-Marc Ela, passionately and eloquently encapsulating the experience and frustration of many, asserts that the eucharist in its current form, far from being a sign of hope and liberation for many, only creates dependence and alienation. He says:

> The case of the eucharist reveals the domination at the heart of the faith as lived in Africa, within a Christianity that refuses to become incarnate in our people. . . . The church ought not to rest but should demand greater flexibility in discipline in order to have more freedom to celebrate the eucharist with matter that will be meaningful for the culture of a given people; it should open itself to the great mass of human beings in quest of liberty and justice. It ought to pay attention to the cry of the oppressed.[27]

The future of Africa and of any local churches can only be left to those churches themselves, and of course the Holy Spirit who is nothing if not unpredictable! Not that the tradition and the catholicity of the church will be forgotten as local needs are addressed, but careful attention *must* be paid to the sign-systems within the culture, whether linguistic, culinary, social, or religious. A tall order? Certainly. But long overdue is the concerted, radical experimentation, that would encourage the local churches without antagonizing them from each other and from the principle of universality. For how can the universal church be credible unless it *gives* the eucharist to local churches, rather than effectively *withholding* or *refusing* it? And though cultures must indeed be challenged and transformed by the Gospel, their response begins from where they are now. As Mercy Oduyoye mourns:

You may come to Baptism with your [African] name;
you may come to be married in [African] clothes;
you may drum and even dance in Church.
But in the Eucharist,
can you use wine made of anything but grapes,
and bread which is made of wheat?
These things do not grow
in most parts of Black Africa.[28]

Yahweh provided food that was not always recognized as such (Ex 16:15). The God who formed humanity and fashioned the genius that created cultures is a provident Creator. In our final section, contemplating the journeys to be made, the terrain still to come, and the paths already trodden, we will try to recognize the food that will sustain us. It is all around, if sometimes unfamiliar.

QUESTIONS FOR THE ROAD

• Do you believe that cultures contain Gospel values even before the arrival of Christianity? Can you identify some?
• Do you think real transformation of culture from within is possible, or does acceptance of Christianity demand repudiation of cultural traditions? What are the implications of your answer for inculturation?
• Several cultural institutions connected with food and ritual are mentioned in this chapter. Would you encourage the linkage of social and liturgical behavior as a way to promote local inculturation? How do you feel about the separation of the Gospel and culture, which is identified in *Evangelii Nuntiandi* as one of the most unhappy circumstances of our age?
• What do you think about the possibility of eucharist without bread or wine for cultures where these are not indigenous?

PART III

JOURNEYS

Chapter 7

Witchcraft, Eucharist, and Hocus Pocus

As the doctrine of Providence can reduce for believers . . . the despair and anguish of blind fate or chance, so theories of evil in Africa can bring an element of courage, comfort and calm resignation. This explanatory function is also intimately connected with ethics.[1]

Witchcraft experiences are real, but since people do not make a clear distinction between the reality of experiences during sleeping and during waking, there is no need to distinguish as relevant, physical anthropophagy and psychic or dream-experience anthropophagy. What to us might be dismissed as a dream or nightmare, depends on our determination of what is "real" experience.[2]

Witch-beliefs, the standardized nightmare of a group.[3]

Hocus pocus: magical formula, trickery, deception; assumed derivation from hoc est corpus.[4]

The bread that I will give is my flesh—for the life of the world.

John 6:51

WITCHCRAFT, DISINTEGRATION, AND TRANSFORMATION

Witchcraft in both a traditional and contemporary sense[5] is one of the great scourges of communities. Where it is believed rampant, a group inexorably becomes demoralized and socially paralyzed. Yet the point of greatest risk is also the point of greatest opportunity. Extreme need tends to produce appropriate resolutions, and witch beliefs not only follow the contours of social values but also vary as social groups vary.[6] Consequently, to

115

study witchcraft in context is to approach a people's value system at its deepest level. In the drama of witch beliefs in action, the people involved are unlikely to be able precisely to articulate the values being threatened and buttressed, yet the astute and informed observer may succeed in mapping the surface behavior onto the deep structures of belief and values. This is our task, but we will go further, seeking a fit between aspects of witchcraft and aspects of eucharist.

Universal and Particular Aspects of Witchcraft

The diagnosis of witchcraft and the steps toward curing its debilitating effects will be described. Witchcraft may be seen here as a metaphor for a social crisis and a subsequent creative response — and, by extension, a partial metaphor for eucharist itself. Though this may sound at first a rather bizarre claim, it should seem gradually less so, especially to those with firsthand experience of certain kinds of witchcraft; to others, a case-study approach may illuminate both the social drama of witchcraft and aspects of the eucharist as a communal ritual.

Earlier we recalled that there is no universal eucharist; every celebration is particular, and in a sense, unique. So it is with witchcraft; universal witchcraft may exist as an idea, but every instance of witchcraft is unique and related to particular persons in a particular context. But just as a person should be able to *recognize* general characteristics of eucharist in a particular eucharistic liturgy (and indeed to recognize a particular eucharist as an example of Eucharist rather than, say, an example of Evensong), so it is with witchcraft.

The example used here is from a particular part of Africa,[7] but though different from other local instances it should be recognizable to anyone familiar with West Africa. Though its details will not mirror witchcraft as institutionalized elsewhere, there should be sufficient resonance for readers to make sense of it, as well as to compare and contrast it with the more familiar.

Witchcraft is believed to be the main cause of child death. People have a certain tolerance of infant mortality inasmuch as they do not immediately suspect a witch when each child dies; they know some medical etiology, and that death comes to everyone sooner or later. But beyond a certain undefined and indefinable point, people begin to get very agitated and feel powerless. When a village becomes increasingly conscious or even obsessed with the thought that far too many babies are dying, the possibility that witches are abroad begins to be whispered. At first, nothing very specific is said, merely that there is a lot of misfortune about. But gradually the fear of witches becomes very openly expressed, and people feel powerless. If a mother believes that voracious witches are in the vicinity, she knows that she can do nothing to save her baby once a witch has decided to "eat" it.

An expatriate who sees mothers in despair and then becoming passive as their children become ill should not conclude that this is normal behavior. Everyone, especially the mothers, knows it is abnormal. But previous events have combined to produce hopelessness or passivity, and unless this is understood, no expatriate will ever appreciate the social dynamics of witchcraft, or anything else. For what is the point in spending money when resources are so scarce if one already knows that the child's sickness is merely an external sign of an irreversible process, when a witch is eating the baby and its physical deterioration simply demonstrates an irreversible process? When mothers reach this stage of hopelessness, nothing can be done save beg for a witchfinder and leave the rest to him, for unless witches are discovered and destroyed, the whole community is in jeopardy.

Chief, Witchfinder, and Community

The custodian of the community is the Paramount Chief,[8] and witchcraft is dealt with at the level of an entire chiefdom, which has a moral and geographical unity. The Chief invites the witchfinder, who is commissioned and sent to every village in turn, to eradicate witchcraft and restore harmony. He will play with emotions and create fear, revulsion, hysteria, and finally relief. He is as much of a celebrity as the Paramount Chief, and such is the importance of his task for whole villages and communities that nobody remains uninvolved in the unfolding drama.

To hinder the witchfinder is an admission of guilt, so everyone is anxious to cooperate. Once within the village, he seals it off from the outside world, simply by hanging cotton threads across every path leading out of the village, forbidding anyone to leave or enter, and threatening dire consequences if the threads are disturbed; it is sufficient.

The village effectively isolated, everyone foregathers, the witchfinder is introduced by the Chief, and the nature of his task is outlined: he will eradicate witchcraft once and for all, in a process that will be frightening and perhaps worse. He addresses the people, reminding them of his dangerous and exhausting task, saying that he must be supported and paid; the laborer is indeed worthy of his hire. Since the witchfinder is the only person capable of halting the infant deaths and arresting malefactors, the people must comply. His apparently exorbitant demands are soon met, but not without a good deal of cathartic grumbling and borrowing and compromise, all of which bonds people together and sets the stage for the drama to follow.

Pregnant women and nursing mothers are sequestered in a small, low hut for the duration; they will be safe there and are not to be accused of witchcraft. But the rest of the village is now a dangerous place. Isolated, affording no escape, it harbors guilty and innocent; since all evil is, in final analysis, personalized (that is, *persons* are responsible), all that remains is to identify the miscreants within!

To show his fairmindedness the witchfinder first grants an amnesty: anyone who possesses any dubious "medicine" or paraphernalia must bring it for public scrutiny and will not be punished. But if anything is discovered later the punishment will be dire. It is easy to imagine the excitement in the village as people rush to divest themselves of "compromising" protective and even destructive medicines accumulated over several years. They dare not risk later exposure, yet are ashamed of the pathetic bric-à-brac they are forced to reveal. But few people are in a position to ridicule others, for it seems that everyone has some reason to be embarrassed. The onlooker might be bemused at the sight of corked bottles, wrapped dried leaves, bits of cloth tied with string, and even an occasional horror like a desiccated human hand. Some of these are the famous "fetishes" of Africa; others are ad hoc fabrications. Through it all people are mumbling apologetic explanations or long-winded excuses. All is grist to the witchfinder's mill. He is quick to draw attention to the fear and hostility that undermine the village: neighbor fears neighbor, wives are jealous of each other, while farmers try to accumulate a little more luck than their fellows. This is the perfect environment for witches and witchcraft!

The amnesty now over, worse is to come! The charms, potions, and protective medicines are now heaved into a large water-filled oil-drum standing on three stones over a fire, the focus of attention, and the only source of light in the encircling gloom.

THE WITCH-HUNT

After a night when sleep was forbidden and talk was hushed and fervent, people are now anxious and self-conscious. Few can remember, and fewer still will discuss, previous witch-cleansings, the most recent of which will have been more than fifteen years previously. The people's confusion seems orchestrated by the witchfinder, whose morning homily recalls what they know only partially: the modus operandi of the witch. *Ndilei* is a word familiar to everyone. It refers to an object unequivocally associated with witches, like a pet (the black cat in popular European tradition); though inanimate, it needs to be "fed" with the blood of babies in order to retain the power which, vicariously, the witch uses for personal enhancement through destruction. *Ndilei* look like a mud-covered ball of string. They are unmistakable; the witchfinder is looking for them. Given the fact that few people have ever seen one, but virtually everyone is hysterically frightened by the mere mention of the name, one can easily imagine the emotional state of the community as the witchfinder points to a house, seemingly at random, and strides purposefully toward it, calling for the owner to open the door.

Probably everyone expects the witchfinder to discover some *ndilei*, but no one is expecting—and everyone is dreading—a personal accusation. So, when the finger of suspicion points at an individual, though that person is probably stunned and frightened, he or she is surely convinced that no *ndilei* will be discovered. Yet within moments the witchfinder has pointed to something suspicious inside the house. Perhaps the simple stick bed and paltry possessions will be unceremoniously thrown out of the door and into public view; maybe the rafters will be searched; a hole may even be dug in the floor; but patently, a *ndilei* will be produced, to the amazement and outrage of the owner.

As one who witnessed this half a dozen times or more, I can affirm the impression that the witchfinder, or one of his assistants, did indeed discover or dig up rather than crudely "plant" the evidence. How it got there in the first place is another question.

Witchfinder, accused person, and everyone together march, stumble, and run back to the village meeting house where the large oil-drum is the focal point. An electrified buzz of conversation is heavy on the air, and the protestations of the accused are already being met by the hardening animosity of a crowd hungry for a scapegoat. The witchfinder recapitulates the drama so far, disclaiming all trickery, and holding up the *ndilei* before the crowd. Cowrie shells, each one representing the deaths of half a dozen babies, are sewn to every *ndilei*. This one has four or five, and the conclusion is clear. Hysteria is mounting as people draw circumstantial conclusions and focus their hostility on the hapless defendant.

As I tell myself that the accused is quite clearly innocent, and that someone will surely provide a character reference, the power of persuasion and social pressure exert themselves in the community. The witchfinder simply employs remorseless logic in his questioning. The *ndilei* was found in your house, was it not? The house has a lock and key, which are in your possession? You saw the discovery of the *ndilei*? The lock had not been tampered with? As the owner, you are responsible for the contents of your house? However much the respondent protests every time the affirmative answer is elicited, the noose draws tighter. The responses become more frustrated and then feebler and less persuasive; finally, as the village waits breathlessly, the improbable happens and a confession is made! Sometimes it seems that the defendant is simply persuaded by the logic itself; at other times the attitude of the villagers hardens perceptibly. But always the witchfinder pushes and persists; he is able to take a reluctant confession, reword it, and have the accused recite it before the implacable judge and jury.

The Extension of Witchcraft

All the witchfinder needs to do is make the conclusions explicit. There is indeed evil in this village. It is under people's very noses. It is in the least suspected places and owned by even the most innocent-looking people! The witchfinder performs a tour de force. But there is much, much more to come. The next day or two see perhaps half a dozen variations on the same theme, as more bemused villagers find themselves confessing, neighbors become scathing of the accused, and no one can think of anything else until the last accusations have been made and proven. The conclusion is that for each accused a *ndilei* has been found (even deep below the undisturbed floor of a mud hut), and that every *ndilei* wears the baleful eyes of incriminating cowrie shells, accounting for dozens (perhaps a hundred in total) of infant deaths over a period of up to two decades. As the *ndilei* are thrown into the great oil-drum, the people sit around transfixed, emotionally battered, psychologically distraught. They have not slept, save for a catnap in the lull of the afternoon, for two or three days; they have scarcely eaten; and some are probably in clinical shock.

Now the denouement, as the witchfinder unmasks the very source and symbol of evil. Witches, it is believed, though antisocial, gather in community to plot their nefarious deeds. But they convene far from the village, in the deepest bush, at night, around the witch pot. This is where the "hocus pocus" occurs, the conjuring of spirits, the plotting of deception and malice. The witch pot is thinly analogous to a sacrificial altar used for the black arts; a witch must return to it periodically to refresh or replenish his or her power. Only when the pot is discovered and destroyed, therefore, will people really be convinced that witchcraft has been eradicated.

In this particular case the accused person identified as the "owner" of the witch pot was the most unlikely person in the world: a kindly old woman, liked by all the village, widowed perhaps a decade before, and the sister of the local chief. But far from standing her in good stead, these testimonies to her character had gone completely by the board when the witchfinder discovered a *ndilei* in her house. Even her brother was quick to accept her guilt: "How tragic that all these years, under our very noses, our sister has been operating as a witch and causing untold deaths." Once again the whole community was drawn into the remorseless web of logic spun by the witchfinder. The old woman must now lead him to the witch pot, and the drama would finally be resolved. Meanwhile the people were told to collect rice and other food for a communal meal on the morrow, and wood for the fire; everyone was involved.

On the Trail of the Witch Pot

After dark, with the whole village gathered in anticipation in the meetinghouse, a tropical downpour added noise, wind, and wetness to the proceedings, which were now only just short of chaotic. The old woman stood, broken and bewildered, before the oil-drum, while the witchfinder explained to the crowd that she would lead him to the pot, hidden deep in the bush. Therefore, some trusty witnesses were required. He nominated a couple, and several voices volunteered me! Much to my surprise, he agreed, and summoned me to come. With the woman leading, mostly because she was being pushed and persuaded by the witchfinder, the bedraggled quartet followed, slipping and stumbling, into the blackness of the night.

At first we might have been on a bush path, but very soon it seemed that we were splashing along in the teeming rain in anything but a clear direction. By the fickle illumination of battery powered flashlights the witchfinder could be seen, just ahead, almost dragging the woman by the arm, but repeating for us all that he was following her. Occasionally he shone his own flashlight into the trees and could be heard asking: "Is that an orange tree?"—a question that seemed faintly ridiculous in the circumstances. But we did eventually come to a small clearing where there was indeed an enormous old orange tree, with a branch extending horizontally about eight or ten feet overhead. The witchfinder seemed satisfied and ordered the uncomprehending woman to tell him exactly where the witch pot was. Then, with arms around her (in the manner of a golf professional teaching a novice) and a hoe in their hands, he ordered her to mark out a circle about ten feet in diameter, which, largely with his help and direction, she managed to do.

I was watching, eagle-eyed and excited, and would have sworn that the earth within the circle had not been touched since the jungle was young. I recall telling myself that if anything were dug up, I would be so confounded that I would probably accept the whole rationale and experience! Yet I was determined to find (perhaps impose?) a rational explanation to satisfy my own intellectual and sensory criteria. So much for objectivity!

Three men with spades appeared from nowhere and began to dig within the circle, while the witchfinder explained that the pot would be buried deep in this lonely place, and that it would be aware by now that it was being hunted. Consequently it would try to escape. The witchfinder was ostentatiously confident, while warning us that unpleasant things might happen. As the hole deepened and the men cut through the roots of the orange tree and dug into compacted earth, the bizarreness of the scene imprinted itself in memory; indeed, it seems in retrospect, it is precisely one of the deepest sociological functions of this entire ritual-drama to be remembered and spoken of for years to come. It was indeed memorable. After midnight, in the lashing rain, surrounded by jungle, soaked to the skin, excited and uncomfortable, expectant yet afraid, this motley crew was committed to digging a hole in undisturbed ground to retrieve a pot hidden by an old woman who could hardly walk and certainly not wield a spade, in order to close the semantic circle formed by infant deaths and maleficent witchcraft. And it seemed entirely appropriate!

Suddenly the witchfinder screamed that the pot was trying to escape. We must drown it, and it would then come to the surface. So the diggers brought water and the rain-sodden earth turned into mud as bucket after bucket was poured into the hole. The witchfinder was now highly excited and stomped around urging more speed and saying that the pot was moving laterally, in the direction of the newly formed pile of soil taken from the hole. Mud and madness were everywhere; the witnesses were spattered and soaked, but the discomfort was more than outweighed by the excitement and expectation. The old woman appeared to be in shock and looked no more substantial than the sodden clothes about her frail body. The witch-finder was as stolid as the orange tree, a five-star general fighting in the dark.

As the laborers attacked the pile of soil and scattered it to reach the witch pot, the whole area under the tree became a morass. The witchfinder walked over it, prodding a pointed stick until it struck a solid mass. Screaming to the diggers—and the suddenly thickened crowd—that they must be prepared to pounce, he went down on one knee in the mud, feeling with his hand. Satisfied, he ordered the three diggers to fling themselves on the spot and grasp the as yet unseen object. This they did, and as one shouted hysterically "it's a pot," there was bedlam. Two of the men tried to escape for fear of the pot, but the witchfinder ordered them not to take their hand off it, saying that they would come to no harm. Indecorously the trio arose from the mud with something in their six hands, half as big as a basketball: a small, iron, three-legged pot, complete with lid and bound by string, but clearly showing a dozen or more of the dreaded cowrie shells. Consternation! Hysteria! Panic! And above the pandemonium the voice of the witchfinder urging the men to carry the pot bravely back to the village, where all would be revealed.

Purification by Fire

It was fifteen mad minutes before order could be restored. Everyone was packed in the meeting house, the fire was roaring, the oil-drum was on the fire, the witch pot was on the central table, and the witchfinder was center stage. The homily was long and appropriate, leaving people in no doubt about the evil of witchcraft, the rampant hostility and fear in the village, and the volatility of a situation which, had he not been there, could have ended in mayhem or murder. The old woman sat, cowering. Having finished his dramatic discourse, the witchfinder bade the people to cook the meal they had prepared in readiness for the finale at dawn, now only a couple of hours away.

Dawn broke over a village gathered for something very special. Everyone was assembled around the witchfinder, the oil-drum, and the old woman with her codefendants sitting under public scrutiny. To one side, between houses, was a roaring fire. The "poison ordeal" followed[9] and served to release much of the tension by convincing the people that the accused were now powerless, while reminding each individual of the virtue and importance of a clean heart.

The oil-drum was manhandled adjacent to the newly stoked fire where it was overturned, spewing forth its turbid water and all the articles gathered in the previous amnesty, including the *ndilei* and the witch pot. Everything could now be seen for what it was, cleaned of mud. And the whole village drew round in a circle, tight enough for everyone to feel the flames.

The witchfinder, resplendent in a clean and colorful robe, stepped forward with hammer in hand, picked up a *ndilei*, placed it on a flat rock, and without speaking raised and brought the hammer down in a single movement. The crowd was pressing around, and some people jumped back in disgust, suddenly spattered by blood from the *ndilei*! One by one *ndilei* were retrieved, placed on the rock, and struck; each time the people recoiled and shrieked. Evidently the blood was proof that babies had been killed to feed the *ndilei*. Evidently, too, explanations and attributions of infant deaths were being provided by this very drama!

Finally, the witch pot was placed on the flat rock for all to see, the strings were cut, and the lid removed. Before anyone saw very much, the pot was in the hands of the witchfinder, who was wordlessly walking round the perimeter of the crowd, thrusting it under people's noses. Grown men and women reeled back at the sight; some even retched. I had little idea of what to expect but was momentarily shocked at what was revealed: it looked exactly like the top of a baby's tousled head, fitting snugly inside the pot! The witchfinder was not quite finished. Walking back to the large stone, he stood the pot on its three little legs, raised his hammer, and brought it crashing down, as gore sprayed everywhere. Then he tossed the pitiful remains of his ferocity onto the fire.

THE CONVERGENCE OF GOSPEL VALUES AND CULTURE

There followed one of the most magnetic sermons one could ever hope to hear, as all the destruction and fear accumulated over years and brought to a head in the previous three days was exorcised and peace was restored to the village. It provided, finally, an overview and a rationale for witchcraft. It was a demonstration of the fact that real healing occurs only in the context of real trauma, and that resolutions are most effectively undertaken by people who have indeed reached their lowest ebb. It was a story of the possibility of conversion, of social and personal transformation.

Witchcraft, we were reminded, festers in lives and in villages when people are less than fully sociable, less than fully openhearted. All wickedness or moral evil is ultimately a reflection of people's own hatred or jealousy or suspicion or fear, unlike the amoral and unavoidable misfortune or disaster of human or natural experience. The latter will finally bring death to everyone, but the former bring premature death, maliciously. Once such malice has taken hold in a community, witchcraft will flourish. And the past few days, the witchfinder reminded us, have produced the obscene fruits of this voracious evil. A catalogue of transgressions can be recited: hostility, envy, covetousness, sorcery, and witchcraft itself. Six people have been found to harbor *ndilei* and to be abroad at night, meeting at the witch pot and feeding on hapless babies.

"Shall we kill or banish these people?" he asks rhetorically. While one or two are provoked into a vindictively affirmative answer, he swoops dramatically on them and on the community in general, bellowing a resonating negative. "No!" he cries, "because that would be to fight evil with evil, to perpetuate the very thing we are trying to eradicate!" Then, more gently, he muses that there can be no peace in the village unless peace is first in the heart of each person. The six have not only confessed but been reduced to impoverishment, suffered humiliation, and taken the poison ordeal; there is no need for further action. In fact, what is now required is magnanimity. So let no one harbor any ill-will against these pathetic individuals. On the contrary, let the people of this village make it their business to see that these six totally destitute people are fed and clothed and housed and able to live out their remaining days in peace.

To all of us who had expected vengeance, this was not only a total surprise but something of a revelation; this was humane to the point of heroic. And now, waxing to his theme of moral and social reconstruction, the witchfinder left his captive audience with a number of injunctions:

• If any of these unfortunates should become hungry or sick on account of negligence or retaliation by the community, then witchcraft would surely return, and the ensuing plague would be worse than the recent one.

• If any married couple had a quarrel, let the husband not beat the wife, and let the quarrel not remain indoors; rather let it be brought into the open so that older and wiser people could adjudicate the merits of the case. Preferably, let forgiveness precede punishment.

• Women were leading men astray. Let no woman therefore go round immodestly dressed; rather, let every woman have, or receive from her husband, an adequate "lappa" or skirt. Husbands should take their conjugal responsibilities much more seriously.

• If babies sickened, let mothers do everything possible to ensure recovery; witchcraft has been driven away, so there is no reason to fear it as a cause of infant sickness.

• Let every person proceed to communal forgiveness, a communal meal, and an evening of dancing and merrymaking!

And as the people, light of heart and purged of ill-feelings, continued their celebrations, the witchfinder, like the Pied Piper of children's stories, packed his things and took his leave: a great celebrity and a rich man.

HOCUS POCUS OR DEPTH PSYCHOLOGY?

Witchcraft is such an emotive word that it can hardly fail to elicit opinions and judgments. Those involved in the mission of Jesus in cultures different from their own cannot fail to encounter witchcraft or something equally exciting and perplexing. The temptation to jump to conclusions or to apply familiar criteria is strong; it must be avoided. Ridicule, unequivocal condemnation, or the use of words like "satanic" or "diabolical" are not only injudicious but quite unhelpful.

Witchcraft has been something of a Gordian Knot to missionaries of the nineteenth and twentieth century. With their curious blend of rationalism and ethnocentrism, piety and pettiness, they are able to take a logical view of some things but are often insensitive to alternative logics; sometimes intolerant of "fetishism," they may nevertheless be steeped in national or denominational devotionalism. Witchcraft, to someone with a binary mentality, is to be avoided or bypassed with an uncomprehending sigh or ferociously attacked head on. But when we need to understand people and to translate the Gospel, denial is no more appropriate than destruction. Anyone who claims that dialogue is impossible is effectively acknowledging an impasse. If dialogue proves truly impossible, we should have the grace to withdraw.

But there is another way, which holds the promise of mutual discovery leading to change and transformation: the old philosophical maxim known as Occam's Razor. This states that one should attempt to explain things by the most simple and direct means rather than by a needless multiplication of hypotheses. Applied to witchcraft, it would mean two things: first, that we pay attention to the particular context and ensure that we do not apply "solutions" from other contexts; and second, that we do not explain witchcraft in occult or supernatural terms if more down-to-earth explanations prove adequate. Clearly, such an attitude would give rise to the possibility of pastoral approaches very different from those which are the fruits of condemnation and confrontation.

Some missionaries give the impression (to local people at least) that they rather enjoy describing other people's beliefs and behavior in the most exotic and extreme terms, as if to prove the fundamental differences between "us" and "them," thus creating a dramatic polarization. Yet such missionaries would never permit the more bizarre tabloid stories from their own culture to be disseminated abroad as representative of their own cultural or religious behavior! To compare the most embarrassing behavior in one culture with the most heroic in another is to fail to compare like with like and to do a grave disservice to people.

The observations offered here are numerous: that witchcraft makes perfect sense on its own terms and within its context; that the processes followed here in recalling the saga of the witchfinder may have much to teach expatriate missionaries; and that unless we understand the sociological processes of witchcraft and undertake an honest dialogue with actual people in real situations and with firsthand experience of witchcraft, then the Good News will fall largely on deaf ears. Furthermore, any attempts to inculturate it deserve to founder because they fail to take local cultures and local people seriously.

In order for these assertions to be substantiated, it is necessary for us to lay aside any "hermeneutic of suspicion" or previously assumed postures about other people's credulity or manipulation, and approach the topic both with committed open-mindedness and with a fundamental belief in the proposition that people (including ourselves) *can* change, be transformed, and be converted. The unfolding drama of witchcraft appears to be proof enough of that proposition. If, therefore, we intend to transmit Good News, we should be careful that it converges with whatever is bad news in people's lives. In the experience and the narrative of witchcraft, we have surely discovered an effective if unlikely context for apostolic discourse.

But we do need to be clear that it would be as false and futile for missionaries to romanticize and glorify witchcraft henceforward as it has been to vilify and slander it heretofore. All social institutions are corrupt or corruptible, but no institution that has survived for as long as the institution of witchcraft can be irredeemably bad. It must contain at least some seeds capable of bearing life. We have already seen this from the perspective of the very end of the witchfinder's accomplishment. We will backtrack now, and see more, as well as signs of the unproductive seed.

The witchfinder, as portrayed in this chapter and as replicated in many analogous figures across cultures, may appear as a clever charlatan or an exploiter of the people. But this would simply trivialize witchcraft and effectively demonstrate an ignorant and superior attitude. Having, over a lengthy period, become friendly with the witchfinder described here, I put this misgiving to him, evidently with a mixture of ignorance and superiority, suggesting that I knew how he accomplished his magnetic performance. With a weary smile he unmasked this ignorance of psychology and social drama and repudiated my implicit charge of hocus pocus.

The power to detect witches was not a common human attribute, he reminded me. He explained how he had received it in a dream (a well-known source of godly enlightenment) through the good graces of his deceased father and thus ultimately from the Creator. The power was a gift, to be used for the good of the community[10]; but when you receive a gift, he said, you must add your own ingenuity and personality before you transmit it. Of course he "planted" the *ndilei* and the witch pot! But this was not deceit, for he knew *where* to place these things, in whose houses, and how to retrieve them. His was the task of showing to the people the undoubted evil of witchcraft, and this he did, clearly and memorably.

He had a point. Even his relative riches and high status were not exploitative or socially divisive—quite the contrary. And the discomfort of the six people was a relatively small price to pay for their subsequent social security (still a source of some discomfort to me, but much more comprehensible than if I had not been present at the denouement to see their rehabilitation).

An outsider adopting a high moral tone and a posture of condemnation, arguing that such collusion between Chief and witchfinder is immoral and that the people were duped and abused, would be not simply naive but quite inappropriate and irrelevant—hardly the basis for dialogue and mutuality! Unless one is prepared and able to take the drama as a whole (played out over each generation), see its social significance, weigh its values and shortcomings, question and challenge the people respectfully, and propose a coherent and comprehensible alternative explanation of the misfortune and evil associated with infant mortality, one would simply be meddling or moralizing in a situation that cries out for an integrated pastoral approach.

Some people (by no means only missionaries) do inhabit a binary universe, with Good and Evil almost personified and aligned as visible enemies opposite each other. But this is a caricature of a world and no basis upon which to build mutual trust and Christian communities. As Rosemary Ruether has said: "A new international culture is needed if we are to have justice and peace. We must dissolve the Manichean dualism. There *is* good and bad, better and worse. But not all on one side or the other."[11]

Applied to witchcraft — a social institution which provides personalistic explanations and punishment of evil — this would imply that to attack it directly is simply to drive it underground; and to assume that a Christian, eucharistic community can continue to function "normally" in the midst of witchcraft accusations and trials is to collaborate in creating dual religious systems and the most unhealthy kind of syncretism.[12]

If the metaphor of witchcraft is eating flesh and drinking blood, no naive superimposition of Christian eucharistic theology is going to help or clarify it! But perhaps a gradual deconstruction of the witchcraft mentality is possible where a Christian community is itself trying to practice forgiveness, justice, commensality, and gift-exchange. This, of course, is a delicate and long-term undertaking that can only bear fruit where there is mutual trust, mutual listening, and mutual forbearance between missionaries and people operating in an ambience of personal causation and invisible agents. It is, however, an agenda not only prima facie worth pursuing, but essential if Christianity is to become more than external decoration applied to people's lives. And it will most probably entail mistakes and modifications, a matter to be explored in the next chapter.

WITCHCRAFT MENTALITY AND EUCHARISTIC LIBERATION

People are not stupid, but they may do stupid things. Yet for an outsider to attribute stupidity to people would itself be rather stupid if it failed to consider the context and to tap the resources available for explanation and reaction: the people themselves. Life in small-scale societies is rather different from the experience of those raised in large democracies with high technology and rapidly developing scientific knowledge. In traditional communities (as, to a degree, in isolated rural communities elsewhere) everyone knows everyone else, and people are accountable to each other. Privacy is either not a recognized state or right, or is jealously cultivated; secrecy is the underside of the public nature of daily life.

Witchcraft, as we have seen here, operates in such a bounded world where people have little access to alternative explanations. By and large there is one way to do things and one explanation for things, and potential deviants become the focus of accusations or mechanisms of social leveling. Witchcraft is able to take root where the microcosm or local world is much more relevant than the macrocosm or world at large. Relatively isolated, homogeneous villages are ideal for the development of witchcraft beliefs, which in turn provide answers to the most fundamental questions of causality: "Why did *my* baby die? Why did that good person suffer? Why did this person become unaccountably rich?"

In such person-focused worlds, "why" questions receive "who" answers; unanswered questions may remain in people's minds for as long as it takes to find an answer. "Why did my baby die?" or "Why did my crops fail?" tends to become "Who caused my baby to die?" or "Who spoiled my crops?" If a person dies unexpectedly, or as *we* might say "accidentally," it may not be understood as an accident so much as posing a further question ("Who was responsible for this apparent accident?") or indeed a final answer to a long-standing question (the person who died unexpectedly must therefore be responsible for the unresolved death in the village or the unexplained crop failure).[13]

The eucharist should epitomize commensality, love, and transformation; as such it meets, theoretically at least, the deepest needs of villages rent by witchcraft fears and accusations. Our question thus is simple, though the answer may be problematic: Is there a "eucharistic" solution to the universal problems witchcraft encapsulates? The difficulty, such as it is, is that any proposed "solution" must make sense not only to its proposers but to those for whom it is intended. It seems that on very many occasions and in numerous communities there has been an inadequate degree of fit between the proposed solution and the perceived problem, or that the solution has been proposed unilaterally and imposed on a context incapable of assimilating it. These assertions need to be examined.

Unless a problem is understood and addressed from the perspective of the person with the problem, any solution will be ultimately inadequate. This is not to impugn the good will of those who earnestly want to solve the problem as they see it, but merely to say that they do not adequately see or experience it. If I tell you my shoes are hurting, you may give me a pair that fit you very well, but don't beat me if they don't fit me—and don't blame me either!

"The missionary mentality" can serve as a heuristic device and a crude characterization; it derives from a Euro-American history and culture that is inseparable from the Enlightenment, rationalism, and the development of scientific technology. But it is also inseparable from an understanding of and commitment to the Christian faith and Jesus Christ. In the same vein, "the witchcraft mentality" derives from a rather different cultural history, a very different social context, and a completely different set of religious ideas. So if there is to be "translation" between these two, it must either be at the expense of one (by "ousting") or by virtue of reciprocity and mutual respect, which will produce modifications in both mentalities.

Ousting, or removing one set of attitudes, is the more clinically attractive option. But as with transplant surgery the host body will and must gather all immunological resources in order to repel the threatening intruder. Not only are people not blank slates; not only can cultural palimpsests not be written naively on people's souls; but persuasion might be less intrusive than presumption. Thereby one party may choose to surrender or repudiate a particular mentality in favor of another. But this is more subtle than it appears, since whoever assimilates something new does so not precisely in the same ways as the one from whom it derives, but in a characteristically personal way.

Ousting or enforced replacement of one thing by another, and assimilation, are two possibilities; there is a third. Gradual change through mutuality may prove possible and life-giving to both parties, though it can take a very long time. This seems to be the way of the evolution of species, and it has many precedents in social terms. But if each generation is cumulatively to provide the next with a "head start," that implies some improvements or simple and gradual modifications over the generations. Yet there are always possibilities, either of false starts or of a more radical kind of change.

For missionaries anxious for quick results, and for those who think that the normal means of church growth is through the multiplication of mature, full-blown Christian communities in a few short years, alternatives will be unattractive and even offensive. But for those who accept conversion and religious transformation as often cumulative and gradual, the implications of what is suggested here will be taken seriously. Time will be allowed both for the missionary and the community to assimilate "the Christian mentality" over a period of time, not perhaps without mistakes, and not without the tensions that arise from syncretic or dual religious forms.

Richard Gray illustrates the potential and the dangers inherent in socioreligious change. In the Mission of Soyo in the Kongo toward the end of the seventeenth century, "Confraternities" became very attractive to new Christians. These offered access to frequent eucharist and members were expected to take advantage of the privilege. But a fundamental attraction of eucharist was actually rooted deep in people's former lives: and confraternities

performed some of the functions of a witchcraft-eradication cult. . . . The mission was incorporating into its structure the deep desires for purification spontaneously expressed [by] members.[14]

And more recently and more widely, the Good News

was interpreted by many Africans as implying the dramatic arrival of a spiritual power who had previously claimed to cleanse the community from the evil of witchcraft. Later generations substantially

modified their approach to the task of witchcraft eradication. Alice
Lenshina [1950s] sought to cleanse her Lumpa church through baptism, prayer and praise, and a similar transformation has been
reported among the Xhosa in South Africa, where the reliance of
Christians on prayer rather than on traditional diviners has assisted
in a radical decline of specific accusations of witchcraft with their
traumatic social consequences.[15]

There is a temptation for architects, social or ecclesial, to rush things, a
temptation to which many missionaries have succumbed. But such a pre-
cipitate step would be violent, or superficial, or both. *Festina lente* ("Make
haste slowly") is called for, yet not laisser faire, which is incompatible with
the urgency of the mandate of evangelization. But, as the examples above
indicate, the missionary is by no means the only agent of religious change.
Respectful dialogue with local communities will minimize unhealthy fission
or a rash of independent churches. There must be challenge and even
confrontation between the Gospel and cultures, but not animosity and violence between peoples. Is there a solution?

The solution proposed here would return to the idea of transformational
rules and deep structures. If we have to wait, with great respect and distant
encouragement, until people with a "witchcraft mentality" develop what
we might clumsily label a "Christian mentality," then not only is it impossible to foresee how long it might take, but there is no reason to assume
that the one will evolve into the other—it might just as well evolve into
rabid individualism. But what if we were to examine what lies at the very
heart of the witchcraft mentality and what is at the heart of the Christian
mentality, with a view to the possibility of a heart transplant? Certainly it
would be risky; certainly there would be concern; certainly we would need
to understand that the "host" culture might try to "reject" the new heart—
even though deemed by others necessary for its continuing life. But these
reactions are normal and expected, and we would need to make provisions
for them. The real question is, are there common deep structures that could
be the lines of communication for the transformation of the witchcraft
mentality into something more in the spirit of Jesus?

The answer, we have to believe, is in the affirmative, and unequivocally
so. The alternative is tantamount to denying the translatability of Christianity, and to arguing for the imperviousness and isolation of cultures, which
is palpably absurd. Yet to answer in the affirmative is not to propose a
simple or an inevitable solution; that would be equivalent to saying that
people are not free to choose an alternative. The witchcraft mentality
breeds where alternative ways of seeing the world are virtually unknown.
Christianity implies an expansion of that world and offers choosable alternatives. But if a person is able to choose Christianity, that person must also
be capable of opting for something else, something incompatible with Christianity. Otherwise Christianity is as "obligatory" as witchcraft was!

We have identified, beneath the surface of the drama of witchcraft, several Gospel values: the desire for peace and harmony; the wish to overcome destructive jealousy and selfishness; the need for trust; the incompatibility of rabid individualism or factionalism with a healthy community. What is Jesus offering if not a new life built on these very virtues and attitudes? Witchcraft, shorn of hocus pocus, *must* logically provide a basis for transformation and translation; otherwise there is nowhere to root Christianity in "foreign" soil. But equally, Christianity must be shorn of its own hocus pocus if it is to be a credible, identifiable, and choosable option, and not simply an alien and "foreign" imposition. Perhaps if Christianity came more openhandedly into contact with those who are not Christian, there would be freedom to take as well as to give, to learn as well as to teach. If we embark on common journeys, we can hardly do less than this.

There is much hocus pocus in every particular cultural exemplification of Christianity; each one is in need of continuous conversion and transformation. The eucharist—not the Western, or Roman, or Latin, for these are only surface structures—can be and surely must be the meeting place where the fearful and the hostile and the needy may come and share, not an ordeal of poison but an ideal of peace. Yet for this to be the case, a gargantuan task must be undertaken. Sadly, this appears to be neither sufficiently wanted nor clearly enough acknowledged as necessary by the institutional church. The task is to move forward boldly yet humbly, fearlessly yet vulnerably, certainly yet tentatively, and with as much trust in the Spirit of God and other people as we have in ourselves and in our institutions.

QUESTIONS FOR THE ROAD

- Are you able to go to another culture or community and to look for a fit between your understanding of the Gospel and what actually happens in the lives of the people? Or do you go very much with your own understanding of what is authentic and with the intention of transmitting that to other people? Or do you try to attempt both? What are the benefits and tensions in the different approaches?
- From a consideration of this chapter do you agree that there are Gospel values in witchcraft? What lessons can be learned about missionary attitudes relative to local culture? What challenges does this pose for you?
- Is there any hocus pocus in your own religious behavior, personal or institutional? How would you deal with other people who perceived hocus pocus where you did not?
- What is your pastoral attitude to witchcraft? Has it changed after reading this chapter?

Chapter 8

Mistakes, Modifications, and Inculturation

Inculturation has obviously its risks. Although prudence . . . is the mother of virtues, a certain risk will always accompany legitimate progress. Take the necessary risk with prudence.[1]

If we take the incarnation seriously, vastly different forms are to be expected and applauded. . . . To accept this may be a traumatic experience for Christians from the West. Even if we have assured ourselves a thousand times that we have been working for a genuine contextualization of the Gospel in the younger churches, we cannot rid ourselves of the nagging fear that, perhaps, they may have missed the real essence of the Gospel.[2]

Third World theologians must be granted the "right" to risk "heresy"; it has been a constituent part of history. Mistakes will probably be corrected in the company, the koinonia, *of other theologians and bishops. If Christology could make use of "pagan" Greek concepts, how can the use of Hindu philosophy be excluded* a priori?[3]

HAPPY FAULTS AND THE DEVELOPMENT OF FAITH IN ACTION

Having emphasized some positive elements in the dramatic events of a witchcraft trial, we have not, for all that, lost our critical faculties. But we might perhaps have been given pause and led to appreciate the limitations of our own wisdom. Yet if we are to continue the journey to transformation, and to understand how missioners can both serve and challenge others and receive graced insights themselves, it is important that we avoid the temptation either to belittle our own contribution or to idealize other cultures.

If the making of mistakes is an essential element in the process of integration and maturation, it is also surely true that not every single person need make every single mistake that everyone else has made previously. So what kind of mistakes, and how many, are constitutive of healthy development? Though there cannot be a specific answer, we may look for certain attitudes to help our assessment. Observing a person or group struggling in unfamiliar situations we may notice excessive or immoderate action such as recklessness or scrupulousness; on the part of the parent or guardian over-protectiveness or irresponsibility may be equally damaging extremes. Striking a balance, both for the callow youth and the experienced sage, is a delicate and difficult matter.

If local churches are to grow to true selfhood yet remain part of the church universal, they cannot but travel the rocky road of experience; if those responsible for the unity of the church are equally respectful of its diversity, they cannot but be concerned about standards and orthodoxy; and if missioners are to provide moral support without smothering, to be edified by legitimate variety without being scandalized by syncretism, they cannot but commit themselves to mission in reverse and the people to the grace and judgment of God. It is not only "the 'necessary' sin of Adam" in which the church exults on Easter night, which may be referred to as *felix culpa*, the happy fault; with the benefit of hindsight there are many aspects of life one might wish to have changed, but they nevertheless contain valuable lessons and even grace. Meanwhile, inculturation must proceed, people must make mistakes, and missioners must learn to trust.

By looking through the history of the development of eucharistic devotion in the West we may find encouragement in the face of mistakes and aberrations. If those of us from the West can appreciate the fact that our history was by no means mistake-free, then perhaps we will be more inclined to trust others and to trust God. Likewise, if we realize that our own understanding of what eucharist is, is determined by the historic and theological threads that we actually trace (personally, denominationally, even nationally or ethnically), then we may more readily acknowledge that there are other threads and consequently other ways of understanding or believing in the eucharist. And if, further, we appreciate that God has many times in the past written straight on crooked lines, then we might more readily expect God to accomplish the same feat in the future, bringing good out of our little efforts.

To begin with a true account (it might be helpful if we first indulge our imagination and only later reflect on our responses, aesthetic and moral):

> The priest, his back to the faithful, raises his hands aloft. He is clearly seen holding a small baby, which he then deliberately kills and dismembers before the watching crowd.[4]

If the context for this ritual were the South Pacific of a hundred years ago, or Central America four centuries past, what might be our reaction and judgment? If it were found today in Haiti or Harare, what scandal would it provoke? Actually, it describes one of the most common "miracles"[5] of the Middle Ages and is intrinsically related to the development of eucharistic theology and practice. So what is our reaction and considered judgment? Our own (Western) culture and institutional church may have come a long way since then—though even that may be open to some discussion—but the journey has led us, not just along highways, but on myriad byways such as this. If we missioners are to consider some of the implications of inculturation, it is important that we be both aware of and candid about the record of the development of eucharistic practice in the West.

It is recorded that St. Hugh of Lincoln was celebrating the liturgy of the eucharist (1196) when

> God in His mercy deigned to open the eyes of a certain clerk and showed him Christ in the likeness of a small child in the chaste hands of the venerable and holy Bishop. Although very tiny, the child was very lovely and of supernatural brilliance and whiteness beyond the imagination. The clerk ... felt great devotion and compassion, and wept continuously from the time of the elevation until he saw it elevated once more to be broken into three portions and partaken of.[6]

So common were these occurrences in medieval Europe that some priests earned reputations because of the frequency or realism of the events that marked their Masses. But Peter of Tewksbury was once accused of cannibalism by a boy who had been at his Mass; the boy swore he had seen Father Peter devour a little child on the chapel altar and feared a similar fate for himself.[7]

Sometimes Jews—victims of anti-Semitic outbursts that branded them as blasphemers and sacrilegious parodyists of the eucharist—were accused of cannibalism or crucifixion. Yet Jews could also be invoked as witnesses to the miracles:

> [In 1400] a Christian travelling with a Jew urges him to wait while he attends Mass. The Jew grows impatient, enters Church just in time for the Elevation, and sees, instead of the host, a fair child which the priest and congregation proceed to devour. He leaves the church in horror, but the Christian soon joins him and claims that the Jew has been subjected to the sight because his forebears killed Christ. The Jew, rather than risk witnessing such an abomination again, immediately resolves to convert.[8]

Centuries before, and worlds away—though the story is as typical of the West as of the East, and of the second millennium as of the first—an old Egyptian monk was having doubts of faith in the eucharistic presence of Jesus. Two fellow monks once accompanied him to church, and when the bread was placed on the altar, all three saw a little boy. An angel of God then stabbed the child with a knife, catching his blood in the chalice. When the bread was broken into pieces the angel cut up the boy's limbs. The doubting monk approached the sacrament and was given bleeding flesh . . . and believed! The flesh resumed the appearance of bread; the three monks took communion; and they went home happily.[9]

These crudely realistic and detailed examples will serve, though they could easily be multiplied, for they recur across time and space and culture, in the oral tradition, in written affidavit, and in mainstream art. Recent interpretative studies are finding the general topic fascinating and enlightening, and disclosing an impressive correlation, specifically between women's spirituality and eucharistic miracles such as these.[10] But how could Christian orthodoxy possibly recover from such palpable aberrations and crudities? Not surprisingly there has been some reluctance, until recently, to publicize such embarrassing incidents in the history of Western Christianity. How fortunate, we might think, that such superstitions have now been rooted out . . .

Far from running from such choice items we will try to face and scrutinize them, for their soil holds our own roots. We should be able candidly to enquire what lessons medieval eucharistic miracles may still hold for us today; what they say about belief, behavior, and authority; and what insights they provide for future explorations in inculturation. Only an institution very obsessive about its infallibility, neurotic about its need to appear in control, afraid to see mistakes as part of growth and maturation, and ignorant of popular piety would worry unduly about such incidents or be ashamed to examine and discuss the record. Only arrogant or very foolish people fail to learn from experience.

By contrast, a church committed to localization and inculturation and aware of the rich diversity of cultures and systems of meaning will find in the past and across the globe a rich repository for building the future and renewing the face of the earth.

CONTEXT AS A KEY TO UNDERSTANDING

It would be as naive and wrong as it is tempting and easy to jump to conclusions and to generalize from specific cases in a bid to learn from the past and apply our knowledge to the future. But only if we understand something of the context of a story or event does it become possible to draw legitimate conclusions and make careful applications. In order to gather some wisdom to apply in new situations of inculturation, therefore, we need to understand, to some degree at least, both the new situation and the relevance and applicability of the knowledge we bring with us for our journey. We must also appreciate their limitations.

We need, then, not only information but a particular context. The wider context for the issues under review here is medieval Europe, mainly from the eleventh to the fifteenth century, and its laity, clergy, and theology; the narrower context is the development of eucharistic belief and practice.

Belief was becoming increasingly formalized, particularly in the face of heresy, while practice was a reflection of, or sometimes a reaction against, the forms in which belief was codified. Far from being shocked and scandalized by bleeding hosts and dismembered babies, people were certainly shocked but also edified, since the miracles vindicated the developing orthodoxy,[11] whether related to the "Real Presence" of Jesus, the Jews as Christ-killers, or the fears that the (mystical) body of Christ was in danger of being torn apart by heretics and infidels.

Eucharistic miracles also posed an undoubted challenge to the intransigence of hierarchy and male dominance (though not necessarily one that was adequately met), since the vast preponderance of them were witnessed, not by the clergy or even by men, but by women who demonstrated a passionate and embodied devotion, which hungered both for Jesus and for justice, for sacrament and for service. The fact that the institutional church did not attempt to belittle or deny these experiences in principle is clear testimony to the fact that even though vouchsafed largely to women, such miracles were not considered to be as insignificant as were the visionaries and witnesses.

But it is as important to acknowledge the undoubted excesses, as it is true to say that the miracles were a powerful means of catechesis and focus for devotion; both scandal and catechesis helped define the boundaries between belief and superstition, orthodoxy and heresy, as these were negotiated by church and people in the Middle Ages. There was a widespread tendency among theologians and commentators over a thousand years of eucharistic miracles to overlook or misunderstand the sociological significance of "popular" devotion; to claim authority to describe the miracles in the language of formal theological discourse; and to censor what were perceived to be excesses. Nevertheless, as surviving records show, not only were non-theologians and indeed critics of clerical laxity often favored with such manifestations, but the shape of medieval piety and eucharistic devotion itself cannot be adequately understood unless great attention is paid to these miracles.

In an age in which belief in the real presence of Jesus in the eucharist came prominently to the fore (though it had never been completely lost); when the skepticism of Berengarius (who would have seen the bread and wine as "only" symbols) was condemned by the papacy and repudiated by the people; and when linguistic, demographic, and ecclesiastical changes left the faithful increasingly deprived of participation in the liturgy and access to communion, and limited to passive roles and "ocular communion"[12]; in such an age eucharistic manifestations powerfully comforted the isolated, supported those weak in faith, and were real miracles of God's abiding presence in the world.

In the earliest autobiography of an English person, Margery Kempe, writing around 1445, records:

One day as this creature [herself] was hearing Mass, a young man and a good priest was holding up the sacrament in his hands over his head, and the sacrament shook and fluttered to and fro just as a dove flutters her wings. And when he held up the chalice with the precious sacrament, the chalice moved to and fro as if it would have fallen out of his hands.[13]

This was not all. Eucharistic miracles of this sort were not only an end but also a means to an end. A certain priest asserted—as Jesus had, to "doubting" Thomas—that Christian merit lies in believing, not only in seeing; such a statement must have posed a serious challenge to contemporary piety after the year 1200 when some holy persons were devoted to rushing from place to place and "seeing" the elevation (this is the meaning of "ocular communion") as many as fifty or more separate times in a single day.[14]

Consideration of the medieval miracles in their context should help us understand what local theology was being done and how it was being assessed and assimilated into mainstream Christianity. It should also notify us of the importance of local people and local communities for the development of doctrine and devotion, no less in our own times than in days gone by. It is on the basis of this kind of contextualized understanding that we might be able to approach and understand the development of devotion and doctrine in other cultures. Without such knowledge we are ill-prepared to be involved in the inculturation of the Gospel.

INTERPRETATION AND APPLICATION

People the world over assume that their point of view is correct, valid, and real; they may defend it as representing objective truth or the way things really are. But there are many people and peoples, each sticking fast to their own truth and reality. So, not only are there many different truths and realities, but people, particularly those living in a binary universe or operating with a strong binary mentality, may brand others as wrong or false, especially when they feel threatened: the more my truth is challenged, the more I must either condemn or respect yours, but I cannot disregard it.

If we open up the notion of eucharist to include those examples of service, ministry, and sharing that mark the life of Jesus, then as we saw, it becomes important to include events such as the feeding of the four and the five thousand, the washing of the apostles' feet, the Emmaus meal, the sharing of broiled fish after the resurrection, and so on. Each of these contributes something to an understanding of eucharist; each has important lessons for Christians and for Christian behavior today. And if we recall the many different rites and eucharistic liturgical forms throughout history and across cultures, we will be reminded that the eucharistic liturgy of the

Roman Rite (as currently expressed in the *editio typica* of the Mass), while the starting point for the inculturation of the eucharist, does not exhaust its meaning as thanksgiving and should not cause us to overlook the significance of other "eucharistic" moments in the life of Jesus.

No single perspective or liturgical expression can fit every time and place and setting; to imagine that it can is to disregard the place of culture and language and tradition in human life. This indeed is one of the reasons for ritual masses, funeral masses, and weekday masses, as distinct from Sunday masses. All of them are different liturgical forms of the Mass in the Roman tradition.[15]

Our greatest service to local churches, therefore, might be precisely *not* to impose our historically and culturally conditioned eucharist on contexts with radically different histories and social forms. The challenge is to transmit the tradition as a living thing rather than as a fossil. In an age of ecumenism and a context of mission it will be as important mutually to affirm the values embodied in Lutheran and Anglican and Roman and other liturgical eucharistic traditions, as it will be to pay real respect to individual cultural and social patterns of praying and playing.

And before everything is accomplished, far more deference and esteem will have to be given to the people of God as a whole: the communities, the believers. Far more experiments, leading to many more mistakes, leading to much more appropriate liturgies, will have to be tested in the fires. If the church is to be both local and universal, across time and space, embracing peoples of many cultural heritages, then who can begin to imagine the authentic and wonderful diversity within the unity for which Jesus prayed? Unless missioners, especially, are committed to learning about the traditions of other Christians and people of cultures different from their own, then their knowledge of their own faith tradition will prove an inadequate tool in the journey to inculturation and the pilgrimage of the people of God.

The integrity of Christian tradition and what we might call the core values of the eucharist, then, must not be undermined. But for a real flourishing of the eucharist across communities and cultures, local theologies must be encouraged to grow free of anything which is not absolutely central and critical to the faith of Christians. If those who do not learn from history are condemned to repeat it, it does not thereby follow that people need to be force-fed the history of all other people and all other times. Why should distant Christian communities relive only the sufferings and perpetuate the history only of a divided and unfaithful church? When will evangelization learn to emphasize the *good* news and unity in Christ and cease to be obsessed by the *bad* news and division in Christendom? This is not to call for a cover-up, or for forgetfulness, but for a new commitment to the Gospel and to the Christian tradition. What a task! What a complex diagnosis!

The intention in examining selected aspects of the history of the eucharist and the development of doctrine is to outline a process and to indicate just how compatible are variety and orthodoxy. By doing this, we should more readily appreciate the utter necessity of diversity for a mature and authentic inculturation of the eucharist across time and territory.

ONE CHURCH, MANY TRADITIONS?

Due to people's need for clarity and security, definitions can sometimes become rather restrictive. How many people habitually think of church in a rather narrow sense and are then irked by other people's equally narrow but somewhat different understandings? Those born and raised within religious enclaves, where one's own denomination was perceived to be coextensive with the church, and other denominations were considered as outside it, know the power of such narrow definitions. Among the many narrow working definitions of "church" is "the Western, Latin Rite, Roman Catholic, English church." In the case of the writer, this "definition" of church is a selective description of *my* church, the church in which I was raised, and thus the church that, for me, retains some strong emotional ties. But apart from its intrinsic limitations, it is a "definition" that would not be accepted by millions and millions of Christians, and it certainly does not adequately define church sociologically or theologically.

To approach inculturation positively we need to recall the reality of the non-Western, non-Latin, non-Roman, non-Catholic, non-English church, in all of its many manifestations.[16]

As early as the fourth century the church in the East was clearly showing its distinctive development, perhaps nowhere more than in the eucharist. In fact, the earliest known eucharistic miracles, associated with themes of sacrifice and blood, come from the East and not the West, and from the fifth century and not the twelfth. The Eastern church is characterized, from St. John Chrysostom (late fourth century) onward, by an attitude of fear and trepidation—one might almost say "holy dread"[17]—which leads, through a physical distancing of the faithful from the eucharist, to a *removal* of the kinds of conditions that gave rise to the ocular miracles in the Western church. Thus in this respect, Eastern and Western church gradually divided. The Iconostasis in Eastern churches ensured that the priest could not be seen, therefore no more "sightings" took place.

Eastern conservatism was very different from the more radical and innovative theologizing of the West. Western Christendom certainly did not lack respect for the eucharist, but its reverence was "tinged with a degree of intimacy."[18] So if, in the West, the scales were weighted against the faithful fully participating by physical reception of the eucharist, a counterweight held up ocular reception as an appropriate eucharistic devotion, giving rise to the Great Elevation of the host around the year 1200, so that everyone was able to see the consecrated bread and make a "spiritual" communion. The danger, it was feared, was that those at the back of church might not know the exact moment of consecration and might thus inadvertently "worship" the wafer! Squints or hagioscopes—small openings in the church wall, giving an unimpeded view of the altar and thus the consecration—became common.

As altars in the East were becoming inaccessible and veiled, approachable only by the priest, so the West was reacting against rood screens and veils, developing devotions that made the eucharist both visible and available in some real sense to all.[19] So it is not surprising that the miracles associated with the eucharist occurred when they did in the West; that is, when doctrine was being formulated and defended, when theologians were ambivalent and inconsistent about frequent communion, when the pious faithful were less and less significant in the structures of the church, but when the involvement of the laity in the liturgy was a major issue, being pressed for and opposed. The situation was, in fact, not so very different, structurally, from that in many parts of the world today.

Yet that was an age of faith, and it was not the 1990s. The Albigensians were denying the doctrine of real presence "in a particularly vicious manner," while the Manichaeans' "fiercest invective was launched against the eucharist."[20] The development of doctrine and practice are not unrelated to events in the wider world, and there may be a "chicken and egg" situation here. Arguably, as the laity became more isolated both from the Latin of the liturgy (vernaculars were developing, and less and less could the laity understand the liturgical language) and from the sacrament of Orders (due to the universal application of the rule of celibacy and the flourishing of monastic life with its heavy emphasis on the role of lay-brothers), the Great Elevation became a rallying point for the marginalized, especially women.

But however easy it may be to relate cause and effect, or to reconstruct history and interpret the past, one point should be emphasized rather than overlooked: from the very beginning the church was not absolutely uniform even in theory, much less in practice. Efforts at inculturation today will be unnecessarily hampered if we forget this. The church has struggled to acknowledge that Gentile sensibilities are as important as Jewish and that Eastern attitudes are as valid as Western. Currently it is challenged to remember that women are the equal of men and that no contemporary culture is less authentic a context for the inculturation of the Gospel than any other. We in our turn may note that the medieval experience is as valid (as "true" or "real") as the modern, and that churches in Africa or Asia, the South or the East, need not and should not be carbon copies of Western eucharistic practice, so long as they remain sharers in the living and vivifying tradition of the church, loyal to Jesus' commands, and visible signs of unity with the universal church.

TOWARD CONTEXTUAL THEOLOGIES

There arose at a particular time (the early twelfth century) and in a particular place (Eastern France and the Western Rhineland), a simple modification in the celebration of the eucharist that brought with it an avalanche of developments both mainstream and heretical. These have colored our own attitudes to the eucharist down to the present day. In tracing the modification and the path of the avalanche, we need to note not only how contextual or contingent these are, but equally, how necessary and legitimate. Then we will be able to see how local variation and error are compatible with, and indeed constitutive of, universality, truth, or orthodoxy, as these continuously develop in the church.

The modification we have identified concerns the so-called Great Elevation, the one among several, which took place at the moment of consecration. This gesture served to freeze the action of the eucharist, make static what had been dynamic, and shift the attitude of the faithful from communal observation of and identification with the liturgy, to personal contemplative devotion in a more passive context for eucharist:

> In certain ways, the priest, not the eucharist, was now the powerful corporate symbol. . . . He *was* the Church; he received for all. . . . He stood for all humanity. . . . Thus, late medieval Eucharistic piety was individualistic.[21]

Not only did the shift of focus to the consecration and the "showing" of the consecrated bread at the elevation cause a modification in personal piety, but it ushered in, over a period of more than two centuries of the high Middle Ages, many additions to the eucharist never previously needed: genuflections, bells, lamps, candles, pyxes, as well as devotions, processions, exposition, and benediction. The elevation, in fact, "initiated the last great cycle of liturgical developments in the Latin Church"[22] until *Mediator Dei* of 1947 and *Sacrosanctum Concilium* of Vatican II in 1963. Important in our consideration of inculturation and contextualization is that this veritable avalanche was generated by a small, local adaptation of the liturgy; it was not inevitable; it occurred when the church was already more than a millennium old; and it need not have spilled across the whole of Europe and thence across the known world. To put it another way: local adaptations are possible in principle; they do not necessarily indicate a betrayal of the Christian tradition; they do not need to be universalized. For ourselves both as loyal Christians and as committed to localization of the church, these should be encouraging thoughts.

So as we look again at these embellishments, we can see them for what they really are: historically, culturally, theologically, and devotionally conditioned and relative, and not intrinsically part of all liturgies for today's global church. If they have become fossilized and fixed in certain places, are we not therefore challenged to look for the living forms elsewhere and work with them toward the development of more truly inculturated liturgies? For if the elevation[23] grew out of a particular set of local circumstances, and if it gave rise to a set of contingent Western practices very different from those in the East, why should efforts to contextualize euchar-ist in other cultures be tied to medieval European practice? Even the ele-vation itself, momentous though it would prove, was not fixed and standardized in 1200; for nearly three hundred years thereafter there existed wide variation and rubrical freedom.[24]

The historical record even prior to this surge also shows not only tol-erance, but actually the cultivation of diversity. Peter Abelard (1079-1142) chastised St. Bernard (1090-1153) for his over-concern with custom, quot-ing the famous letter from Pope Gregory I to Augustine, the evangelizer of England (written in A.D. 599 or 600). Gregory, who had demurred when asked to override his bishops on the grounds that it was pointless to have them in the first place unless they had full authority, had said simply to St. Augustine and the evangelizers of England:

> I approve of thy selecting carefully anything thou hast found that may be more pleasing to Almighty God, whether in the Roman Church or that of Gaul or in any Church whatever, and introducing in the Church of the Angli [English], which is as yet new in the faith, by a special institution, what thou hast been able to collect from many Churches. For we ought not to love things for places, but places for things. Wherefore, *choose from each several Church such things as are pious, religious and right, and, collecting them as it were into a bundle, plant them* in the minds of the Angli for their use.[25]

So, despite the conservatism of people like Bernard, there was in the twelfth century church great variety, attested to both in the Sacramentaries themselves and in the fact that many local churches, without such common standards as Sacramentaries, consequently fostered local custom. Perhaps the point for serious consideration is that Rome did try to control orthodoxy at a universal level, but was also practical enough to realize that with poor communications and long distances, control was not always possible and that the emphasis should be placed squarely on unity rather than on divi-sion. Thus the *Canon of the Mass* remained the focal point of orthodoxy, not the rubrics or local variations. And though East and West went their separate ways, each remained part of the one church by virtue of their centering on the words of consecration and the almost completely scriptural context within which they remained.

It is very likely that the emphasis on the elevation in the Latin Church was as much a response to the piety of the faithful as it was simply a creation of theologians or hierarchy; it can be seen as an example of local churches producing acceptable and viable local forms. If this were a rule of thumb for today's emergent local churches, there would be a new psychological approach to many ecclesial issues, one which would, without totally remov-ing deviance or error, contribute mightily to the strengthening of local churches, which are an intimate part of local life in a wider society. Perhaps then the gap between the Gospel and culture could be more directly addressed.

But dare we think of a eucharist without an elevation? It is hardly outrageous. Think of many of our small group eucharistic liturgies today where face-to-face celebration and intimate community make an elevation intrusively ostentatious. In any case, eucharist "in the round" or with the presider facing the people has made the elevation, and thus attendant bells, unnecessary. Yet in our larger churches many of the medieval accretions, not only bells but smells, decorations, and devotions, cling tenaciously. For some of these, at least, their time has surely passed, notwithstanding worthy claims about symbolic and ritualistic significance. Yet in the absence of an elevation, many of those accretions could be allowed to atrophy. Then perhaps we would be able to move closer to a deeper contextualization of local liturgical forms and a eucharistic action that could truly be an embodiment and an incarnation of the local community of faith. But these things do take time; parasites do cling tenaciously to the vine; and all things old-fashioned or nostalgic are by no means thereby to be condemned or removed.

POPULAR AND UNPOPULAR PIETY

The term "popular religiosity" is often used with a decidedly pejorative flavor by those who find it intensely *unpopular*, with themselves and with "the church" for which and for whom they presume to speak. It is perhaps time the word "popular" was reinstated and used without prejudice to mean simply "of the people," for "popular piety" in the sense of "what the people of God are actually doing to express their faith" is the most widespread and valid indicator of faith in action.

Here is an attempt to diagram (Roman Catholic) Christianity; many refinements can be made to this model, but it has the virtue of simplicity. We start by drawing an imaginary line running from left to right. At the extreme left (X) is "superstition," and at the extreme right (Z) is "heresy." Around the middle (Y) is the broad band of "orthodoxy." But there are various forms of orthodoxy. We may characterize these at their most simple as "clerical orthodoxy" (y1) and "lay orthodoxy" (y2). This line and its constituents can be represented thus[26]:

$$
\begin{array}{c}
\text{y1 - clergy} \\
\text{X-(superstition)————Y-(orthodoxy)-Y————(heresy)-Z} \\
\text{y2 - laity}
\end{array}
$$

This may look somewhat complicated but it really is not. We should, however, notice the following:
- there is a *difference* between y1 and y2;
- both "orthodoxy" and "power" reside principally in y1;

- the faithful are *theoretically* powerless;
- the faithful are far more numerous than the clergy;
- people characterized as X or Z *still* live in the same world as everyone else.

The importance of the people's religion (the People of God, rather than simply the clergy) will be obvious to anyone working in unfamiliar cultures or at the margins of their own. If the church wishes to proclaim and to call to transformation, it is imperative that its emissaries understand the behavior and motivation of those without formal theological education or social mobility. So here are five observations on "popular religion," which seems preferable to the more loaded word, "religiosity."

1. If we want to know what people find relevant we should check what they actually do and what they avoid, what they are comfortable with and what makes them concerned or afraid. We need to know what motivates and inspires people, and how they react to the "official" or "clerical" form of religion. It is insufficient for us to bemoan the gap between proclaimed orthodoxy [y1] and public behavior [y2, X, or Z]; we should know *why* this gap exists and whether it is growing.

2. If the church supports inculturation, the consequences of this will need to be acknowledged and welcomed. They include *variety* or *variation* in people's responses to the Gospel and in the way they reorganize their lives as communities and individuals. People respond differently because they think and perceive differently; this in turn is due to differences in language, culture, and socialization processes[27]; and transformation or conversion operates precisely within those parameters. But we cannot predict the variety of human response in detail. People no longer live in the isolated groups of earlier centuries. But for all the urbanization of today, to enforce the homogenization of peoples or cultures would be a sin. David Bosch, in the passage quoted as an epigraph to this chapter, says that

> different forms of indigenization and contextualization are to be expected and applauded. . . . It is presumptuous for persons of one culture and tradition to dictate the "normal" signs of conversion for another culture and context. [This fact] makes our own views and convictions vulnerable. It de-absolutizes them.[28]

3. If variety is in principle accepted, we will recognize that in the development of doctrine (as in the development of science or of personality) there will, must, and should be mistakes, excesses, and aberrations. Such false starts not only cannot be avoided but—while not exactly being encouraged—may be subtly tolerated as part of a halting process toward a full-blown inculturation. Certainly, neither people nor doctrines are served by simply labeling them as "crude and objectionable," by intolerance, or by pouring scorn on "popular credulity."[29] It seems more appropriate to

endorse the sentiments of Walbert Bühlmann, who is also quoted at the head of this chapter:

> Outright denial of a dogma of the faith is one thing, but exploration, the discovery of hidden dimensions, is something else. . . . No one who understands the genius of Hinduism would think to question the orthodoxy of a Christology incorporating Hindu elements.[30]

4. Without positive encouragement from the centers of power, local churches will be expected to exist as clones of a monocultural universal church, with little or no identity of their own. But they will discover they cannot survive in such an alien environment and without adequate support systems. If that should happen, not only diversity but fundamental disarray will result. Current experience in Africa and Latin America provides a cautionary tale.

5. Many Reformed traditions are no strangers to the reality of diversification in local church practice. Much may be learned from their experience, positive and negative. Yet we also need the reminder that federations, or boards, or multiple membership in a global "communion" is not without its own problems relative to orthodoxy or to tradition.

POPULAR RELIGION, EUCHARIST, AND CATECHESIS

Western medieval miracles were not the only examples of popular local development; there were a great many others. During the eighth century, relics, said to be of the true crib, were used as an altar on which the pope consecrated the bread at the Christmas Mass.[31] In the early thirteenth century Francis of Assisi was central to a practice of restaging the nativity along with the eucharist: stable became church, manger was altar, and the beasts were compared to communicants, while Francis himself "tasted" the child. Medieval miracle plays, too,[32] are a magnificent source for any study of popular religion; they retell and reenact the whole history of salvation. Among their themes is the identity between the baby born once in Bethlehem and the Christ "reborn," as it were, in the daily eucharist.

Such devotions were legion; they vitalized and helped transmit the faith. They also tended to reflect socioreligious developments. For example, as the Middle Ages waned and communion for the laity became rarer and rarer, many devotional exercises and reenactments like miracle plays with their strong and explicit eucharistic motif, or the richly decorated and painted church facades and interiors which provided stage and scenery, helped catechize the faithful and unite them in respect for the eucharist, which remained, in a real if increasingly symbolic sense, the center and summit of their lives. The importance of such catechetical resources cannot be overlooked by those committed to inculturation. There is no justification for depriving Christian communities of the eucharist, but to curtail popular devotions, especially among eucharistically "deprived" people, is tantamount to fossilizing their religious expression and experience. To do so would betray both a lack of sensitivity and an ignorance of human psychology.

Missionary catechesis may have something significant to learn from the European Middle Ages and from this brief excursus into popular religion. Very widely in non-Western cultures, Western missionaries have made impossible demands on the people they evangelized; and Western theological formulations and expressions have remained culturally conditioned, inappropriate, and often counterproductive. The eucharist, intended to unite, to focus, and to uplift the community, was often perceived as irrelevant to daily life and the daily struggle for survival and harmony, *because* it divided, stratified, excluded, and humiliated members of communities. Primal or traditional religious systems may have been much more holistic in their view of the world, monistic rather than dualistic (as were Western perceptions and theology), and inclusive rather than exclusive in their thinking. But because different from the worldview of missioners they were deemed unsuitable and condemned, or at best ignored. And then Christian missioners tried to propagate a way of life without a context and a form of worship with little perceived relevance to people's lives.

Naturally the development of medieval eucharistic theology was related to the prevalent knowledge-system or epistemology. To that extent it was contextual or local. Since realism was a major issue, the church at every level "filtered in" devotions and arguments supporting the developing articulation of theology, and "filtered out" what was deemed incompatible (and there were *dozens* of "heresies," "superstitions," and "unorthodox practices"). Consequently, the few teachings that opposed the doctrine of the Real Presence were crushed. But popular piety and devotion were allowed to continue inasmuch as they *endorsed* the doctrine, even though there were what we would now consider rather gross examples of realism in the eucharist, as typified by the Flemish mystic Hadewijch (c. 1230), who said that "he eats us; we think we eat him, and we do eat him, of this we can be certain."[33]

It seems fairly clear that in the Middle Ages, what later might be called mistaken zeal or worse was allowed if it was basically compatible with orthodoxy. And if orthodoxy was somewhat less rigidly defined in an age without mass literacy and its support systems, still the attitude has a strong appeal for the situations in local churches today.

But the Middle Ages were not all sweetness and experimentation. In trying to bring God to earth and to touch God,[34] the Western church became alienated from the first millennium of its own history, just as that same medieval church would become alien to what we might call the Religions of Transcendence such as those widely encountered throughout the East and elsewhere in the world. Though many useful questions were indeed addressed during the medieval era in the West, they may be almost totally beside the point for twentieth-century churches in the cosmopolis. The medieval church is thus no unequivocal example of inculturation, though it manifested some of the characteristics that would be very useful today.

We know very well that in many contemporary non-Western (though "Latin") communities, the eucharist is inappropriate because its "celebration" perpetuates the fragmentation of the community and imposes expatriates on situations that cry out for local ministry. It is not convincing to assert that the eucharist is the center of Christian life if a majority of adults are unable to participate, if it is infrequently available, and if it is held hostage to "foreign" clergy or local clergy with "foreign" ways.

The eucharist seems to be at a crisis point worldwide, and the reasons are not far to seek. But if we look closely at particular patterns of local or popular belief and practice, we can see what is really happening and at least make a prognosis, or offer recommendations that might point toward more fruitful dialogue between the church and cultures.

Is the eucharist, then, in danger of turning into a fossil of strictly antiquarian interest? In the West church attendance and numbers of clergy continue the steep decline. In Africa the epidemic proportion of AIDS is beginning to be felt like the Black Death right across the board—in laity, clergy, religious, and potential recruits. Meanwhile, modified devotions, "alternative eucharists," "agapes," and "priestless Masses" multiply. Beyond the West, in local churches the eucharist is often unavailable or little used. Unless the artificial "lack" of ministers is reversed, and unless the perceived irrelevance of many eucharistic liturgies is addressed, then all the liturgical reforms and all the fancy theologizing and all the wonderful anthropological insights will be impotent. The faithful, the People of God, the believers, the community—the church—is getting hoarse, while the eucharist, far from being bread for the journey, is more like "Care Packages" of "Overseas Aid," which fail to prevent malnutrition, though they appear to meet people's needs and people are expected to be grateful for them.

We are, palpably, at a decisive moment in the history of Christianity—what Rahner referred to as the beginning of a truly world church—as it seeks to grow and flourish in non-Western garb and non-Western localities. The two thousand years of that history are full of examples of diversification, adaptation, and experimentation. They are also heavy with examples of freedom or repression of laity, "popular" or "elitist" ministry, centralized or localized government, and dogmatic or charismatic leadership. The history of the church is not only the history of anathema, inquisition, and heresy but of reform, prophecy, and martyrdom. The Vatican II decree on Eastern Churches praises and affirms "individual Churches," "variety," and "equality," yet fails to convince of its commitment to real dialogue. The windows opened by John XXIII seem to have been slammed shut in recent years by concerned but fearful pastors who approve of "dialogue" only when "we" make it clear to "them" from the outset that "we" are right and will not change! This is not dialogue, and not even subtle. The church we know remains very Western and—for Roman Catholics—very Latin, very authoritarian, very besieged, and very hierarchical in language, ecclesiology, and liturgical practice. The way forward is unclear, the journey hazardous.

Bühlmann[35] offers the imaginative yet reasonable suggestion of five "Pentarchates" rather like Patriarchates, one for each continent, which might facilitate the discovery of a new authenticity for the church. But an "elevation-bound" theology (that is, a theology focused on a distant and inaccessible eucharist) exported by the West still remains dominant in mission practice. It is packaged with a static, almost magical focus on eucharist as transubstantiation, as sacrifice, as esoteric drama, and as dependent on a priestly caste. It may be inhibiting a life-giving celebration and remembering: an *anamnesis*.

But Pentarchates will be no advance if they are simply four copies of a single, unchangeable blueprint. An "elevation-bound" eucharistic theology is reactionary; a more relational understanding of the community as the body of Christ has been at the center of liturgical theology for years now and would need to be widely encouraged. Somehow the limitations of current thinking must be transcended. Somehow the people of faith must be encouraged—not silently to bow but loudly to proclaim, not distantly to observe but closely to participate, not passively to "receive" but actively to appropriate and to share. Somehow the kernel or the core—the deep structures—of the eucharist and the faith must be rediscovered and transformed into living and life-giving liturgies and lifestyles in a thousand cultures and ten thousand communities. Then we will be able to break bread that nourishes and, haltingly and tentatively, but with great faith and greater hope, undertake journeys together.

QUESTIONS FOR THE ROAD

- The South African theologian David Bosch had strong words to say about inculturation. Discuss Bosch's statement quoted in the second epigraph to this chapter.
- What is your reaction to the medieval miracles? Do you consider that they have a positive side, something to contribute to the development of belief in action? How would you apply your conclusions about them to the issue of the development of indigenous liturgies and theology?
- Would you like to see inculturation without mistakes? How might this be undertaken? What are the benefits and dangers?
- Do you think that "popular religion" or "popular religiosity" is inferior? Is it unorthodox? Does it have any place? How might it relate to inculturated forms of Christianity?

Chapter 9

Mission on the Margins

Since they are members of the church by virtue of their baptism, all Christians share responsibility for missionary activity.

Redemptoris Missio, 77

Each member of the faithful and all Christian communities are called to practice dialogue.

Redemptoris Missio, 57

The poor are not our problem; we are theirs.

Anonymous

Never be condescending, but make real friends with the poor.

Romans 12:16

The coming of the Realm of God does not admit of observation and there will be no one to say, "Look here! Look there!" For you must know, the Realm of God is among you.

Luke 17:20-21

PASTORAL CARE AND MISSION

Some people (those afflicted with binary mentality-ism) jump at the opportunity to distinguish, separate, and polarize "pastoral" work and "mission" activity. But whoever reflects on the Gospel challenge must recall that all mission should be pastoral and all pastoral activity should have a centrifugal missionary dimension. Yet some have thought that this is to merge and absorb what should be separated and distinguished. However, it is quite feasible to separate analytically what should be combined existentially; and we can certainly do that in this instance. The fact that some pastoral work fails to live up to the challenge of mission is regrettable but not inevitable. But the idea that activity can be truly missionary without it also being truly pastoral is surely fallacious.

The recent encyclical puts this very starkly:

The boundaries between pastoral care of the faithful, new evangelization, and specific missionary activity are not clearly definable, and
it is unthinkable to create barriers between them or to put them into
watertight compartments (*Redemptoris Missio*, 34).

But what if the problems are due to our tendency to put *ourselves* and
our undertakings into "watertight compartments"! The suggestion in these
pages has been consistent: to the extent to which someone, having identified
some personal boundaries or limitations, moves through them in faith and
in the name of Jesus Christ and the Gospel with a view to witnessing and
proclaiming the Lordship of Christ and the faith of the church, to that
extent a person is moving toward engagement in mission.

Mission is not to be defined geographically as "over there," though there
remains in some theological discourse a tendency to distort it in this way.[1]
But if this were an adequate understanding of what mission is it would
effectively preclude most Christians from what is stated as their baptismal
right and duty: to be involved in mission. Similarly, we know, sadly, that it
is possible to go many leagues from one's home yet not engage in authentic
mission, due to a regrettable tendency to recreate a "home away from
home," which effectively ensures our comfort and privacy, allows us to
retain control, and insulates us both from the importuning of people and
from the demands intrinsic to evangelization.

But mission is not about comfort or privacy, nor is it about constructing
our lives "rationally." It is about dialogue and martyrdom, proclamation
and risk, discipleship and ministry. It is about uncertainty and trust. And
this brings us back to personal boundaries. First we must identify elements
of our selfishness, ethnocentrism, prejudice, or fear (no easy matter, nor
does it come quickly; rather, given who we are, it is a lifetime's pursuit).
Then, rather than hiding behind these barriers or bulwarks and staying
within a familiar world, we must both seek to move through them and allow
ourselves to be pulled, perhaps with some resistance, by those on the other
side.

Someone afraid of persons of another race or sex or religion, who stead-
fastly refuses to be called to an encounter with them, is not yet in mission.
A person who avoids people of another social class or whose ministry is
only among like-minded people, and who does not venture beyond nor
invite the stranger and the outsider, has not yet discovered the missionary
dimension of pastoral work. And one who speaks honeyed and spiritual
words to other believers but resists facing the hostility or criticism or simple
challenge of those of another faith (or of none) has not yet discovered the
centrifugal thrust of mission.

In every case Jesus is our exemplar. He journeyed along the borders
between countries and people, letting himself be sidetracked and put upon
(Lk 17:11ff). He dared to ask the most unlikely people what they would
like him to do and to meet their requests (Mk 10:46ff). He engaged and

encountered a variety of sinners and outcasts, and he entrusted himself to people whom he did not intentionally seek (Mk 7:24ff; Jn 12:1ff). The examples are so numerous as to make individual references merely random exemplifications of a whole attitude and a whole way of being; that is, Jesus' entire life was directed toward engagement with people and with negotiating and transcending their boundaries but also his own, the latter, gradually and cumulatively as his understanding of his mission became clearer, partly through the challenge he received from those he met.

And so it is with each of us. But we have to be committed to the call to mission, to the lure and the demands of the boundaries or margins. Unless we seek the margins and the people who live there, a dimension of our Christian lives will remain unexplored and a whole vista of mission will remain unseen, out of sight. The wonderful thing is that the vista is visible almost from where we are; just a short, committed, faith-filled step across our margins is all that is required.

THE "OUTCAST" AS AGENT OF EVANGELIZATION

Many times we have emphasized the need for our own conversion, whether in terms of the radical disjunction of St. Paul's experience or by virtue of a more radical continuity with our original calling. But who will aid the Spirit in the accomplishment of that task? If it is possible for us to be evangelizers, then given the fact that the Spirit of God is available to every single person, it is in principle possible for anyone in the world to be an agent of our own evangelization. And in actual fact the Good News might make an impact on us through some rather unlikely persons, if only we encounter them! Here are some examples that typify the situations in which we can be called to conversion and from which new ways of being church can be experienced.

Saints, Sinners, and the City

In Chicago there is a house just across the road from Wrigley Field where the Cubs try to play baseball and their fans continue to believe, contrary to the record and the evidence, that they will succeed! Genesis House is where women try to rebuild their lives and where their supporters struggle, against the odds, to convince them that they are worthwhile and loved.

Genesis House is a place of nurturing, and those who feel at home there are women trying to mend lives broken on the wheel of prostitution and associated addictions. More than 90 percent of them come from abusive relationships and situations, something which not only victimizes them but so traumatizes them that one wonders whether apparent recovery can ever be permanent. Like the little priest made famous in a Graham Greene novel, they feel betrayed and abandoned, especially by church, frequently by family and erstwhile friends, sometimes by God.

Genesis can only accommodate four or five women at a time; the limited space is also occupied by a staff of social workers, therapists, counselors, and volunteers. But in less than a decade it has provided short- or long-term hospitality for hundreds, and now thousands, of women.

The Thursday evening meal is "open house." Former residents, women passing through, hungry staff, friends, supporters, women on their way to "outreach" programs with others currently in prostitution—all are likely to be gathered around the table. A meal for the hungry it certainly is, but it is more. This is a haven, a home, a meetingplace, a "drop-in," a center of affirmation, a focus for community. One of the residents, or perhaps a guest, prays over food and family, giving thanks to God and other benefactors, asking for continued help, mentioning successes and goals reached, articulating faith and hope and love. It is impossible to be complacent or bored at the table-grace or table-companionship. It is a breaking of bread, a communion, a type of eucharist.

Now it is surely important that one neither romanticize what happens around the table nor claim formal resemblances to the Christian sacrament of the eucharist. But the word of blessing is not sentimental and is clearly a word of grace; the breaking of bread together—the table-companionship—is not superficial but poignantly striking. What is occurring here is a multileveled drama: to some of those present it is an example of mission in reverse; to some it gently calls to a commitment to a greater inculturation of the eucharist; to some it is mission on the margins. The transforming power of God, working in and through real people in a rather unlikely situation far away from normal expressions of church, is striking. The presence of the Spirit, and the faith and wisdom that flourish at the margins of society and the visible church, are palpable. And it does raise questions about a fragile church and a flourishing mission, which can be found, like tenacious weeds, in the cracks, at the edges, on the borders.

In a certain sense Genesis House needs the church much less than the institutional church needs this community. Genesis House exists like a silent (and sometimes a rather noisy) invitation to the church to become more involved in its mission, to rise to the challenge of the God of the woman taken in adultery and of all the prostitutes and sinners loved by Jesus. But a church planted at the center may take a long time to notice the weeds in the cracks; the mute invitation may not be understood.

Yet in another sense Genesis House *is* the church in microcosm. It is a local community that wants to belong but not to lose its identity; it is a local community that knocks, and seeks, and asks. But if the door is not opened, if compassion is not found, if questions are not answered, what then? And if those who knock are left waiting or sent round to the back door; if those who search are too far away from the centers; and if those who ask are silenced and told to listen, then where is the hope and where is the sacrament of salvation? Communities such as this tend to arise in the shadow of the official church, since institutionally at least, it has contributed to the alienation and victimization that mark the community itself.

But actually, the need—of Genesis House and of the church—is real; it is mutual even if unexpressed, even if unknown. For it was Jesus who prayed that all may be one, and "all" is inclusive, absolute. It does not stop at the margins. So wherever there is disunity, fragmentation, mutual hostility, vilification, or hurt, there is need for common bread and common commitment to common journeys, so that all may be one. "The breaking of the bread is at once the point of departure and the point of arrival of the Christian community," says Gustavo Gutiérrez.[2] At Genesis House simple people break bread simply and together; some of those gathered around the table have glimpsed eucharistic possibilities not yet dreamed of by many "legitimate" eucharistic communities.

Yet there was a time when the church was a defender of people like the women of Genesis House and when a litany of saints could have been compiled from among women who had once practiced the world's oldest profession. Perhaps that time is here again. Certainly the women of Genesis House, like the Samaritan woman (Jn 4), extend hospitality to all who knock, seek, and ask. And she who only gave a cup of cold water was "co-missioned" and sent back to announce the Good News to her people.

But for mission to grow in such situations and for mission in reverse to flourish, the last must become first, teachers must become learners, givers must receive, and those at the centers must move to the edges. People familiar with "normal" pastoral roles and ministries will have to be transformed.

Wisdom in West Africa

We met the witchfinder in Chapter 7 and we told an incomplete story. Here is its completion.

Although the town has been declared free of witches, there remain half a dozen people accused of some very serious crimes. They have indeed made a full confession, and the witchfinder declares that if they are sincerely repentant then the town will be once again free of the scourge of witchcraft. But is their confession a real sign of true contrition? It is for the whole group to determine.

Early in the morning every member of the community gathers. The witchfinder explains that the self-confessed witches must undergo a "poison ordeal" to prove the integrity of their confessions: if really contrite, they will not suffer poisoning. In this highly charged and rather frightening situation, everyone falls quiet. But one of the six, a frail old woman, speaks up: what if there is no evil in her heart but poison in the food? It is well said. The witchfinder smiles and pulls a piece from the dough-ball he intends to offer to the putative felons. He eats contentedly, at a leisurely pace. He has made his point. Only the deceitful and unrepentant will suffer poisoning. And now he pulls off another piece, and another, and hands them to each of the six people before him. One by one they bring it to their mouths, and very slowly they chew. The crowd is hushed, breathless. One by one they swallow, gingerly, and then they smile, tentatively. Finally, each one has eaten, there are no ill effects, and everyone relaxes.

The witchfinder now concludes his homily (see Chapter 7), cautions the whole village against evil and impenitence, and shares food with everyone in the village. The six have partaken with the rest; everyone is united in breaking and eating. They are companions, communicants.[3]

To an onlooker, the parallels with the Christian sacrament are indeed striking. The passage from the First Letter to the Corinthians comes to mind, that to eat and drink unworthily is to eat and drink condemnation: "That is in fact why many of you are weak and ill and some of you have died" (1 Cor 11:20). In the experience of the onlooker, many Sunday eucharists in Christian churches have not come close to the seriousness and social importance of this one. Here are people breaking, taking, and eating as if their lives depended on it! And the whole community is vitally involved in the action, since the whole community is vitally involved in life and living, and because each member of the community depends on the group as a whole. On occasions like this we may glimpse what our own eucharists may yet become.

This is neither to accept uncritically all local behavior nor, we should reiterate, is it to argue that such social dramas, unreconstructed, qualify as crypto-eucharistic liturgies. An easy cultural syncretism is not the way to authentic inculturation of the Gospel. But the story is told in order to call for respectful attention to the Gospel values embedded in cultures. It is intended to urge that inculturation begin with the experience and the behavior of local people, and neither belittle nor ignore it.

A postscript should be added. Several months later I passed through the villages whose witchcraft trials I had witnessed. In each one the accused and "repentant" defendants were happier than for many years! Every day someone would bring them food. Every day they would be visited and checked to see if they were well. Every day they would be sure of not being neglected. A witchcraft trial is surely an extreme way of identifying all the old and unattached people in the village, but it certainly resulted in an excellent form of social security in the long term! We who abandon or institutionalize so many old and isolated people could learn a thing or two!

There is another lesson. By looking at such examples of local behavior and by absorbing some of the wisdom of other peoples, we might begin to perceive just how shallow and unconvincing some of our own liturgical behavior can be, and can appear to others. We profess our repentance, yet we are such recidivists; we break bread and share it yet, we fail to be companions. But, as we try to meet others where they are, so Jesus calls us from where we ourselves are. He challenges us to accept each other with trust; to meet people and to journey with them to a place new to both of us; to find bread for our journey and to break it together; and to recognize in the breaking the one who makes our hearts burn and who abides with us on all our journeys. Mission in reverse is indeed full of surprises!

Funeral Festivities

Winter is brutal. Survival is a social affair requiring friends and food, shelter and warmth, luck, money, and a purpose.

Josie was homeless and unbalanced, hardly noticed through many of her fifty-four years. She died one winter's night, frozen to the street. Josie had been looking for food outside McDonald's. She must have slipped and fallen, and in the sub-zero temperature her frail body offered little resistance to the biting cold. She was the first to die like this, that year. It was the second day of January.

The city keeps unclaimed bodies for a while, accumulating them. Then it buries them in batches in a common, unmarked grave. Many homeless people fear this fate; for them there is no dignity, even in death. But a kindly funeral director, swift advocacy, hasty preparations, and Josie would have a proper funeral! Word went out that her death would be modestly remembered and her life belatedly celebrated: too little, too late, but all the people from the streets were welcomed and invited.

Homeless people are not mute, though their voices are rarely heard; they are not stupid, though their wisdom passes largely unnoticed; they are not unfeeling, though they have learned to be numb. They came to Josie's funeral. The memory of the emotion as they sang "The Old Rugged Cross" will remain forever with those who were present. This dead, anonymous, forgotten woman was brought back to life and given an identity through the recollections and stories, the prayers and the singing that day—a kind of *anamnesis* even. Homeless people dared to hope that they too might get a proper burial, and those with homes to go to glimpsed the black hole of homelessness.

Afterwards, there was a meal, a joyful, wholesome, comfortable, human, social meal. It was not just food, but good meat and real vegetables and hot gravy and fresh, warm bread: in memory of her. A hundred and fifty people sat down and were fed; and there was much food left over.

We must ask, where was the church? The church—the *ekklesia*, the gathering, the assembly—was surely there in the community of faith gathered to remember Josie and Jesus. But it was a tenacious, angry, fierce, and blazing faith, kindled into flame around the casket and fanned in the warm companionship of the meal. The voices were those of the voiceless, and the wisdom came from the foolish of this world, and the margin was at the center that day; there were reversals and transformations in the air. And though one or two of the more "respectable" members of the church were there too, they were given the grace of silence before the mystery.

We must ask, where was the eucharist? The eucharist—bread for the journey, bond of companionship, sacrament of justice—was surely there in the community of faith gathered to remember Josie and Jesus. Food and drink were reverently shared by people of faith gathered in the shadow of death and the old rugged cross. And nourishment was given to body and spirit touched by life and the hope of resurrection. There was remembrance of God's fidelity in the powerful witness of prayers of intercession. And there was certainly giving and thanking, taking and breaking, sharing, and caring.

The people who gathered on that frigid day would never have come together in any other circumstances. The only common thread was the spent life of the one they mourned. Most had never known her well; many did not know each other. But Josie was the catalyst for conversations between rich and poor, for companionship between outcasts and professionals, for community of homeless people and ordained ministers. No church building could have embraced that event; no formal eucharistic liturgy would have been possible. Many of the participants would have been afraid of a church building, just as some of the ministers in attendance were a little frightened by the faith they witnessed.

The only way for Josie's funeral to have happened was according to the needs and initiatives of the local people; the only way it could have been arranged was by starting from the existential situation, not by appealing to custom or precedent. But it happened because in a certain sense it had to happen, because people need to express their common humanity and their faith. An attitude such as we have described as mission in reverse would awaken sensitivity in all who venture to the edges of their own experience in order to trust those whom they encounter there, to look for and encourage local initiatives, to become freed from stifling thinking and fossilized behaviors, to offer presence and moral support before wordy advice and complicated directives, to be edified at the palpable fact that God is very present, far from the centers.

THE PROPHET OF LOONGOJO[4]

Ashumu, the young prophet, has a large following. From all over Maasai country groups of men and women come to spend a day or two in his village. They come to listen to him and to be blessed by him. His message is always the same: return to our ancient traditions; grasp our time-honored values of clan and family; put your trust in God, the source of all good things.

Two years ago the prophet came to our church to hear what we were preaching. He was taken with the message of Jesus, seeing it as one with his own. He felt that somehow Jesus must be the source of his vocation. He wanted to know all about the son of God called Jesus and his teaching. The Ngorongoro Maasai Christians organized themselves, and have been instructing Ashumu for the last year and a half. Every Saturday at least one elder and often more have made the four-hour trek to the village of the prophet high in the mountains to teach him and the people of his village the way of Jesus.

Now the great day of baptism had arrived. Our group of more than fifty Ngorongoro Christians were singing with great gusto as we approached the village. We arrived just as the sun was setting and stood in a half-circle some distance from the cattle-gate. The people of the village were expecting us. Out they came, first the elders, then the warriors, finally the women and children. They formed a half-circle singing songs of welcome. After a few minutes the two groups came together in a single circle. Our hosts then passed among us extending their hands in greeting—like children to adults, since in a real way they were the children of our Ngorongoro community. Finally a warrior passed among us collecting all the sticks, clubs, and short swords. These would have no place in the Christian rites about to take place. They would be put away and returned to us next day on our departure.

The villagers welcomed us into their homes for a meal of heavily sugared tea and boiled corn meal. Later everyone gathered in the moonlight-bathed enclosure for more singing. The final act of the day was to extinguish the fires in all the houses of the village. New fire would be ritually kindled at dawn with traditional fire sticks and carried to all the houses, signaling new life in Jesus.

In the cold light of dawn all gathered around a new fire, heaped with green leaves. Three old men joined me in its blessing with milk and honey beer. I signed all with the cross on their foreheads using a chalk-like rock commonly used in Maasai ritual. Finally, one by one, the eighty catechumens sat on the skin of a ritually slaughtered bull. They were baptized with water, called "living" by the Maasai, since they had dipped it from a flowing spring. Finally I liberally anointed the newly baptized with oil using the fat of the sheep ritually slaughtered just hours before.

The ceremonies were not over. Now there was to be a wedding. It was said that the prophet would never take a wife, but during the course of his baptismal instructions he had decided otherwise. This morning warriors had brought his bride, and she was baptized with the rest of his family. Now we would bless the couple. All gathered again around the fire, with Ashumu the prophet and his bride standing on the holy skin. First we asked the traditional questions: Will you stand by your wife in the dry season as well as the rains? Ashumu, will you care for her and her children even when the milk cows are dry and the country is dust and the sun burns like fire? Will you always receive your wife's mother and father with respect and help them when they are in need? Naarmai, will you stand by your husband even in sickness when he can't care for you? Will you take his father and mother as your own, respect them and care for them in their old age?

We smeared fat on the thin bridal chain she would wear attached to her ear all her married life and placed it around her neck. The bridegroom's traditional necklace of blue beads was then smeared with the fat and placed around his neck. Finally I anointed their linked right hands with fat, signing their union and our desire that their marriage be successful in every way. Two elders from the Ngorongoro community, one from his own family, and I, then blessed their union and the entire assembly with milk and honey beer and many words. Then we sang and sang and sang songs of blessing and thanksgiving.

The people formed themselves into age-group clusters. They shared the meat of the large ox slaughtered for the occasion and drank the milk brought by the many guests. They sipped the honey beer brewed for the occasion . . .

[Though not present for these ceremonies, I myself was privileged to spend some time with the Ngorongoro community. I felt then, as I feel recording this, the vitality of their faith, the power of their liturgy, and the warmth of their welcome. For many years the Maasai people of Tanzania and Kenya were considered unevangelizable!]

WALKING ON THE WATER

The mental picture of Peter's brave, foolhardy, and faltering steps as he tried to walk on the water (Matt 14:29ff) is a powerful image of the call to mission. There is something compelling about the call, but water is not the normal surface for human progress; in fact, it is clearly impossible to walk on!

Peter, unsure of the stranger's identity, makes the outrageous request: "Lord, if it is you, tell me to come to you across the water." According to the Gospel of Matthew it is Peter's idea; Mark's and John's Gospel are more discreet, and Luke's account says nothing. But Jesus, always sensitive to the requests of others, utters the enabling word, "Come."

"Come," "come to me," and "come follow me" precede "go," "go your way," and particularly "go, teach all nations." We may need to be reminded of this because sometimes it seems we have not heeded this sequence. But only if we have come to Jesus, only if we are currently following Jesus, can we in turn go out and make disciples (Matt 28:19). Disciples (*mathētēs*) are those who learn; we must first have learned from Jesus before we can presume to call others to learn from us.

If we are first to come and follow Jesus then, like the two disciples in John's Gospel (1:38-39), we must come and see where he lives: among the lost sheep, with outcasts and sinners, in the outlying towns and villages. Sometimes he has nowhere to lay his head. Here is one at the margins more than at the centers, as often in the company of sinners as in the synagogue. So Jesus' invitation would appear to point us, too, in the same direction.

If we follow Jesus, how will we communicate? The poor, the blind, the downtrodden and dispossessed do not speak our language. But since it is their territory and their lives on which we encroach, it is more correct to say that it is we who do not speak their language. We are the outsiders. We need to learn to communicate; they already can. The only way we can credibly communicate with those who live on the other side of our own borders is to undertake to learn from those who live there. That makes us, in a significant sense, their disciples!

Far from being fanciful and naive, this is simply to describe the way Jesus approached and responded to people, time and time again. The woman at Bethany was upbraided by the disciples, but Jesus responded, "Leave her alone. Why are you upsetting her?" (Mk 14:6). This was typical of one whose whole ministry was built on fostering relationships and show-ing respect. The effectiveness of this approach may be gauged by the num-bers of people who came to him; contrary to popular belief, poor and marginalized people who retain their self-respect do not throw themselves at passing strangers, but they may respond to gentleness, compassion, and respect.

To follow Jesus to where he lives, and to follow his example of com-municating in the vernacular of the outcast, is to undertake a daunting task. It is like walking on water; it cannot be done. We may dream of being all things to all people and of gaining the respect of the powerless and exploited, just as we may dream of walking on water, but deep down we fear it is not only difficult but impossible. And of course this is correct to a point. But to respond to mission is precisely to undertake the impossible. If it were within our own capabilities we could engage in mission and expect to succeed. If it were within our own capabilities we could plan it rationally and assess our effectiveness objectively. Only when we know that it is beyond us and possible only to God can we respond as Peter responded, ask the Lord for a call, and then get out of the boat, step into the unknown, and start walking on a volatile and unfamiliar surface. The rest is a matter of faith.

Faith is the key to all the healing that Jesus accomplishes; lack of faith explains lack of healing. With faith, everything is possible. Fear is useless. Only faith matters; faith saves. Not surprisingly perhaps, we, like many of those who came before Jesus, fail to measure up; our lives are witness to the times we have sunk already, or fear that we shall. And so it becomes rather difficult for us to clamber over the side, let go of our firm ground, and move beyond our boundaries and narrow limitations. The temptation is always to remain in the boat or stay on dry land; after all, it is unrea-sonable, maybe irrational, to do otherwise. But the invitation is always to get out of the boat and to walk on the water; after all, the one who calls has overcome the world. And if our pusillanimity is stronger than our faith, then we need constant encouragement lest we forget that the invitation is continuous. To forget the invitation or to look to our own devices is to shirk the impossible mission to which we are called. Mission is nothing if it is not on the margins, and one sure thing about margins is that they are some way from the centers.

THE MARGIN AS EPICENTER OF MISSION

How often in a world of rank injustice, violence, and greed does the Good News we presume to speak turn to bile in our mouths? How often, in the face of unspeakable suffering and tragedy, do the words we utter sound hollow even to ourselves? If the salvation wrought by Jesus Christ really is such wonderful news, why do so many not hear it, and so many more not respond? If the word of God is really "alive and active," something that "cuts like any double-edged sword but more finely" (Heb 4:12), why has it not cut deeper into people's lives, bringing surgical correction and new life? We cannot force people to hear the word of God, and their conversion is not a matter that we can control or judge, so how should we respond to hostility or indifference? So many questions.

It seems axiomatic to say that if we are not attracting people it is because we are not attractive; if we were, we might. How could we become more attractive and persuasive? Only, surely, by reflecting to an increasing degree the attractiveness and attraction of Jesus. Rather than expending our energies on trying to make other people see things our way, perhaps we simply need to become more imbued with the spirit of Jesus. "Blessed are those who hunger and thirst for justice"; in a culture of "snackers" and "grazers" perhaps we have not developed an edge to our appetite nor an honest thirst.

The naked and imprisoned, the persecuted and mourning, the strangers and the sick—these are the really hungry and thirsty ones, and not occasionally but as a way of life. They are the outcasts of society, the biblical "sinners." And they are indeed "more sinned against than sinning." Most of them are caught in the cracks and cannot escape; many are stepped on by passers-by. And we presume to teach them about hunger and thirst and about justice! They are capable of teaching us so much, about passion and the need for compassion, whether rationally or through their anger and frustration. They could be the first to show us where injustice is deep-rooted and where conversion needs to begin.

It should not be surprising, then, that Jesus responded to just this kind of situation. When we look carefully at his pastoral missionary outreach, we see his "preferential option" for such people in just such conditions. It is precisely they, the furthest from the centers and from respectability, who extend to him the challenge to live his mission to the utmost. Far from being impartial, Jesus is partial and quite biased; since the "religious" people have the consolation of institutional support while the outcasts are judged irredeemably beyond the righteousness of God, it is explicitly to the latter that Jesus goes. By no means does he exclude the (self-)righteous from love and forgiveness: people like the rich young man/ruler (Mk 10), or well-disposed scribes and Pharisees. Jesus' point is precisely that *no one* is outside God's love. Yet he clearly and painstakingly seeks out "the lost sheep" and announces the Good News to those in whose life there is very little that is good. Jesus *becomes* the Good News!

Second, he is clearly affected both by the condition and by the response of those at the margins: women, the ritually impure, public sinners, physically and mentally broken people, collaborators. These are people for whom — according to those who interpreted the law — there is no possibility of conversion. These are the people who begin to recognize him, to name him, to have faith in him, and to believe, through him, in themselves. And they in turn "enable" Jesus: they ratify him, affirm him, and like the Syrophoenician woman they are not afraid to challenge him.

For the follower of Jesus (the disciple, the learner) his biased choosing of the outcast becomes a compelling example. Jesus is doing the will of God; we, through following Jesus, do likewise. God hears the cries of the poor; God heals the brokenhearted (Is 61:1). This is part of the passage of scripture that Jesus makes his own "mission statement" at the beginning of his public life (Lk 4:18). And for the disciple there is more. In our following of Jesus we are made whole, and in our encounter with the broken our brokenness finds healing. "The ministry of healing" is a description of the call of Jesus' followers.

The preferential option that we are called to make cannot be the result of a communal decision, if that dilutes our personal response. Radical discipleship goes beyond; our own conversion cannot be the outcome of consensus.[5] The more religion is institutionalized the more stifling it becomes, the further removed from life-giving revelation it is, and the less responsive to the charisms of martyrdom, prophecy, and healing it proves. These are not private gifts, though individuals may be their custodian on behalf of the community; but only in communities that resist institutionalization, hierarchy, and centralization, and try to retain a certain spontaneity can such charisms flourish for the good of the church. Our preferential option is no less than a commitment to Jesus' preferential option: a choice biased in favor of those unjustly deprived. Such a choice must make us attractive purveyors of the Good News; such an engagement makes us vulnerable to God's converting grace.

MISSION OF TRANSFORMATION, TRANSFORMATION OF MISSION

Surely there can be no doubt that Jesus was a revolutionary in the sense that he wanted to rock the world, and society, on its heels. He was set for confrontation, for the falling and the rising of many (Lk 2:34). He was planning to make all things new in God (Rv 21:4). He was gentle with the wounded and only excoriated the hardhearted. But his was a single purpose: to unite all things and all persons. As St. Paul has it:

The old creation is gone, and now all is new. It is all God's work. It was God who was reconciling (*katallaxantos*) us to God's self through Christ; and God gave us the work of handing on this reconciliation (*katallages*) (2 Cor 5:18).

The general tenor of this statement and the words used are very clear and fit well with our overall theme. The Greek verb translated by the English "reconcile" refers to an act of exchange. In reconciliation, a relationship changes from enmity to friendship. But there must be some mutuality, since reconciliation or forgiveness demands the consent of the recipient of the reconciliation or forgiveness; they cannot be achieved simply by the good will of one of the parties.

In Chapter 5 we considered the implications of eucharist as an act of exchange. Certainly the initiative is not entirely our own, but equally certainly, unless we become involved in the eucharist and learn to become morally responsible eucharistic people, then its potential remains unrealized. Likewise with reconciliation. Our response is required. St. Paul says that we who have been reconciled now have the responsibility for handing on this reconciliation. This is rather reminiscent of those exchange relationships exemplified across a range of societies; it demands not simply that we do something *to* or even *for* others, but *with* them. The mission we undertake in the spirit of Jesus is a mission that transforms all who are involved; in fact, the mission has as its very purpose the transformation of all things and persons, to bring them into closer conformity with Christ.

It is fashionable in some quarters today to minimize the transformational nature of mission and the seriousness of the call to conversion on the grounds that we must respect people where they are. Again, this smacks of a binary mentality. Certainly we have to respect people in the concrete, but mission is inseparable from movement, and the *terminus a quo* or starting point is not the *terminus ad quem* or point to which the movement is directed. This is as true of conversion of heart as it is of inculturation of the liturgy: we are, all of us, on a journey, a pilgrimage; we are not simply standing around, waiting for something to happen.

What is required, then, is *both* respect for people in their existential situation *and* also the proclamation of the Gospel, the latter being a crucial component of evangelization and intended to effect the "reconciliation" or exchange of which Paul speaks. Each of us will therefore need to be convinced about the faith we profess and committed to the proclamation of the Good News, yet without prejudice to the deep respect we owe to people and cultures. But sometimes our declarations of esteem for others may mask our own weakness of faith, our lack of conviction about the power of the Good News, and our consequent reluctance to speak out. Since this missionary undertaking is not without delicacy or pain, we who are involved in the exchange must also undertake to provide moral support for others and to entrust ourselves to those among whom the mission of Jesus takes us. To do any less is to be mere messengers, not ambassadors.

If transformation (affecting ourselves, other recipients of the proclamation, and relationship between people and peoples) is intrinsic to the missionary enterprise, then the enterprise itself (both as philosophy and as practical undertaking) needs to be constantly challenged and exposed to transformation. We cannot therefore cling to well-laid, long-term plans irrespective of a changing context, expecting them to work and ourselves to implement them; one of the variables is the people themselves and another is the Spirit of God. There has been a tendency in the history of Christian missions to discover a "plan" that works, to assume that it is transplantable anywhere, and to await the same vigorous harvest in a completely different context. But this is to belittle local conditions and the genius of local peoples. A single, universal plan is worthless, and very frustrating; however global the strategy, the tactics must be local. Paul knew the importance of adaptation and claimed to have become "all things to all people."

The future of mission is not laid out clearly before us in every detail. Our fidelity is to the God of Jesus Christ, not to a grandiose plan; sometimes our plans can actually inhibit the mission we espouse. And as biblical studies are helping us to see Jesus less as a king who comes in glory and more as "one who serves" (Lk 22:27), so our attitudes to mission have started to become rather less triumphalistic and more servant-like. But the transition from positions of authority and prestige to positions of service and low status is not easy. It is a clear example of the transformation of mission.

Every Christian who responds to the call of Jesus to "come follow me" and to "be healed," and is then commissioned by the mandate to "go" and to "heal," is swept up into a mission of pilgrimage and transformation; every disciple who undertakes to go to the nations both to announce the Good News and to be converted by the God whose grace works in other persons and other places undertakes a journey and is part of a movement committed to the transformation of mission itself. In a world touched by the incarnation, there must be pilgrims, there will always be journeys, and the bread will surely be sufficient.

"Send forth your Spirit, and renew the face of the earth."

QUESTIONS FOR THE ROAD

- "The Church is missionary by its very nature." What do you understand this to mean? Does it not demean the notion of mission? How can the church and its members become more missionary?
- Do you accept that grace may be mediated through the "outcast" and the "sinner"? Or is this just a fanciful way of speaking? How might it impinge on our own conversion? What might it imply about God's Providence?
- What is your overall impression of the stories and incidents related in

this chapter? Do they affect the way you have understood mission? Might they affect your future approaches?
- If you were working to evangelize the Maasai people, how would you use the information in this chapter? Is there anything you find potentially applicable to a wider field?
- Explore the image of mission as "walking on the water."

Notes

INTRODUCTION

1. The theme of alien and stranger is examined in chapter 5 of Anthony Gittins, *Gifts and Strangers: Meeting the Challenge of Inculturation* (Mahwah, N.J.: Paulist Press, 1989).

2. Stanley Hauerwas and William H. Willimon, *Resident Aliens* (Nashville, Tenn.: Abingdon, 1989).

3. Stanley Hauerwas and Will Willimon, "Why *Resident Aliens* Struck a Chord." *Missiology* 4 (1991): 419-29. See page 419.

4. Hauerwas and Willimon, "Why," p. 419.

5. Hauerwas and Willimon, "Why," p. 425.

6. Hauerwas and Willimon, "Why," p. 420.

7. Hauerwas and Willimon, "Why," p. 421.

1. MISSIONARY JOURNEYS

1. Bruce Chatwin, *The Songlines* (New York, N.Y.: Viking, 1987), p. 304.

2. Wilkie Au, *By Way of the Heart* (Mahwah, N.J.: Paulist Press, 1989), p. 90.

3. T. S. Eliot, *Little Gidding* (1942), pt. 5.

4. Margaret Miles, *Carnal Knowing: Female Nakedness and Religious Meaning in the Christian West* (Boston, Mass.: Beacon, 1989), p. 30 and passim.

5. H. McKennie Goodpasture, ed., *Cross and Sword in Latin America: An Eyewitness Account* (Maryknoll, N.Y.: Orbis Books, 1989).

6. People with "borderline personalities," unsocialized people, and those who have been traumatically abused, may not yet be able to engage in mission. "Be healed" precedes "heal." The Gerasene demoniac is a good example of a broken and needy person encountering Jesus and being healed and then "commissioned." It may be important to remember this when we are too judgmental or demanding of others.

7. See Chapter 4 and associated references.

8. Claude-Marie Barbour, "Jesus, Shalom, and Rites of Passage: A Journey Toward Global Mission and Spirituality." *Missiology* 3 (1987): 299-313. See page 304.

9. Ernesto Cardenal, *Gospel in Solentiname* (Maryknoll, N.Y.: Orbis Books, 1982). This work consists of four volumes of dialogue homilies brilliantly capturing the insights of a small community in Nicaragua, reflecting on and breaking open the word of scripture, united in the Spirit. It contains numerous insights and discloses a whole style or approach to evangelization.

10. Vincent Donovan, *The Church in the Midst of Creation* (Maryknoll, N.Y.: Orbis Books, 1989), pp. 84-85.

11. Jon Alexander, "What Do Recent Writers Mean by Spirituality?" *Spirituality Today* (1980): 247-56.

12. William Stringfellow, *The Politics of Spirituality* (Philadelphia: Westminster, 1984), pp. 19-26.

13. This refers to a quotation that recurs in Vatican II. It is from the encyclical *Mediator Dei* of 1947: "The summit, we may also say the center, of the Christian religion is the Mystery of the Most Holy Eucharist" (para. 70).

2. SPIRITUALITY, EUCHARIST, TRANSFORMATION

1. Patrick L. Carroll and Katherine M. Dyckman, *Chaos or Creation? Spirituality in Mid-life* (Mahwah, N.J.: Paulist Press, 1986), p. 24.

2. Miles, *Carnal Knowing*, pp. 31,41.

3. Lamin Sanneh, *Translating the Message: The Missionary Impact on Culture* (Maryknoll, N.Y.: Orbis Books, 1989), p. 64.

4. From a talk by Professor A. Walls at the University of Cambridge Divinity School, England, 1989.

5. Johannes Arndt, *True Christianity*. Classics of Western Spirituality (Mahwah, N.J.: Paulist Press, 1979), p. 22.

6. Gustavo Gutiérrez, "A Spirituality of Liberation." In *Conversion: Perspectives on Personal and Social Transformation*, ed. Walter Conn (New York, N.Y.: Alba House, 1978), pp. 307-8.

7. Walter Hollenweger. In *Concilium* 114, *Evangelization in the World Today* (New York: Seabury Press, 1979), pp. 40-41.

8. Gutiérrez, "A Spirituality of Liberation," p. 309.

9. This is dealt with extensively in Miles, *Carnal Knowing*.

10. This point is argued by Edward Schillebeeckx in *Ministry: A Case for Change* (New York, N.Y.: Crossroad, 1981), pp. 50-55. He acknowledges that there is "only one explicit piece of evidence that if need be, a layman too could preside at eucharist"; and cites Tertullian who "writes that in normal circumstances presiding at the eucharist is, by definition, a role for the leader of the community" (p. 51). But, says Tertullian, "where no college of ministers has been appointed, you, the laity must celebrate the eucharist and baptize; in that case you are your own priests, for where two or three are gathered together, there is the church, even if these three are lay people" (*De Exhort. Cast.* 7,3). Schillebeeckx avers that "in exceptional circumstances, the community itself chose its president, *ad hoc*; and that Augustine denied communities that right" (p. 153).

11. Chapters 5 through 7 consider some possibilities for eucharist to be catalytic for socio-religious change, and for cultural practices to be catalytic for transformation and inculturation.

12. "The BEM Document" and the responses of various churches are most enlightening here. The document itself, also called "The Lima Document," is a Faith and Order Paper officially titled "Baptism, Eucharist, and Ministry: The Agreed Text." World Council of Churches Geneva, Switzerland, (1982). See also: *Churches Respond to Baptism, Eucharist, and Ministry Text* (Geneva, WCC, 1986-88), 5 volumes. A point strongly emphasized is that many Christian churches are

acknowledging their historical overreaction against the eucharist and their determination to reinstate it at the center of their communities' life.

13. A "sentence" (a *theoretical*, perfect, grammatically correct, non-redundant construct) differs from an "utterance" (an *actual* piece of speech, inclusive of hesitations, solecisms, and redundancies). People do not speak sentences; the utterances we do produce are more numerous than the underlying perfect sentences.

14. People who learn a few phrases before traveling abroad have virtually no flexibility or control over language. They are unable to "generate" *a variety* of speech forms but are virtually limited to what they have explicitly learned. Yet native speakers do not learn all the "sentences" of their language; still, they can produce a quasi-unlimited stream of new creations. Language can be said to have been acquired when a speaker has such creativity, which we call fluency.

15. Just as we do not speak "sentences" but "utterances," so "deep structures" are *theoretical* constructs, postulated to underlie the surface structures that are realized at a syntactic level. The notion of "deep structure" is helpful as a heuristic device, and as such may be compared to "root metaphors" underlying behavior or "Ur-structures" beneath narrative. Another helpful image — though not identical — is that of the skeleton which supports the living body. We do not have instant access to the skeleton, but we can know a good deal about it by observing physical movement. A standard reference is John Lyons, *Introduction to Theoretical Linguistics* (Cambridge, U.K.: University Press, 1967); also Noam Chomsky, *Syntactic Structures* (The Hague: Mouton, 1957).

16. Ambiguity can only be explained adequately by reference to something beneath the surface. "Flying planes can be dangerous" is ambiguous. But if the complete verb-form underlying *can* is identified, we can disambiguate. The phrase may mean either that flying planes *is* dangerous, or flying planes *are* dangerous. Without access to the deep structure, there is no way to clarify.

17. This is the basis of "dynamic equivalence," by which one attempts to translate meaning and not simply words. It can readily be understood if we consider idioms, which cannot be translated *literally* from one language to another ("She was at death's door" translates in French as "she was [at] two fingers from death."). A dynamic translation requires knowledge of underlying meaning, which is a function of relationships at a deep structural level.

18. See Sanneh's excellent work *Translating the Message*.

19. "The BEM Document," section E26, p. 25

20. "The BEM Document," section M3, p. 29.

21. Mercy Oduyoye, "The Eucharist as Witness." *International Review of Mission* (1983): 228.

22. Arthur Vogel, *Is The Last Supper Finished?* (New York, N.Y.: Sheed and Ward, 1968), p. 134.

23. In the official responses to "The BEM Document" *Faith and Order Paper 129: Churches Respond to BEM*, ed. Max Thurian, p.13.

24. Beverly Wildung Harrison, "The Power of Anger in the Work of Love." *Union Seminary Quarterly Review*, vol. 36, *Supplementary* (1981):41-57. This quotation is from page 50.

25. Aylward Shorter, *Jesus and the Witchdoctor* (Maryknoll, N.Y.: Orbis Books, 1985), p. 29.

26. The symbol [!] indicates a "click" sound. See Richard Katz, *Boiling Energy:*

Community and Healing among the Kalahari Kung (Cambridge, Mass.: Harvard, 1982).

27. Chapter Seven will take up this theme, as we look at the sociological and pastoral significance of witchcraft.

28. Thomas Ogletree, *Hospitality to the Stranger: Dimensions of Moral Understanding* (Minneapolis, Minn.: Fortress Press, 1985), pp. 3,57.

29. See for example, Victor Turner, especially *The Ritual Process: Structure and Anti-Structure* (Ithaca, N.Y.: Cornell, 1977).

30. R. Wynne, "The Eucharist Converts!" *International Review of Mission* (1983): 241-42.

3. THE CONVERSION OF THE MISSIONARY

1. St. Augustine, *Sermon*. 128.3.5; See also *City of God* 10.3.2. Quoted in Margaret Miles, *Practicing Christianity: Critical Perspectives for an Embodied Spirituality* (New York, N.Y.: Crossroad, 1988), p. 148.

2. Soren Kierkegaard, *Journals*. In *An Anthology of Devotional Literature* (New York, N.Y.: Harper, 1959), p. 543.

3. José Comblin, *Retrieving the Human: A Christian Anthropology* (Maryknoll, N.Y.: Orbis Books, 1990), p. 3.

4. Stephen Neill, *A History of Christian Missions* (Harmondsworth, U.K.: Penguin, 1964), p. 512. The term was first applied to and by the Jesuits in the sixteenth century.

5. Anthony J. Gittins, "Call and Response: Missionary Considerations." *Louvain Studies* 3 (1985):264-85.

6. David Bosch's magisterial *Transforming Mission: Paradigm Shifts in Theology of Mission* (Maryknoll, N.Y.: Orbis Books, 1991), is the current reference work. But also see his "The Structure of Mission: An Exposition of Matthew 28:16-20." In *Exploring Church Growth*, ed. Wilbert R. Shenk (Grand Rapids, Mich.: Eerdmans, 1983), pp. 218-48.

7. Robin Horton, "African Conversion." *Africa* 41/2 (1971); idem, "On the Rationality of Conversion." *Africa* 45/3,4 (1975).

8. David Bosch, *A Spirituality for the Road* (Scottdale.: Herald Press, 1979), p. 20.

9. Orlando Costas, "Conversion as a Complex Experience." In *Down To Earth: Studies in Christianity and Culture*, ed. J. Stott and R. Coote (London: Hodder and Stoughton, 1980), pp. 173-91.

10. Victor Turner, *Revelation and Divination in Ndembu Ritual* (Ithaca, N.Y.: Cornell, 1975).

11. Carolyn Walker Bynum, "Women's Stories, Women's Symbols: A Critique of Victor Turner's Theory of Liminality." In *Anthropology and the Study of Religion*, ed. R. Moore and F. Reynolds (Chicago: University of Chicago, 1984), pp. 105-25.

12. Quoted in Richard Gray, *Black Christians and White Missionaries* (New Haven, Conn.: Yale, 1990), pp. 74-75; from K. G. Molyneux, *African Christian Theology*, Ph.D. thesis, University of London, 1988, p. 157.

13. Gray, *Black Christians*, pp. 77-78.

14. Bynum, "Women's Stories," pp. 114-15.

15. Mary Douglas, *Natural Symbols: Explorations in Cosmology* (New York, N.Y.: Pantheon, 1970).

16. I pursue this theme in "Toward Integral Spirituality: Embodiment, Ecology, and Experience of God." In *Common Journey, Different Paths: Spiritual Direction in Cross-Cultural Perspective*, ed. Susan Rakoczy (Maryknoll, N.Y.: Orbis Books, 1992), pp. 44-54.

17. Comblin, *Retrieving the Human.*

18. See Anthony J. Gittins, "The Dance of Life: Liturgy and Ethics in Cross-Cultural Perspective." In *Living No Longer For Ourselves: Liturgy and Justice in the Nineties*, ed. Kathleen Hughes and Mark Francis (Collegeville, Minn.: Liturgical Press, 1991), pp. 185-202.

19. Constance Noyes Robertson, ed., *Oneida Community, An Autobiography* (Syracuse, N.Y.: University Press, 1970).

20. Boka di Mpasi Londi, "Symbol in Art and Worship," *Concilium* 132 (New York: Seabury Press, 1980), pp. 56-62.

21. Michael Jackson, *Paths Toward a Clearing: Radical Empiricism and Ethnographic Enquiry* (Bloomington, Ind.: Indiana University Press, 1989).

22. The source of this quotation has escaped me, though the sentiment is increasingly current. See (23) below.

23. Harrison, "The Power of Anger," pp. 46-49.

24. Michael Jackson, *Paths*, p. 135.

25. Arthur Vogel, *Is The Last Supper Finished?*, pp. 74-83.

26. Miles, *Practicing Christianity*, p. 111.

4. MISSION IN REVERSE

1. Peter Hebblethwaite, *National Catholic Reporter*, 18 August 1990.

2. J. J. Thierry, ed., *Epistle to Diognetus* (Leiden, Brill, 1964).

3. Claude-Marie Barbour, et al. "Shalom Ministries: An Urban Base Community Comes of Age." *The Chicago Seminary Register* vol. 81, no. 1 (Winter 1991): 42-49.

4. Claude-Marie Barbour, "Seeking Justice and Shalom in the City." *International Review of Mission* (July 1984): 304.

5. Eleanor Doidge, "The Spirituality of 'Mission-in-Reverse.'" Unpublished paper, p. 21.

6. John T. Boberg, "The Missionary as Anti-Hero." *Missiology* 4 (1979): 418.

7. Sharon Welch, *A Feminist Ethic of Risk* (Minneapolis, Minn.: Augsburg Fortress, 1989).

8. Comblin, *Retrieving the Human*, p. 43.

9. Marcel Mauss, *The Gift: Forms and Functions of Exchange in Archaic Societies* (London: Cohen and West, 1970), p. 64.

10. Sara Maitland, *Virgin Territory* (London: Michael Joseph, 1984), pp. 26-27.

11. This theme is pursued in Gittins, *Gifts and Strangers,* chap. 5.

5. EUCHARIST: EXCHANGE AND TRANSFORMATION

1. Walbert Bühlmann, *With Eyes To See: Church and World in the Third Millennium* (Maryknoll, N.Y.: Orbis Books, 1990), p. 57.

2. Donovan, *The Church in the Midst of Creation*, pp. 88, 91, 92.

3. David Power, "Response: Liturgy, Memory and the Absence of God." *Worship* 57 (1983): p. 328.

4. *Sacrosanctum Concilium*, 10.

5. The word "Mass" is used here, both to distinguish it from the other forms of eucharist (sometimes referred to as "eucharistic devotion outside Mass") and as "shorthand" for the full eucharistic liturgy as used by Christian churches, including "The Lord's Supper" or "The Holy Communion Service."

6. This is stated in *Sacrosanctum Concilium*, 22,3. The *editio typica* of the Roman Rite of the Mass is the *terminus a quo* of liturgical adaptation. The *terminus ad quem* is the vernacular translation. See Anscar Chupungco, *Liturgies of the Future: The Process and Methods of Inculturation* (Mahwah, N.J.: Paulist Press, 1989), especially chap. 2. It is clear that the Mass needs to be widely inculturated, and my hopes had been to write on this specific subject. But given the more practical nature of this book, it seemed best to consider other kinds of eucharistic devotions and the general meaning of eucharist. Official support for inculturation of the Mass appears less than enthusiastic and is painfully slow, yet it remains critically necessary.

7. The best-known case has been in Zaire (which, however, has not been able to produce its own rite, but only the Roman Rite of the Zairean Mass). This, and other attempts in the Philippines, India, and the Cameroons, can be traced in the following sources: Chupungco, *Liturgies*, pp. 87-94; Philip Tovey, *Inculturation: The Eucharist in Africa* (Nottingham, U.K.: Grove Books, 1988).

8. *Sacrosanctum Concilium*, 40; Chupungco, *Liturgies*, pp. 21ff., cites this with its attendant qualifications.

9. *Sacrosanctum Concilium*, 14. See Chupungco, *Liturgies*, pp. 9, 22 and footnote; this echoes *Mediator Dei*, 84: "It is therefore important . . . for all the faithful to understand that it is their duty and highest privilege to take part in the Eucharistic Sacrifice; and to take part in it, not passively or negligently or with distracted mind, but with such active devotion as to be in the closest union with the High Priest."

10. Chupungco, *Liturgies*, p. 23.

11. See note 5, above.

12. Chupungco, *Liturgies*, pp. 37-38.

13. See Gittins, "The Dance of Life," pp. 185-202.

14. Paul Bradshaw, *A New Dictionary of Christian Worship*, ed. J. G. Davies (London: Sheed and Ward, 1980), pp. 227-29.

15. Bradshaw, *New Dictionary*, p. 227.

16. Karl Rahner, *Theological Investigations*, vol. 14 (New York: Seabury, 1976), p. 170.

17. Bradshaw, *New Dictionary*, p. 228.

18. See note 9, above.

19. *Mediator Dei*, 119, 121. But see also para. 84 (footnote 9, above), which urges "active devotion."

20. We will pursue this in Chapter 8.

21. *Lex orandi lex credendi*: "The church's prayer is the church's faith." See David Power, epigraph to this chapter; footnotes 3, 9, 18; and *Sacrosanctum Concilium*, 14 ("full and active participation") and 26 ("liturgical services are not private functions, but are celebrations belonging to the church").

22. R.P.C. Hanson, "Tradition." In *A New Dictionary of Christian Theology*, ed. A. Richardson and J. Bowden (London: SCM Press, 1983), pp. 574-76.

23. Hanson, "Tradition," p. 574.

24. Hanson, "Tradition," p. 576.

25. Nathan Mitchell, *Cult and Controversy: The Worship of the Eucharist Outside Mass* (New York, N.Y.: Pueblo, 1982).

26. "Introduction to Holy Communion and Worship of the Eucharist Outside Mass." *The Rites of the Catholic Church* (New York, N.Y.: Pueblo, 1983), p. 475.

27. Sanneh, *Translating the Message.*

28. Chupungco, *Liturgies*, p. 32.

29. Chupungco, *Liturgies*, pp. 27-28.

30. Gregory of Nazianzen, *Orationes*, 38, 13.

31. Not "commerce" but "exchange." It is a term denoting moral relationship and not purely contractual. See footnotes (32) and (36) below.

32. I refer to pre-capitalist or traditional societies. There are problems for contemporary capitalist societies with their acquisitive, contractual mentality, but then perhaps eucharist is incompatible with such a mentality! *"Prestation"* in the French is not the same as *"don"*; the latter may translate as "gift" in the sense most commonly used in English, but "prestations" are part-gift, part-loan, part-self-interest, that is, indicators of an ongoing relationship.

33. See Gregory Dix, footnote (45) below.

34. There is not only a single deep structure for eucharist, any more than there is only one deep structure underlying language; there are a number. But here we are pursuing a single theme: exchange.

35. Mauss, *The Gift.*

36. "Gift-exchange" is the translation of the term Mauss renders by *"prestation,"* which means not just a giving of gifts but a moral system that endures over time and is found in non-capitalist societies and residually in capitalist societies. It is not to be confused either with "gift" or with "exchange" as these are normally used in English.

37. This seems to be on the basis of a selective and decontextualized reading of Acts 20:35.

38. Someone (A) gives something (X) to me. I give (X) to another person (Y), who returns a gift (G) to me. This gift (G) is both the spirit of the original gift (X) and the extension of that gift. Therefore (G) really belongs to (A).

39. This is Mauss's discovery (p. 9); but see below (1 Cor 11:29-30), and footnote (40).

40. A point made by A. Fossion, "The Eucharist As Act of Exchange." *Lumen Vitae* 4 (1980): 411-16.

41. I owe this helpful insight to my colleague Gilbert Ostdiek, OFM.

42. We might recall the relationship between parents and children as one of reciprocity. Yet its fundamental inequality of status does not exclude sentiments of real affection and gratitude.

43. Some people seem to think that their cast-off or unwanted possessions constitute a gift when offered to others. But why should a person be grateful for something the donor deems of no value? If Jesus offers gifts to us, they must be worthy gifts, gifts of real value. And we in turn must be able to receive them— which implies our ability to refuse or decline them, too. Without such freedom, there is no true gift.

44. A stunning example of the kind of social institution that seems very compatible with some kind of eucharistic inculturation is given by Katz in *Boiling Energy*. It is about a group of Bushmen who have a form of institutionalized social suffering;

some of their members discover that they have the capacity to suffer (in trance) great pain and privation in order to bring healing to the whole community. The healing dances last for several hours, through the night, as often as every few weeks. Significantly, however, unless the community is already committed to its own well-being, such "ministers" are unsuccessful and the healing sessions will be cancelled as inappropriate, pending some basic signs of social concern among the wider community.

45. Gregory Dix, *The Shape of the Liturgy* (San Francisco, Cal.: Harper & Row, 1945, 1982), p. 48.

46. Chupungco, *Liturgies*, pp. 37-38.

47. Dix, *The Shape*. Interestingly, Dix's fourth action (the communion: bread and wine together) would appear to mark single-species communion as an anomaly and not part of the tradition! This is something still very widespread in Roman Catholic communities, particularly in what is still sometimes called "the Missions." It needs to be addressed promptly.

48. See below, Chapter 8.

49. B. Thompson, *Liturgies of the Western Church* (New York, N.Y.: World Publishing, 1961); A. King, *Liturgies of the Past* (Milwaukee, Wis.: Bruce Publishing Co., 1959).

50. Nathan Mitchell, *Cult and Controversy*, pp. 51-53.

51. Chupungco, *Liturgies*, pp. 36-40.

52. Thomas W. Goodhue, "Do We Have to Lose Our Uniqueness When We Merge?" *Journal of Ecumenical Studies*, 22, 1, (1985): 127-30; quoted in "Mennonite Footwashing: Identity Reflections and Alternate Meanings," *Worship*, 66, 2 (1992), p. 148.

53. For the theme of foot washing in relation to social systems of exchange, see Genesis 18:4 (Abraham and the three men); 19:2 (Abraham and the two angels); and commentaries.

54. Pedro Arrupe, quoted by Eugene Hillman in *Commonweal*, January 1991.

55. See epigraph (*Evangelii Nuntiandi*, 20).

56. Hughes and Francis, *Living No Longer*.

6. PLAYING WITH FOOD AND PRAYING WITH FOOD

1. Attributed to Saint Vincent de Paul (1581-1660).

2. Eugene Uzukwu, "Food and Drink in Africa, and the Christian Eucharist." *Afer* 37 (1980): 371.

3. More accurately though less felicitously, we should say "eatings" and "celebratings."

4. Mary Douglas, "Accounting for Taste." *Psychology Today* (1979): 44-51.

5. Peter Farb, *Consuming Passions* (Boston, Mass.: Houghton Mifflin Co., 1980), p. 202.

6. Gillian Feeley-Harnick, *The Lord's Table: Eucharist and Passover in Early Christianity* (Philadelphia, Penn.: University of Pennsylvania, 1981), p. 2.

7. Peter Farb, *Consuming Passions*, p. 111.

8. This does not imply that the eucharist should be compromised, but simply that an appropriate response is required. So, if grape juice is valid matter (it is), then limiting its use in the eucharist to priests with alcohol-related problems, on

condition that they ask permission, is less than subtle. Since it is valid matter, should it not be commonly used in situations where alcoholism is a known risk in the community as a whole? If it were, a significant pastoral point would be made thereby.

9. Once, as we gathered for Mass in an African village, a thoughtful though theologically unsophisticated man brought forward a fowl "for the sacrifice," as he said! How does one respect people's wish to participate, if their offerings are deemed inappropriate or unacceptable? How does one respond pastorally, without compromising the eucharist?

10. Mary Douglas, "Accounting for Taste" p. 51.

11. In linguistics one can only apply a rule if the rule is applicable, not randomly. A rule that turns an active into a passive string can only operate where there is a certain string of elements in the active voice.

12. Peter Farb, *Consuming Passions*, p. 12.

13. Peter Farb, *Consuming Passions*, pp. 8-9.

14. Peter Farb, *Consuming Passions*, pp. 155-56.

15. Peter Farb, *Consuming Passions*, p. 9.

16. Peter Farb, *Consuming Passions*, p. 158. Is this a counter-example to universal gift-exchange? Apparently, yet there must be some form of social exchange even within this society, otherwise life simply could not continue.

17. Peter Farb, *Consuming Passions*, p. 159.

18. Peter Farb, *Consuming Passions*, p. 161.

19. "Popular" is not used here in a pejorative sense but simply referring to "what people actually do."

20. See Chapter 8, relative to the developments in the Western eucharist before the fifteenth century.

21. Gospel values are cultural values compatible with or exemplified in the Gospel story. Though not rooted in explicit faith in Jesus, they are nevertheless capable of transformation into explicit examples of faith in action.

22. Peter Farb, *Consuming Passions*, pp. 147-48 (abridged).

23. Recall that gift-exchange is often a relationship that endures over many years.

24. Michael Young, *Fighting With Food* (Cambridge, U.K.: Cambridge University Press, 1971), pp. 228-33 (abridged).

25. Robert Luneau, "Une Eucharistie Sans Pain et Sans Vin . . . ?" *Spiritus* 48 (1972): 3-11.

26. Uzukwu, "Food and Drink," pp. 370-85.

27. Jean-Marc Ela, *African Cry* (Maryknoll, N.Y.: Orbis Books, 1986), pp. 5-7.

28. Mercy Amba Oduyoye, *International Christian Digest* (February 1987): 17.

7. WITCHCRAFT, EUCHARIST, AND HOCUS POCUS

1. Richard Gray, *Black Christians and White Missionaries* (New Haven, Conn.: Yale, 1990), p. 101.

2. Anthony J. Gittins, *Mende Religion* (Sankt Augustin, W. Germany: Steyler Verlag, 1987), p. 165.

3. Monica Hunter Wilson, "Witch Beliefs and Social Structure." In *Witchcraft and Sorcery*, ed. Max Marwick (Harmondsworth, U.K.: Penguin, 1970) p. 263.

4. These are dictionary references, from the *Oxford English Dictionary*.

5. Not including Satanism or the cults widely found in the contemporary West. "Witchcraft" here is used in the classical anthropological sense, and refers to a central social institution and not a marginal or aberrant cult.

6. Wilson, "Witch Beliefs," pp. 252-63.

7. The example can be found in full in Gittins, *Mende Religion*, pp. 184-201.

8. Chief (large "C") refers to a Paramount Chief, who has authority over all villages in a chiefdom. There may be as many as seventy local village-chiefs (small "c"). The Chief concerned in this story of witchcraft had fifty-six village-chiefs in the chiefdom, and the witch-cleansing took a year or so to complete.

9. See the section in Chapter 9, "Wisdom in West Africa" for the continuation and completion of this part of the story.

10. This, coming from the witchfinder, is a surprisingly good working definition of a charism, theologically!

11. Rosemary Radford Ruether, "Religion and War in the Middle East." Talk given in Chicago, 1991.

12. See Robert Schreiter, *Constructing Local Theologies* (Maryknoll, N.Y.: Orbis Books, 1985), chaps. 7 and 8.

13. An old man fell from a tree and was killed. An accident? No, the people talked about it for a while and finally concurred that his own unusual demise proved that he himself was responsible for an unsolved death in the village. Only later did I discover that the "unsolved" death had taken place about thirty years before! The outstanding unattributed crime was paired with this unexpected death and the circle was completed. Presumably, if there had been no unattributed unexpected death to account for, the fall would itself have been explained not as a solution to a previous death but as the result of another's malice. Then steps would have been taken to find the person responsible. It would be remembered as a problem awaiting a solution, half of a pair awaiting its mate.

There are no pure accidents in such a world. Every effect must have a personal cause, and if a cause is not immediately found the "unsolved" death can remain, like a cloud of suspicion, over the village or community. It is not surprising that in small villages with high morbidity and mortality, social "dis-ease" is not far from the surface, or that ceremony and ritual are so often and so visibly employed.

14. Richard Gray, *Black Christians*, pp. 45-46.

15. Richard Gray, *Black Christians*, pp. 81-82, and ff.

8. MISTAKES, MODIFICATIONS, AND INCULTURATION

1. Chupungco, *Liturgies*, p. 33.

2. David Bosch, "An Emerging Paradigm for Mission." *Missiology* (1983): 483.

3. Walbert Bühlmann, *The Church of the Future* (Maryknoll, N.Y.: Orbis Books, 1986), pp. 156-57.

4. L. Sinanoglou, "The Christ Child and Sacrifice: A Medieval Tradition and the Corpus Christi Plays." *Speculum: Journal of Medieval Studies*, vol. 48, no. 4 (1973): 491.

5. Quotation marks are used here to indicate that people commonly perceived these occurrences as miracles, rather than to claim objectively that they are. Subsequent references will discard the use of quotes.

6. Sinanoglou, "The Christ Child," p. 492.

7. Sinanoglou, "The Christ Child," p. 492.

8. Sinanoglou, "The Christ Child," p. 493.

9. Sinanoglou, "The Christ Child," p. 492.

10. Carolyn Walker Bynum, *Holy Feast, Holy Fast: The Religious Significance of Food to Medieval Women* (Berkeley, Cal.: University of California Press, 1987).

11. Bynum, *Holy Feast*, p. 64.

12. See Mitchell, *Cult and Controversy*.

13. *The Book of Margery Kempe* (Harmondsworth, U.K.: Penguin, 1986), chap. 20.

14. Bynum, *Holy Feast*, p. 55.

15. See Chupungco, *Liturgies*.

16. The use of "non-" is deliberate. The purpose is to indicate how such terminology can subtly inject normative criteria into the narrative: Western, Latin, Roman, and so on. Though difficult to avoid, all "non-" terms are loaded.

17. I have been unable to find the date for this citation. It is by G. Grant, and the piece is "The Elevation of the Host: A Reaction to Twelfth Century Heresy," which can be found in *Theological Studies*, pp. 228-30. Perhaps 1940.

18. Grant. "The Elevation," p. 228.

19. To appreciate fully the reality of ocular communion we need to grasp the medieval understanding of the physics of sight and vision, in, for example, Roger Bacon. See Margaret Miles, *Image as Insight* (Boston, Mass.: Beacon Press, 1986).

20. Francis Clark, *Eucharistic Sacrifice and the Reformation* (London, U.K.: Darton, Longman & Todd, 1960), p. 323.

21. Bynum, *Holy Feast*, p. 65.

22. Grant, "The Elevation," p. 231.

23. Bynum, *Holy Feast*, pp. 54-55.

24. Grant, "The Elevation," pp. 238-40.

25. *Epistles of Gregory*, Book XI: Ep. LXIV, ad Q. 3. In *Nicene and Post-Nicene Fathers*, vol. 13: 75 (Grand Rapids, Mich.: Eerdmans, 1956), p. 11.

26. Michael Singleton, "Let the People Be: Popular Religion and the Religion of the People." *Pro Mundi Vita Bulletin* 61: 4 (1976). I am heavily dependent on Singleton's thoughts and diagram.

27. See Nathan Mitchell, *Cult and Controversy*, pp. 118-19; 86; 90.

28. David Bosch, "An Emerging Paradigm," p. 476.

29. Francis Clark, *Eucharistic Sacrifice*, pp. 214, 228.

30. Bühlmann, *The Church of the Future*, pp. 156-57.

31. Sinanoglou, "The Christ Child," p. 496.

32. Throughout the Middle Ages in England there were three kinds of vernacular drama: miracle plays, mystery plays, and morality plays. They evolved (in Latin) during the eleventh and twelfth centuries, from the liturgical Offices, and were performed to enhance the festivals of the liturgical calendar. By the thirteenth century they had been widely vernacularized and were performed by Guilds at public festivals, as entertainment but crucially also as a form of catechetical instruction. There are several play cycles extant. Mystery plays cover the history of salvation; miracle plays and morality plays are self-explanatory. All indicated the confluence of the Divine and the human, the sacred and the secular, the religious and the profane.

33. Bynum, *Holy Feast*, p. 156.

34. Mitchell, *Cult and Controversy*, p. 373.
35. Bühlmann, *The Church of the Future*, p. 138.

9. MISSION ON THE MARGINS

1. The recent encyclical, *Redemptoris Missio*, is a case in point: "Visiting the missions is commendable, especially on the part of young people who go there to serve and to gain an intense experience of the Christian life" (para. 82). This is to dichotomize "missions" and "home" in a rather unhelpful way, and to beg the question of how Christians acquit their baptismal responsibility in terms of their response to mission.

2. Gustavo Gutiérrez, *We Drink from Our Own Wells* (Maryknoll, N.Y.: Orbis Books, 1984), p. 134.

3. As with the previous material cited on this topic, the source is Gittins, *Mende Religion*, pp. 184-201

4. Ned Marchessault, C.S.Sp., has been evangelizing the Maasai people in Tanzania for more than twenty years. I was privileged to stay with him, to accompany him, and to meet members of the Ngorongoro Christian community. The narrative here is his own and is used with permission; clearly, it speaks for itself.

5. Consensus within a Western, democratic community of individualists is rather different from agreed common action within a (traditional) local community. In the latter case a decision, intended for the common good, is taken by a single person and accepted by the community: not "individually" but "communally."

Though people ("individualists") within certain types of ("Western-type") community might be able to live creatively through abiding by common decisions, we are not absolved from making a specific, personal option for our own radical transformation and conversion. Moving passively "with the flow" is inadequate for discipleship. And prophets and their voices are not part of a mainstream community or crowd; they do not await consensus before acting and speaking.

Index

Aaron, *biblical patriarch*, 89
Abuse, 25, 165
Accused, 118-120, 122, 126-128
  scapegoat, 119-120, 126; witchcraft, 118-120, 126
Action, 23, 48, 61-62, 73, 78, 82-84, 99, 101, 108, 116, 124, 133, 141, 154
  hostile, 82; liturgical, 73, 78, 108; passivity, 84, 116; patterned 82
Adaptation, 47, 50, 73, 84, 98, 107, 147, 163
  liturgical, 47, 50, 73, 84
Addiction, 69, 91
Affection, 171
Affirmation, 89
  meal, 89
Africa, 108-111, 115-118, 129-130, 145, 147, 158, 170
  AIDS, 147; Lumpa, 130
Age, 15, 42, 47, 52, 108
  Faith, Age of, 46; Reform, Age of, 46; spirituality, 52
AIDS, Africa, 147
Albigensians, 140
Alienation, xviii, xix, 69, 84, 110, 131, 165
Alliance, Perpetual, 84
Altar, 88, 91, 120, 122, 134, 140, 145
  relics, 145; table, 88; tomb, 88; witch pot, 120-122
Ambiguity, 17, 21, 56, 98, 101-102, 167
American Society of Missiology, ix
Amnesty, 117-118, 122
  witchcraft, 117-118, 122
Anarchists, 3
Anawim (Hebrew), 63
Ancestors, 105-106
Angels, 43, 45, 134-135
Angry, 26, 160
Animals, 3, 97

migratory, 3; sedentary, 3
Anguish, 115
Anthropology, ix, 59, 66-67, 108
  anthropologists, 67-69, 108-109; cultural, ix; interpreters, 67
Apathy, 45, 51, 69
Appeal, 42
  esthetic, 42
Apostles. *See* Missioners
Architects, 130
  ecclesial, 130; social, 130
Arndt, Johannes, 22
Arrogance, 26, 67, 70, 95
Arrupe, Pedro, S.J., 89
Art, ix, 120, 135
Ashumu, the prophet of Loongojo, 156-158
  baptism, 156; Ngorongoro Maasai Christians, 156; vocation, 156; wedding 157-158
Assembly, 45-46, 77
Assumptions, 28-31, 57, 65, 70-71
  ethnological, 31; intellectual, 71; theological, 71
Atonement, 81
Attention, 58-60, 63, 67, 95, 100, 104-105, 118, 125, 136
Attitudes, 43, 49, 56-61, 64, 67, 83, 91-92, 104, 119, 125-126, 129-133, 140-141, 151, 163
  Eastern, 140; evangelistic, 59; ignorance, 126; missioners, 131; offical, 92; social, 49; superiors, 126
Au, Wilkie, 17
Augustine, of Canterbury, *Saint*, 142
Augustine, of Hippo, *Saint*, 19, 34-35, 81, 166
  eucharist, 1
Authority, 12, 60, 73-75, 135, 148, 163, 174